ROGET'S THESAURUS

For home, school and office

A-Z for easy reference

Clear & easy-to-read format

Key words in bold type

A dictionary of synonyms and antonyms

KAPPA Books

Visit us at www.kappapuzzles.com

INTRODUCTION

A thesaurus is a collection of synonyms (words with the same meaning) and antonyms (words with the opposite meaning). This thesaurus is organized in dictionary form — that is, on the pages of this book, we have listed entry words (typed in bold) in alphabetical order. Next to each such entry, we have given its part of speech, followed by a list of its synonyms and near synonyms. Synonyms for different senses of the entry word are separated by semicolons. Where appropriate, we have also included antonyms for the entry word.

You will find this book handy in many ways. You can use it as you would a regular dictionary to quickly get a sense of the spelling or meaning of an unfamiliar word, but it is especially valuable as an aid to good writing. If you are working on a term paper or writing a letter, an e-mail, a poem, or a story, and you need to find just the right word to convey your meaning, the thesaurus will provide you with a menu of choices.

GUIDE TO ABBREVIATIONS

adj. — adjective	n. — noun
adv. — adverb	prep. — preposition
conj. — conjunction	v. — verb

A

abandon, v. desert, forsake, forego, discard, relinquish. Antonyms: maintain, continue.

abase, v. degrade, dishonor, reduce, humiliate.

abdomen, n. belly, paunch.

abduction, n. kidnapping.

abide, v. dwell, stay, continue, remain.

ability, n. competence, efficiency, aptitude, capacity.

able, adj. competent, qualified, capable, talented, clever.

abnormal, adj. irregular, exceptional, unusual.

abode, n. residence, habitation, dwelling, sojourn.

abolish, v. annul, nullify, invalidate, revoke, destroy. Antonyms: confirm, establish.

abound, v. be plentiful, teem, swarm.

abridge, v. shorten, diminish, curtail.

abrupt, adj. hasty, rough, rude, curt, jagged, rugged.

abscess, n. ulcer, fester.

absence, n. nonattendance, want, destitution, privation.

absolute, adj. unconditional, unrestricted, uncontrolled, supreme; consummate, faultless.

absorb, v. engulf, overwhelm, swallow up; suck up, engross, occupy, monopolize.

abstain, v. refrain, withhold, deny one's self. Antonym: indulge.

absurd, adj. ridiculous, preposterous, irrational, inconsistent.

abundance, n. sufficiency, plenty, profusion, exuberance, overflow.

abuse, v. misapply, misuse, desecrate, violate, profane.

acceptance, n. approval, favorable reception. Antonym: rejection.

accessory, adj. accompanying, subservient, subsidiary.

accommodation, n. adaptation, adjustment; complaisance; favor, kindness.

account, n. calculation, record, tab; registry, register; recital, relation, narrative, report, portrayal, description, opinion; value.

accumulation, n. hoard, aggregation, accruement.

achieve, v. accomplish, realize, effect, attain.

action, n. agency, operation, activity, deed, lawsuit. Antonyms: inaction, inactivity.

active, adj. brisk, nimble, agile, sprightly, spirited; strenuous, diligent. Antonyms: inactive, passive.

actual, adj. real, veritable. Antonyms: potential, nominal.

adapt, v. adjust, conform.

adequacy, n. sufficiency. Antonyms: inadequacy, insufficiency.

admissible, adj. allowable, permissible. Antonym: inadmissible.

adorn, v. decorate, beautify, grace, garnish, beset. Antonyms: disfigure, mar, deform.

advance, v. progress, increase; promote, elevate; enhance. Antonyms: retreat, decline.

advantage, n. superiority, mastery, ascendancy; benefit, avail. Antonym: disadvantage.

adversary, n. enemy, foe, opponent, antagonist. Antonyms: ally, friend.

advice, n. counsel, information, report.

advise, v. counsel, warn; inform, notify.

advocate, n. defender, apologist, upholder, promoter.

affectionate, adj. devoted, fond, loving, ardent.

afflict, v. persecute, distress, trouble, harass.

agency, n. operation, action, mediation, means.

agent, n. representative, substitute, procurator, proctor, solicitor. Antonyms: principal, chief.

aggravate, v. intensify, enhance, increase; irritate.

agree, v. concur, accord, chime, harmonize; accede, comply, assent, consent, grant. Antonyms: disagree, differ.

agriculture, n. farming, geoponics, agronomy.

ailment, n. disorder, complaint, illness.

alarm, v. terrify, scare, appall, unnerve, frighten.

alienate, v. transfer, demise, assign; estrange, wean.

alleviate, v. mollify, lessen, moderate, relieve.

allow, v. permit, consent to; suffer, endure, let.

allowance, n. permission, admittance, tolerance, sufferance, assent. Antonyms: disallowance, refusal.

allude, v. refer, advert, suggest.

amaze, v. astonish, astound, surprise, stagger, dumfound, awe.

ambiguous, adj. indefinite, vague, doubtful.

amiable, adj. gracious, benign, good-natured, obliging, friendly.

amuse, v. entertain, recreate, please.

analogy, n. similarity, agreement, correspondence.

anatomy, n. dissection; body, structure, skeleton.

ancestor, n. forefather, primogenitor, forbear.

ancient, adj. old, archaic, antique, primitive.

angelic, adj. cherubic, celestial, heavenly, divine.

anguish, n. agony, distress, torture, misery, remorse.

animate, v. vitalize, quicken, inspirit, rouse.

animosity, n. rancor, hatred, virulence.

announce, v. proclaim, publish, advertise, trumpet. Antonyms: suppress, reserve, withhold, hush-up.

annoy, v. trouble, bother, pester, aggravate, chafe.

antagonist, n. opponent, foe, adversary, rival.

anterior, adj. prior, before, previous.

anticipate, v. expect, preclude, obviate.

anxiety, n. apprehension, solicitude. Antonyms: indifference, assurance.

anxious, adj. apprehensive, concerned, worried. Antonyms: unconcerned, assured.

apathy, n. dispassion, indifference, unconcern.

apparent, adj. visible, manifest, obvious, evident; seeming, specious.

appendage, n. pedicle, appendix, attachment.

appetite, n. hunger; desire. Antonyms: aversion, distaste.

applause, n. acclaim, cheers. Antonyms: hooting, derision.

appliance, n. device, facility.

applicant, n. candidate, petitioner, suitor.

apply, v. utilize, practice.

appreciate, v. value, esteem, prize.

apprehend, v. arrest, seize; understand, consider, believe.

appropriate, adj. fitting, proper, apposite, pertinent. Antonym: inappropriate.

aptitude, n. proneness, propensity, leaning, inclination. Antonym: inaptitude.

ardent, adj. zealous, warm, passionate, fervent, enthusiastic.

aristocracy, n. peerage, nobility, patrician order. Antonyms: commonalty, peasantry.

armory, n. arsenal.

aromatic, adj. fragrant, balmy, spicy, savory.

arouse, v. excite, rouse, stimulate, awaken, revive.

arrest, n. apprehension, capture, detention; custody, duress; stoppage, restraint.

arrogance, n. insolence, haughtiness, lordliness.

article, n. thing, commodity; portion, clause, stipulation.

artifice, n. finesse, craft, guile, diplomacy.

ashamed, adj. confused, mortified, disconcerted. Antonyms: unashamed, brazen-faced.

aspect, n. appearance, look; view, scene, prospect.

assent, n. consent, agreement, concurrence. Antonyms: dissent, declension.

assert, v. affirm, state, say, predicate, maintain.

assets, n. resources, property, effects, possessions.

assign, v. allot, appoint; transfer, make-over, convey.

assistant, n. helper, deputy, aide, ally, accomplice, subsidiary.

assurance, n. surety, promise; confidence, conviction, assuredness; audacity.

asylum, n. retreat, sanctuary.

atrocious, adj. heinous, felonious, infamous, outrageous.

attain, v. achieve, compass, gain.

attend, v. guard, look after; accompany, escort.

attention, n. regard, consideration, alertness, watchfulness, courtesy. Antonyms: inattention, slight, disregard.

attitude, n. posture, position, pose.

attract, v. allure, entice, draw, decoy, interest, engage, induce. Antonyms: repel, repulse.

attribute, v. impute, assign, refer, trace.

audacious, adj. presumptuous, impudent, brazen, unabashed.

authentic, adj. genuine, trustworthy, credible.

author, n. creator, originator, writer.

authorize, v. empower, commission; sanction, warrant, justify, confirm.

automatic, adj. self-propelling, self-moving.

auxiliary, n. assistant, helper.

average, adj. medium, ordinary, mediocre, middling.

aversion, n. dislike, antipathy, loathing.

avoid, v. evade, shun, elude, shirk, parry.

awaken, v. wake, awake, rouse, arouse, excite.

aware, adj. conscious, apprised, mindful.

awkward, adj. clumsy, ungraceful, gawky, ungainly, inelegant, klutzy, unskillful, embarrassing. Antonyms: graceful, courtly, elegant.

awry, adj. distorted, wry, crooked, perverse.

axle, n. shaft, spindle.

B

baby, n. infant, babe, newborn.

back, adj. posterior, dorsal, neural; remote, distant, frontier; rear, reverse.

backbone, n. spine, spinal column, chine.

backslide, v. break faith, relapse, regress, desert, fall away.

backward, adj. reversed, regressive; retrospective; reluctant, loath, unwilling; dull, inapt.

bad, adj. evil, wicked, immoral, corrupt, sinful, demoralized, sinister, vicious.

badge, n. device, emblem, ensign, star, insignia.

badinage, n. raillery, banter.

baffle, v. balk, disconcert, frustrate, thwart, circumvent.

bag, n. sack, pouch, knapsack, pocketbook, satchel, suitcase, purse, tote, gunny sack.

baggage, n. luggage, suitcases.

bail, n. security, surety.

bait, n. lure, enticement, temptation, decoy, allurement.

balcony, n. gallery, terrace.

balk, v. frustrate, baffle, foil, disappoint.

ball, n. sphere, globe, orb, pellet.

ballast, n. steadiness, self-control, stability, judgment.

balm, n. ointment; nepenthe, balsam.

banal, adj. commonplace, hackneyed, trite.

banality, n. platitude, commonplace.

bandage, v. swathe.

bandit, n. outlaw, brigand, desperado.

banish, v. exile, expatriate, relegate; drive away, dismiss.

bank, n. mound, pile, ridge, dike, heap, drift, embankment; brink.

bankrupt, adj. insolvent; depleted, impoverished.

banner, n. flag, standard, ensign, banderole, colors, pavilion.

banquet, n. junket, regalement, feast.

banter, n. joking, jesting, pleasantry, badinage, chaff.

barbaric, adj. barbarous, savage, rude, uncivilized.

barbarous, adj. uncivilized, barbarian, inhuman, brutal.

bare, adj. naked, nude, undressed, unveiled, exposed, undraped, unadorned, empty.

barefaced, adj. unmasked, undisguised, glaring, shameless, audacious.

bargain, v. stipulate, agree, barter.

bark, v. bay, yelp, yap.

barrel, n. cask, hogshead, keg.

barren, adj. sterile, unprolific; unproductive, unfruitful, unfertile.

barrier, n. obstruction, impediment, obstacle, hindrance, barricade.

barter, n. traffic, exchange, trade.

base, n. basis, bottom, foundation, groundwork.

basement, n. cellar.

bashful, adj. over-modest, diffident, coy, sheepish.

basis, n. foundation, source, origin.

bask, v. luxuriate, revel.

basket, n. hamper, creel, hanaper, canister, bassinet.

batch, n. quantity, lot, assortment, collection.

bath, n. ablution, lavement.

bathe, v. lave, wash, cleanse.

baton, n. staff, wand.

batter, v. smite, pelt, assault; demolish, shatter.

battle, n. engagement, fight, encounter, skirmish, contest, combat, strife.

bauble, n. trinket, plaything.

bay, n. firth, fiord, bayou; recess, alcove, sinus.

beach, n. shore, strand.

beacon, n. balefire, signal fire; signal, pharos.

beak, n. bill, nib, mandible.

beam, n. girder, joist; ray, gleam.

bear, v. endure, tolerate, stand, undergo, brook, submit to, suffer, carry.

beard, n. whiskers; goatee.

bearing, n. mien, carriage, demeanor, air, deportment; endurance.

bearish, adj. discourteous, boorish, rude; ursine.

beast, n. brute; quadruped; monster.

beat, v. forge, whip, hammer; belabor, maul, buffet, flagellate.

beau, n. lover, sweetheart, gallant, swain, flame, wooer.

beautiful, adj. fair, lovely, handsome, elegant, exquisite. Antonyms: homely, ugly, repulsive, hideous, inelegant.

becloud, v. dim, cloud, obscure.

becoming, adj. appropriate, fit, seemly, befitting. Antonym: unbecoming.

bed, n. berth, bunk, couch, cot; pallet, mattress; cradle.

bedim, v. obscure, becloud, overcast.

befall, v. happen, supervene.

befitting, adj. suitable, proper, seemly, meet, applicable.

befuddle, v. confuse, mystify.

beg, v. beseech, implore.

beget, v. procreate, generate.

beggar, v. impoverish, ruin; exhaust, surpass, go beyond.

begin, v. commence; arise, spring, originate.

beguile, v. ensnare, mislead, lure, deceive, cheat.

behave, v. deport one's self, act.

behead, v. decapitate, execute.

beholden, adj. obliged, indebted, bound.

being, n. existence, entity. Antonyms: nonexistence, nonentity.
belfry, n. bell tower.
belief, n. persuasion, faith; conviction, assurance, confidence; creed, opinion. Antonyms: doubt, disbelief, skepticism.
belittle, v. decry, disparage.
belligerent, adj. at war, militant; bellicose.
bell tower, n. belfry, campanile.
belly, n. abdomen, paunch.
belly-ache, n. colic, gripe.
belonging, n. possession, appendage, appurtenance.
below, adv. under, beneath, underneath.
belt, n. girdle; girth; zone.
bemoan, v. lament, deplore.
bend, v. curve, flex, crook; direct, turn, apply; stoop, incline; yield.
beneficent, adj. benevolent, charitable, magnanimous.
benefit, n. avail, profit, behalf, service.
benevolence, n. beneficence, bounty, charity.
bent, adj. crooked, flexed, hooked; determined.
benumb, v. stupefy, blunt.
bequeath, v. devise, will.
berate, v. upbraid, rate.
beseech, v. entreat, implore.
beset, v. besiege, obsess, environ, encompass; perplex.
besiege, v. obsess, environ, beset, encompass.
betoken, v. foreshadow, portend, foreshow, indicate.
betray, v. seduce, mislead, delude, beguile, reveal, disclose.
betroth, v. affiance.

better, adj. improved, enhanced, superior; healthier, recovered. Antonym: worse.
better, n. superior.
better, v. improve, enhance, advance.
betterment, n. improvement, promotion, reformation.
between, prep. betwixt.
bewail, v. deplore, lament, bemoan.
bewilder, v. confuse, perplex, confound, mystify.
bewitch, v. charm, fascinate, captivate, enamor. Antonym: repel.
bias, n. bent, proneness.
bibulous, adj. absorbent; intemperate.
bickering, n. contention, wrangling, sparring, quarreling.
bid, v. offer, proffer; order, direct, enjoin, command; invite, ask; wish, greet.
big, adj. large, huge, bulky, massive, immense, gross, voluminous, capacious.
bigot, n. fanatic, zealot.
bile, n. choler, bitterness, anger, spleen, rancor.
bill, n. circular, placard, dodger, poster; statement; beak, nib, mandible.
bin, n. crib, bunker.
bind, v. tie, fasten, secure, gird, confine, restrict, retrain; bandage. Antonyms: unbind, loose.
bird, n. avian; fledgling, nestling; squab.
birth, n. nativity; origin, beginning, genesis; extraction, lineage; regeneration.
bishop, n. diocesan, prelate; met-

ropolitan.

bit, n. morsel, fragment, scrap, crumb; mite, ace, particle, whit, jot, iota.

bite, v. champ, nibble, chew; sting, smart, tingle; take hold of, adhere; nip, blast.

bitter, adj. poignant, intense; calamitous distressing, virulent.

bizarre, adj. fantastic, whimsical, grotesque.

blab, v. tattle, gab, spill the beans, chatter, gossip, tell tales, leak.

black, adj. sable, ebony, inky.

blacken, v. darken, char, begrime, tarnish, discolor; defame, malign.

blackguard, n. scoundrel, rascal, villain.

black-hearted, adj. villainous, abandoned, reprobate, base.

blacksmith, n. ironsmith, farrier, horseshoer.

blade, n. buck, gallant, dandy.

blamable, adj. culpable, censurable, blameworthy.

blame, v. censure, reproach.

bland, adj. suave, mollifying, affable, complaisant; soothing, emollient.

blank, adj. void, empty, unfilled; expressionless, vacant, nonplused, astounded.

blarney, n. palaver, blandishment, cajolery, flattery.

blasphemy, n. sacrilege, profanity.

blast, n. squall, gust; peal, blare, clang; explosion.

blatant, adj. brawling, clamorous, bawling, braying.

blaze, n. flame.

bleach, v. whiten, blanch.

bleak, adj. windswept, cheerless, raw, penetrating, desolate, dreary.

blemish, v. deface, mar, disfigure, sully.

blench, v. flinch, recoil.

blend, v. intermingle, fuse, merge, combine, mix.

blessing, n. benediction, benison, beatitude.

blight, v. blast; ruin, frustrate, thwart.

blind, adj. unseeing, sightless; oblivious, undiscriminating, unmindful; unintelligible, obscure.

bliss, n. felicity, transport, rapture, beatitude, ecstasy.

bloat, v. inflate, distend.

block, v. obstruct, blockade.

bloodsucker, n. leech.

bloodthirsty, adj. truculent, ferocious, cruel.

bloom, n. blossom, blow; prime, vigor, flush; fuzz.

blossom, n. flower, florescence, bloom.

blot, n. stain, blemish.

blow, n. whack, knock, rap, thump, assault, stroke, wallop; misfortune, setback, upset.

blow, v. puff, exhale, gust, waft; bluster, rage.

blue, adj. azure, cerulean, sapphire, amethystine, turquoise, ultramarine; sad, morose, depressed, melancholy.

bluff, v. deceive, mislead, trick, con, pretend.

blunt, adj. dull, obtuse; abrupt, brusque, uncivil, ungracious, discourteous; stupid.

blur, v. dim, obscure; sully, blemish, befog.

bluster, n. swaggering, boasting;

wind, storm.
boast, v. brag, crow.
belittle, v. disparage.
boat, n. water craft, launch, ship, yacht.
bob, n. pendant, float.
bode, v. forebode, foreshadow, tract, presage, betoken.
boding, adj. ominous.
body, n. torso, trunk; physique; bulk, mass.
boggle, v. hesitate, stickle; baffle.
border, n. verge, edge, margin, brink, skirt, rim, brim.
bogus, adj. counterfeit, fictitious, sham, fraudulent, forged, mock, false.
bore, n. perforation; caliber; tiresome person.
bore, v. tire, weary, irk; penetrate. Antonym: interest.
boil, v. seethe, simmer.
boisterous, adj. noisy, turbulent, unrestrained, rude.
bold, adj. daring, brave; forward, immodest, rude, brazen, saucy, insolent. Antonyms: modest, coy, bashful, shy, timid.
boldness, n. impudence, botch, presumption, impertinence.
bolster, v. prop up, support, maintain.
bolster, n. cushion, pad.
bolt, v. leave suddenly; gulp.
bona fide, adj. in good faith, real, actual.
bond, n. band, tie.
bondage, n. servitude, slavery, captivity, bond service.
bonnet, n. headdress, chapeau.
bonus, n. premium.
booklet, n. pamphlet, brochure

boring, n. tedious, tiresome, dull.
boss, n. superintendent, director, employer, foreman, overseer.
bother, v. trouble, annoy, bungle, fiasco, worry.
bothersome, adj. troublesome, perplexing, annoying.
bottle, n. vial, cruet, flask, decanter, tankard, carafe.
bottom, n. foot, base; nadir; foundation, groundwork, basis, base, pedestal.
bough, n. branch, limb.
bounce, v. spring, bound, rebound, recoil, dismiss.
bound, v. limit, enclose; leap, spring, bounce.
boundary, n. circumference; limit, border confines, precinct.
bounteous, adj. bountiful, generous, liberal.
bouquet, n. nosegay; boutonniere.
bout, n. round, turn; contest, set-to, conflict.
bower, n. arbor, grove.
bowman, n. archer.
box, n. receptacle, chest, case, coffer, carton, casket.
boxing, n. sparring.
boyhood, n. youth, juvenility, minority.
brace, v. prop, support, fortify, buttress, stay, shore; strengthen.
bracket, n. console, corbel, strut, cantilever.
brag, v. boast, vaunt, vapor. Antonyms: disparage, decry, belittle.
braid, n. plait; queue, pigtail.
braid, v. plait, plat, entwine, interlace.
brain, n. mastermind; egghead; smarty-pants.

brake, v. decelerate, curb, damp, deter, control, restrain.

branch, n. bough, limb; shoot, sprout, sprig, spray, twig.

brand, v. stigmatize.

brash, adj. quick-tempered, irascible.

brassy, adj. brazen; bold, impudent, forward.

bravado, n. blustering, swaggering.

brawl, n. quarrel, dispute, fight, rumpus, uproar.

brawny, adj. muscular, sinewy, robust, strong.

breach, n. breaking, rupture; infraction, violation, trespass, nonobservance.

breadth, n. width, latitude; liberality, tolerance.

breakdown, n. downfall, collapse, crash.

breaking, n. fracture, rupture, breach, infraction.

breakup, n. disruption, disorganization.

breed, v. generate, procreate, engender, nurture, train.

breezy, adj. airy, windy; light.

brew, v. foment, concoct, hatch, plot.

bribe, n. hush-money, boodle.

bribery, n. subornation.

bridal, adj. nuptial, conjugal.

bridge, n. trestlework, culvert, pontoon, bridge.

bridle, n. restraint, curb, check.

bridle, v. restrain, curb, check, control.

brief, adj. short-lived, transient, transitory; terse.

brigand, n. highwayman, bandit, outlaw, robber.

bright, adj. luminous, gleaming, lustrous, radiant, intelligent, apt, acute, clever. Antonyms: dull, lackluster, obscure, dim, opaque, murky, tarnished.

brilliant, adj. sparkling, glittering, dazzling, gleaming, flashing; splendid, glorious; intelligent, exceptional.

brim, n. rim, border, margin, edge, brink, bank.

bring, v. fetch.

brink, n. edge, border, verge.

brisk, adj. lively, spirited, spry, agile, rapid.

brittle, adj. frangible, crisp.

broad, adj. wide; extensive, extended, vast, wide-reaching, comprehensive; liberal.

broil, v. grill.

broken, adj. fractured, splintered, shattered, interrupted; impaired; subdued. Antonyms: inviolate, intact, whole.

broker, adj. agent, factor, middleman, go-between.

brood, v. incubate, sit; meditate.

brook, n. rivulet, runlet, rill, creek, streamlet.

brotherhood, n. fraternity, fellowship.

brow, n. forehead.

brown, adj. dusky, tawny, dun.

bruise, n. contusion; injury; shiner.

brush, n. brushwood; thicket, underbrush; grazing.

brutal, adj. inhuman, cruel, ruthless, unfeeling; beastly, bestial, brutish.

brute, n. beast; fiend, monster, ruffian.

buck, n. ram; beau, fop, blade, dandy.
bud, v. pullulate, germinate.
build, v. erect, construct, raise.
building, n. erection, construction; edifice, structure, pile, architecture.
businesslike, adj. pragmatic, professional.
bulging, adj. protuberant, convex, gibbous.
bulldoze, v. intimidate, browbeat.
bully, n. blusterer, swaggerer, roisterer, rowdy, rough.
bulwark, n. rampart, fortification.
bump, v. jolt, jounce, thump.
bundle, n. parcel. package, bale, pack, budget, packet.
bunker, n. bin, receptacle, crib.
burden, n. load, cargo; incubus, encumbrance, weight, impediment, trial.
burial, n. interment, inhumation, sepulture. Antonyms: disinterment, exhumation.
burlesque, n. travesty, farce.
burn, v. scorch, scald, singe, char, sear, cauterize, brand.
bury, n. inter, inhume, entomb, sepulcher; hide, secrete, conceal. Antonyms: disinter, exhume.
bush, n. shrub; thicket, jungle, boscage.
business, n. vocation, calling, pursuit, craft, trade, occupation, profession; avocation.
bustle, n. stir, agitation, ado, commotion.
busy, adj. occupied, engaged, employed, engrossed; diligent, industrious, active.
buttress, n. support, stay.

buy, n. bargain; acquisition, purchase.
buy, v. purchase, procure.
buzz, n. hum, murmur,.
bystander, n. spectator, onlooker, witness.

C

cabin, n. hut, hovel, shanty, shack, cottage.
cage, v. confine, coop up.
cajole, v. beguile, wheedle, blandish, flatter.
cake, v. harden, solidify, coagulate.
calamitous, adj. disastrous, deplorable, baleful, ill-fated, untoward, dire.
calamity, n. disaster, catastrophe, misfortune, adversity, mischance.
calculate, v. compute, reckon, estimate; forecast.
calendar, n. almanac; list, schedule, register, docket.
call, v. summon, bid, evoke, invite; convoke, assemble, convene.
call, n. summons, invocation, entreaty, appeal, invitation; signal; requirement, demand.
callous, adj. unfeeling, insensible, hardened.
callow, adj. unfledged, immature, green.
calm, n. lull, tranquillity, quiet, placidity.
calm, adj. still, serene, motionless, undisturbed, unruffled, pacific, placid, tranquil. Antonyms: excited, stormy, agitated, ruffled, perturbed.
calm, v. lull, allay, hush, becalm,

still, compose, quiet, appease.

camouflage, n. disguise, blind, deception, illusion.

camouflage, v. disguise, blind, deceive, hide, conceal, veil, dissemble, mask.

camp, n. encampment; bivouac; quarters.

cancel, v. annul, abrogate, rescind, nullify, abolish. Antonyms: confirm, approve, enforce, maintain.

cancellation, n. annulment, abrogation, rescission, nullification.

candid, adj. impartial, unbiased, fair; frank, ingenuous, unreserved. Antonyms: disingenuous, reserved, subtle.

candidate, n. nominee, postulant, office-seeker.

candor, n. impartiality, disinterestedness; frankness, openness.

candy, n. confectionery, bonbon, confection, lollipop, caramel, fudge, fondant, praline, sweets, goodies.

canker, n. corrosion, erosion.

canny, adj. cunning, crafty, wary, shrewd, prudent.

canoe, n. pirogue, dugout.

canon, n. law, regulation.

canopy, n. covering, awning, tilt, tester, pavilion.

cant, n. slope, tilt, turn; bias, impulse; prating: idioms, vocabulary: affected piety, hypocrisy; slang.

cant, v. tilt, tip, incline.

cantankerous, adj. perverse, contentious, contrary.

canvas, n. tarpaulin.

canyon, n. gorge, ravine.

cap, n. topper, hat; lid.

capability, n. ability, capacity, qualification, proficiency, efficiency.

capable, adj. able, qualified, competent, efficient.

cape, n. promontory, headland.

caper, n. dido, trick, prank.

caper, v. gambol, frisk, cavort, leap, skip, prance.

capital, adj. principal, leading, chief, cardinal.

caprice, n. fancy, whim, notion, quirk; whimsy, fickleness.

capricious, adj. fanciful, whimsical, vagarious, inconstant, fickle.

capsize, v. upset, overturn.

captain, n. commander, chieftain, leader, chief: skipper, master, foreman.

captious, adj. critical, carping, censorious.

captivate, v. enchant, subdue, bewitch, fascinate, entrance, infatuate.

captivity, n. bondage, servitude, vassalage, slavery.

capture, v. seize, catch, apprehend, arrest, corral.

capture, n. prey, prize; apprehension, arrest, seizure, catching.

car, n. cart, vehicle, chariot, caboose, tender, cage, coach, tram, truck.

cardinal, adj. principal, chief, superior.

care, n. concern, anxiety, worry, apprehension; oversight, charge, management, custody.

careful, adj. cautious, watchful, provident, attentive, considerate, prudent, wary, mindful.

careless, adj. negligent, unconcerned, indifferent, inattentive, regardless, lax, remiss.

cargo, n. freight, load, burden, lading, last.

caricature, n. exaggeration, burlesque, take-off, travesty.

carousal, n. revel, wassail, jamboree.

carouser, adj. reveler, debauchee.

carp, v. cavil, censure, nag, complain.

carriage, n. carrying, bearing, behavior, deportment; air, demeanor; vehicle, coach, gig, buggy, sulky, surrey, chaise, sedan.

carrier, n. messenger, conveyer; porter, bearer.

carry, v. convey, transport, bear, tote.

cart, n. vehicle, wagon, carriage; lorry, truck.

carte, n. menu, bill of fare.

carve, v. sculpture, chisel, engrave, fashion.

case, n. sheath, covering, capsule, quiver, chest; event, happening, instance.

cash, n. coin, currency.

cast, v. fling, hurl, throw, pitch, sling; direct, deposit, place.

castaway, n. outcast, pariah, derelict.

castigate, v. chastise.

castle, n. fortress, citadel, palace, mansion, chateau.

cast off, v. discard, reject.

cast-off, adj. discarded, rejected.

casual, adj. chance, accidental.

cat, n. feline, tabby, puss, kitten, kitty.

catalogue, n. list, register, schedule, index.

cataract, n. waterfall, cascade.

catastrophe, n. disaster, calamity.

catch, v. seize, grasp, clutch, gripe, nab; apprehend; arrest.

catch, n. capture, seizure, arrest; hook, clasp.

catchword, n. cue, cliché, byword, truism.

category, n. class, state, condition, division.

cater, v. purvey, supply, furnish.

catholic, adj. universal, general, tolerant; Roman Catholic, Roman. Antonyms: local, narrow.

cause, n. origin, source; motive, incitement, incentive.

cause, v. occasion, induce, effect, originate.

caustic, adj. burning, virulent, cutting, satirical.

caution, n. wariness, forethought; advice, warning.

caution, v. forewarn, admonish, warn, advise.

cautious, adj. circumspect, prudent, wary.

cave, n. cavern, grotto, den, catacomb, crypt.

cavil, v. carp, criticize.

cavil, n. objection, criticism.

cease, v. discontinue, stop.

cede, v. surrender, grant.

celebrate, v. commemorate, observe.

celebration, n. commemoration, observance, solemnization.

celebrity, n. fame, renown.

cellar, n. basement.

censor, n. inspector, reviewer, critic; caviler.

censorious, adj. carping, captious, critical.

censurable, adj. reprehensible, blamable, reproachable.

censure, n. reprehension, blame, reprimand.

censure, v. reprove, rebuke, reprehend, chide.

center, n. middle, midst.

central, adj. middle, centric.

ceremonious, adj. formal, precise. Antonyms: informal, free and easy.

ceremony, n. rite, form, ceremonial, solemnity; formality.

certain, adj. sure, assured, confident, convinced, satisfied, undoubting; undeniable, irrefutable. Antonyms: indefinite, uncertain.

certainty, n. sureness, confidence, assurance, fact, truth.

certify, v. assure, attest, testify to, vouch for.

chafe, v. rub, gall, irritate; fret, fume, rage.

chagrin, n. mortification, abashment, vexation, confusion, discomposure.

chagrin, v. mortify, abash, vex, confuse, humiliate.

chain, v. fetter, restrain, shackle, enslave, trammel.

chair, n. seat; professorship.

chalice, n. grail.

challenge, v. defy, dare, brave.

challenge, n. defiance; objection.

champion, n. defender, vindicator, protector, paladin; winner, hero.

chance, n. fate, fortune, luck, fortuity, hap, casualty, accident; possibility.

change, n. variation, alteration, transition, mutation, conversion, innovation. Antonyms: contin-uation, stability, conservatism, permanence, monotony, continuance.

change, v. alter, transmute, shift, modulate, reverse, reform, vary. Antonyms: continue, persist.

changeable, adj. mutable, variable, inconstant, unstable, reversible.

changeless, adj. permanent, immutable, inexorable, invariable, undeviating, unvarying.

channel, n. water-course, canal, aqueduct, gutter, runway, conduit, duct.

chant, v. intone, recite.

chant, n. intonation, mantra, hymn.

chaos, n. confusion, disorder, melee.

chap, n. lad, youth, boy, stripling.

chapel, n. oratory, chantry, bethel.

chapter, n. branch.

character, n. personality, nature, individuality.

characteristic, n. trait, feature, attribute, idiosyncrasy.

characterize, v. distinguish.

charge, n. accusation, complaint, allegation, indictment, imputation, crimination.

charge, v. impose, load, encumber; exhort, enjoin, instruct; commit, entrust.

charitable, adj. benevolent, benign, beneficent, magnanimous; liberal, tolerant. Antonyms: uncharitable, intolerant.

charity, n. benevolence, good will, love, benignity, bounty, philanthropy, tolerance.

charlatan, n. pretender, quack, impostor, fraud, cheat.

charlatanic, adj. pretentious, empirical.

charlatanry, n. quackery, pretension, empiricism.

charm, n. spell, incantation, enchantment, amulet, talisman; glamour, attraction, illusion. Antonyms: disenchantment, repellence.

charmer, n. enchanter, magician, sorcerer; siren.

charming, adj. bewitching, **captivating**, enchanting, enrapturing, magical. Antonyms: charmless, repellent.

chart, n. map, plat.

chary, adj. frugal, careful, saving, cautious.

chase, v. track, hunt, pursue; scatter, expel, dispel.

chasm, n. abyss, gap.

chaste, adj. virtuous, pure, continent, inviolated, innocent; classic, pure. Antonym: unchaste.

chasten, v. discipline, correct, punish; refine, purify.

chastise, v. castigate, chasten, punish, whip.

chastisement, n. castigation.

chastening, n. punishment.

chastity, n. purity, virtue.

chat, n. confabulation, talk, conversation.

chat, v. gab, chatter, chew the fat, converse, gossip, yak, shoot the breeze.

cheap, adj. inexpensive, low-priced; inferior, mean, mediocre, of small value.

cheapen, v. depreciate; belittle, lower.

cheat, n. fraud, trick, finesse, imposition, imposture, swindle, humbug.

cheat, v. swindle, defraud, trick, hoax, hocus, beguile.

check, n. obstacle, restraint, curb, bridle, damper, barrier, repulse, delay.

check, v. restrain, impede, curb, bridle, checkmate.

checkers, n. draughts.

checking, adj. repressive, restraining, curbing.

checkmate, v. defeat, vanquish, conquer, baffle.

cheek, n. jowl; nerve, audacity.

cheeky, adj. audacious, bold, impudent, unabashed, nervy.

cheer, v. inspirit, elate, exhilarate, encourage, console, revive; applaud.

cheerful, adj. cheery, buoyant, sunny, vivacious, optimistic, sanguine, elated, jubilant.

cheerfulness, n. cheeriness, elation, exhilaration, light-heartedness, optimism.

cheering, n. applause, plaudit; ovation.

cheerless, adj. dismal, somber, dreary, gloomy, desolate, sad, hopeless, despairing.

cheery, adj. cheerful, pleasant, sunny, blithe, jovial.

chemise, n. shirt, smock, shift.

cherish, v. treasure.

chest, n. box, case, trunk, hutch, receptacle.

chest, n. thorax, breast.

chew, v. masticate, munch; crunch, champ.

chewing, n. mastication; rumination.

chic, adj. in good taste, neat.

chicanery, n. trickery.

chicken, n. fowl; hen; rooster; pullet; capon; scaredy-cat, coward.

chicken, adj. timid, fearful, cowardly, scared, frightened, apprehensive.

chide, v. admonish, censure, upbraid, scold.

chief, n. boss, head, leader, captain, commander, chieftain.

chief, adj. leading, supreme, main, head, principal, prime, major, foremost.

child, n. progeny, offspring, issue; infant, babe, baby, tot.

childbirth, n. parturition, lying-in, labor.

childhood, n. nonage, infancy, minority, pupilage.

childish, adj. juvenile, infantile, immature, babyish.

childishness, n. juvenility, immaturity.

children, n. offspring, progeny, issue, posterity.

chilly, adj. cool, chill, raw.

chimera, n. delusion, phantom.

chink, n. crack, cranny.

chipper, adj. lively, vivacious.

chivalrous, adj. gallant, knightly, valiant.

chivalry, n. knighthood, gallantry.

choice, n. selection, option, election, preference, volition. Antonyms: compulsion, indiscrimination.

choice, adj. select, rare, careful, sparing. Antonyms: indiscriminate, common.

choke, v. strangle, throttle, stifle, suppress.

choleric, adj. irritable, testy.

choose, v. select, elect, prefer, pick out.

chop, v. hack, mince, hash.

chosen, adj. selected.

Christmas, n. Noel, Yule, Yuletide.

chronic, adj. habitual, lingering, inveterate.

chronicle, n. record, account, diary, history.

chum, n. companion, intimate, associate, friend, pal, buddy.

church, n. temple, sanctuary, cathedral; chapel, bethel, tabernacle, chantry.

churchly, adj. ecclesiastical.

churl, n. rustic, hind, lout.

churlish, adj. boorish, rude.

cigar, n. stogie, cheroot.

cinch, n. tight grip.

cipher, n. zero, naught, nothing; nobody; device.

circle, n. ring; circumference, periphery; circuit; clique, set, class.

circuitous, adj. roundabout, devious, indirect.

circulate, v. disseminate, promulgate, diffuse.

circulation, n. dissemination, diffusion, propagation.

circumference, n. periphery, circumscription, girth.

cite, v. quote; specify, mention, name, refer to.

citizen, n. resident, inhabitant, native.

city, n. municipality, town, metropolis.

civil, adj. civic, political, municipal; courteous, obliging, polite. Antonym: uncivil.

civility, n. courtesy, politeness. Antonyms: incivility, discourtesy.

claim, v. demand, pretend.

claim, n. pretension, demand.

claimant, n. claimer, pretender.

clamor, n. uproar, racket.

clamorous, adj. noisy, uproarious, bawling.

clandestine, adj. hidden, stealthy, surreptitious.

clannish, adj. narrow, exclusive.

clap, v. applaud.

claptrap, n. nonsense, hogwash, rubbish, drivel, baloney.

clarity, n. clearness.

clash, v. collide, hurtle, crash together; contend, disagree; clatter.

clasp, v. grasp, grapple, clutch, seize; embrace, hug.

class, n. division, rank, category, order, group, grade; refinement, taste, elegance, style, flair, panache.

classification, n. grouping, disposition; taxonomy.

clause, n. article, stipulation, provision.

claw, n. talon.

claw, v. scratch, lacerate.

clean, adj. unsoiled, unsullied, immaculate, cleanly, neat; chaste, pure, virtuous.

clean, v. cleanse, scrub, purify, wash, scour.

cleanse, v. purify, deterge, wash, disinfect.

cleanser, n. abstergent, detergent, purifier.

cleansing, n. purification, purgation, lustration, expurgation.

clear, adj. transparent, diaphanous, lucid, crystal; plain, evident, obvious.

clear, v. clarify; explain, interpret, acquit, absolve, vindicate; disengage, disperse.

clearing, n. clarification, clearance, dispersion; interpretation, explanation, acquittal.

clearness, n. clarity, distinctness; transparency, lucidity, perspicuity, translucency. Antonyms: opacity, ambiguity, vagueness.

cleave, v. adhere, cling, be loyal; split, rive.

cleft, adj. split, divided.

clergy, n. ministers, the cloth, ecclesiastics, clergymen. Antonym: laity.

clergyman, n. minister, divine, ecclesiastic, priest, pastor, parson, preacher, rector. Antonym: layman.

clerk, n. salesperson, recorder, registrar, bookkeeper.

clever, adj. adroit, skillful, expert, ingenious, deft.

cliff, n. crag, bluff.

climax, n. culmination.

climb, v. clamber, scale.

climbing, adj. ascendant.

cling, v. adhere, cleave, hold fast.

clip, v. shear, snip, cut, shear, trim, prune, curtail.

clique, n. coterie, circle.

cloak, n. mantle, coat, dolman, pelisse; pretext, blind, mask.

cloak, v. conceal, mask, hide.

clock, n. timepiece, timekeeper, horometer.

clodhopper, n. bumpkin, boor, clown.

clog, v. impede, hamper, encumber, restrain.

cloister, n. monastery, nunnery.
close, adj. oppressive, uncomfortable, muggy, unventilated; narrow, cramped; secretive, reserved.
close, v. shut, stop, occlude; conclude, finish, end, terminate.
close, n. conclusion, end; peroration; grapple; court, area, enclosure, yard.
close-mouthed, adj. wary, secretive, reserved.
closeness, n. nearness, proximity, adjacency; density; intimacy.
closing, adj. concluding, final.
closing, n. stopping up, obstruction, blockade.
clot, n. coagulation.
cloth, n. fabric, material, drapery, textile, texture.
clothe, v. dress, attire.
clothes, n. garments, vesture, attire, drapery, costume, garb.
cloud, v. overcast, becloud, obscure, shade, tarnish.
cloudy, adj. overcast, lowering, murky, obscure, sullen, hazy, dim, blurred.
clover, n. trefoil.
clown, n. jester, merry-andrew, zany, harlequin, droll, punch, mime.
clownish, adj. boorish, ungainly, awkward, churlish.
cloy, v. satiate, glut, pall.
club, n. cudgel, truncheon, bat, mace, staff, bandy; society, association.
club, v. cudgel, beat, pommel.
clue, n. intimation, hint.
clump, n. cluster, tuft, bunch, thicket.

clumsy, adj. ungraceful, lumbering, unhandy, inapt.
cluster, n. bunch, clump, tuft; raceme, panicle; bevy, crowd.
clutch, v. seize, grasp, grip, clench, grab, snatch.
clutch, n. grasp, seizure.
clutter, n. litter, disorder.
cluttered, adj. disordered, littered, jumbled.
coach, n. stage; trainer.
coal-miner, n. collier.
coarse, adj. crass, gross, unrefined, rude, unpolished, indelicate, homespun, vulgar.
coast, n. seashore, seaboard, shore, strand, beach.
coat, n. sack, jacket, frock, cutaway, ulster.
coat of arms, n. armorial bearings, arms, crest.
coating, n. layer, veneer, glaze.
coax, v. wheedle, cajole, entice.
cock, n. rooster, chanticleer; weather-cock, vane; chief, leader; faucet.
cocky, adj. pert, saucy.
coddle, v. parboil; pamper, fondle, humor, indulge.
coerce, v. constrain, compel.
coercion, n. compulsion, restraint, force, constraint.
coffeehouse, n. cafe.
cog, n. cam, catch; trick.
cogent, adj. convincing, conclusive, forcible.
coherent, n. consistent.
coin, n. specie, cash; medallion.
coin, v. mint; invent, create, lay claim to.
coinage, n. minting; fabrication, invention.

coincide, v. concur, correspond, agree, tally.

coincidence, n. concurrence, agreement.

coincident, adj. concurrent, contemporaneous.

coiner, n. minter; neologist.

cold, adj. cool, chilly; frigid, gelid, icy; nipping, bleak, raw.

cold, n. coldness, frigidity, chilliness, algidity.

cold-blooded, adj. deliberate, cruel, callous, merciless, unfeeling.

collar, n. neckband, ruff.

collar, v. nab, arrest, capture

collect, v. assemble, accumulate.

collection, n. assemblage, accumulation, aggregation, heap; offering, offertory; anthology.

collision, n. clashing, concussion, interference.

colloquial, adj. conversational, familiar, informal.

colony, n. settlement, dependency.

color, n. hue, shade, tinge, tincture, tint; pigment, paint, dye, stain.

color, n. ruddiness, redness, flush, blush, rosiness; semblance, pretext; variety.

color, v. dye, tinge, stain, imbue, tint, tincture; falsify, pervert.

colorable, adj. specious, plausible, palliated.

colored, adj. tinged, dyed, tinted, stained, discolored.

coloring, n. dyeing, staining, tinting.

colorless, adj. uncolored, faded; pale, pallid; neutral.

colossal, adj. enormous, gigantic, huge, prodigious.

coltish, adj. frisky, sportive, wanton, playful.

column, n. pillar, post, shaft; file, line, row.

comb, n. crest, caruncle.

combat, n. contest, bout, struggle, contention, fight.

combatant, n. contestant, fighter.

combative, adj. pugnacious, contentious, bellicose.

combination, n. union, alliance, federation, confederacy, syndicate, league, merger.

combine, v. unite, incorporate, merge, blend.

combine, n. combination.

combined, adj. united, confederated, federated.

come, v. arrive, approach; come from, issue, proceed, ensue, flow, originate.

come after, v. follow, succeed. Antonyms: precede, antecede.

come again, v. return, recur.

come and go, v. alternate.

come between, v. intervene, interpose, interfere; cause estrangement, disaffect.

come down, v. descend, alight.

comely, adj. good-looking, handsome. Antonyms: plain, homely.

come to, v. revive, recover, awaken; consent, yield, accede; arrive at, reach; amount to.

come to a head, v. mature; culminate.

comfort, v. console, solace.

comfortable, adj. cozy, relaxed, at ease, comfy, snug; well-off, affluent.

comfortless, adj. disconsolate,

desolate, distressed.

comical, adj. funny, humorous.

coming, n. approach, arrival.

comity, n. politeness, courtesy, civility.

command, v. order, direct.

command, n. order, mandate, charge, injunction, requisition, direction; authority.

commanding, adj. authoritative, mandatory, imperative.

commence, v. begin.

commend, v. commit, consign, entrust; praise, recommend.

commendable, adj. praiseworthy.

commendatory, adj. laudatory.

comment, v. remark, descant.

comment, n. remark, observation; commentary.

commentator, n. critic, observer, analyst, reviewer.

commerce, n. traffic, barter, business, trading; course.

commercial, adj. mercantile.

commit, v. entrust, consign; perpetrate, do.

common, adj. public, general; customary, usual, ordinary, commonplace, inconspicuous.

commonalty, n. populace, proletariat, rank and file.

commonly, adv. ordinarily.

common man, n. commoner, proletarian, plebeian.

commonplace, adj. ordinary, banal, trite, prosaic.

commotion, n. agitation, tumult, turmoil, riot.

communion, n. participation, sharing, fellowship.

compact, adj. close, solid, dense, crowded, impenetrable.

compact, n. covenant, pact, agreement, treaty.

companion, n. associate, comrade, intimate, consort, partner, fellow, mate, chum.

companionable, adj. affable.

companionship, n. association, intimacy, fellowship, society.

company, n. guest, visitor; fellowship, companionship, association, society. Antonyms: seclusion, loneliness, host.

compare, v. collate, liken.

comparison, n. collation; illustration, simile.

compass, n. extent, reach.

compassion, n. pity, sympathy, commiseration, mercy.

compel, v. force, make, drive, oblige, overpower, coerce.

compelling, adj. forcible, coercive, imperative. Antonyms: elective, optional.

compendium, n. epitome, compilation, anthology.

competency, n. fitness, ability, efficiency, proficiency, capability.

competent, adj. qualified, capable, efficient, proficient. Antonym: incompetent.

competition, n. emulation, rivalry, contention, strife.

competitor, n. rival, contestant, opponent.

complain, v. murmur, repine, grumble, croak.

complaining, adj. murmuring, repining, discontented.

complaint, n. murmur, lamentation; ailment, disease; allegation, information.

complete, v. finish, perfect.

complete, adj. entire, whole, integral, unabridged, intact.

completion, n. consummation, integration, elaboration, finishing, realization.

complex, adj. composite, compound, mixed; complicated, intricate. Antonyms: simple, straightforward.

complexity, n. intricacy, entanglement, complication.

compliance, n. yielding, obedience, submission.

compliant, adj. yielding, obedient, tractable.

complicated, adj. complex, intricate, involved.

complication, n. intricacy, entanglement, involution, snarl, Antonym: disentanglement.

composure, n. self-possession, calmness, sedateness.

compound, n. combination, mixture, concoction, intermixture, conglomeration, medley.

comprehend, v. understand, fathom, grasp; embrace, contain.

comprehension, n. understanding. Antonym: incomprehension.

comprise, v. comprehend, include, embrace, involve.

compulsion, n. constraint, coercion, obligation. Antonyms: discretion, volition, election.

compulsory, adj. constraining, coercive, obligatory. Antonyms: optional, elective.

compunction, n. qualm, contrition, remorse, regret.

compute, v. reckon, calculate, rate, estimate.

comrade, n. associate, companion, mate.

comradeship, n. association, friendship.

concave, adj. curved in, bowl-shaped, hollow, dished. Antonym: convex.

concealed, adj. hidden, latent, secreted, disguised.

concealment, n. secretion, hiding; secrecy, privacy, seclusion; suppression.

conceit, n. idea, conception, fancy; whim, caprice, freak; vanity, egotism.

conceited, adj. egotistical, vain, bumptious, self-conceited.

concept, n. conception, notion, idea.

conception, n. imagination; idea, concept, notion.

concern, n. business, affair; moment, importance, interest, weight; solicitude, anxiety.

concerned, adj. solicitous, worried, anxious, troubled. Antonyms: unconcerned, indifferent.

concerning, prep. regarding, about, respecting, touching.

concert, n. accordance, harmony, musicale.

concise, adj. epigrammatic, succinct, pithy. Antonym: diffuse.

conclude, v. decide, determine, resolve; close; infer; effect.

conclusion, n. decision, determination; inference, deduction, illation; close, end, finale.

concoct, v. compound, mix; devise, contrive, invent.

concrete, adj. solidified; specific,

special.

condemn, v. denounce, curse, execrate, reprobate, doom, ban. Antonyms: exonerate, vindicate, absolve, justify.

condemnation, n. denunciation, execration, ban.

condemnatory, adj. denunciatory.

condense, v. abridge, epitomize; reduce; compress.

condescend, v. deign, patronize.

condition, n. state, plight, category, predicament, situation; stipulation, term.

conditional, adj. contingent, subject, provisory.

conduct, v. lead, pilot, escort, guide, attend, convey.

conduct, n. guidance, management, leadership, administration; behavior.

confederate, adj. confederated, federated, allied, leagued.

confederation, n. coalition, federation, league, union.

confess, v. acknowledge, own, admit, avow; divulge, reveal.

confession, n. acknowledgment, admission; shrift.

confidence, n. reliance, trust, faith; certainty. Antonym: doubt.

confident, adj. sure, reliant, undoubting, undaunted.

confine, n. boundary, border.

confine, v. restrain, limit, restrict, circumscribe, enclose, bound; immure.

confinement, n. restraint, imprisonment, durance, duress, incarceration, limbo.

confines, n. borders, precincts, outskirts.

confirm, v. ratify, verify, corroborate. Antonym: abrogate.

confirmation, n. ratification, substantiation.

conflict, n. clashing, encounter.

conflict, v. clash, interfere, collide, be contradictory.

conflicting, adj. contending, contrary, opposing.

confound, v. confuse, disconcert, abash, nonplus.

confounded, adj. confused, disconcerted, abashed.

confuse, v. disconcert, perplex, abash, fluster, embarrass, chagrin, pose, bewilder.

confusion, n. disorder, turmoil, disarray, jumble, chaos; babel, pandemonium, commotion.

confute, v. refute, disprove.

congenial, adj. kindred; suited, suitable, agreeable, genial.

congratulate, v. felicitate, applaud, commend.

congratulations, n. felicitations, salutations, compliments.

conjecture, n. surmise, supposition.

conjecture, v. surmise, guess, speculate.

conjuration, n. incantation, enchantment, spell, sorcery.

conjurer, n. sorcerer, wizard, diviner.

connect, v. join, link, couple, attach, unite.

connected, adj. joined, coupled, linked, affiliated, related.

connection, n. union, alliance, relationship, junction, affiliation, association. Antonyms: disconnection, isolation, incoherence.

conquer, v. defeat, overpower, down, vanquish, triumph, conqueror, subdue, overthrow.

conqueror, n. subjugator, victor.

conquest, n. subjection, victory, mastery, triumph, reduction, overthrow.

conscientious, adj. scrupulous, just, upright, high-minded.

conscionable, adj. reasonable.

conscious, adj. cognizant, aware, sensible; sentient, knowing.

consecrate, v. dedicate, hallow.

consent, v. agree, accord, concur, yield, assent, comply, permit. Antonyms: dissent, disagree.

consent, n. concurrence, compliance, approval.

consequence, n. result, effect, issue, event, sequel, outcome, upshot; pursuance.

conservation, n. preservation, keeping.

conserve, v. save, preserve.

consider, v. meditate on, ponder, contemplate; regard.

considerate, adj. thoughtful, heedful.

consideration, n. deliberation, advisement, contemplation; motive.

console, v. comfort, cheer, solace.

consolidate, v. solidify, compress; unify, merge.

consolidation, n. unification, union, combination.

conspicuous, adj. salient, noticeable, prominent.

conspiracy, n. plot, intrigue, collusion, scheme.

conspire, v. plot, connive.

constancy, n. steadfastness, stability, resolution, loyalty, fidelity.

constant, adj. permanent, unchanging; unwavering, unshaken, steadfast, loyal, faithful. Antonym: inconstant.

consternation, n. dismay, terror, alarm, panic.

constitution, n. structure, physique, temperament.

constitutional, adj. inborn, innate, organic, inbred.

constrained, adj. involuntary, forced, unnatural.

constraint, n. compulsion, force, pressure, restraint.

consultation, n. conference, council, advisement.

consummate, adj. perfect, supreme, complete.

consummation, n. fulfillment, perfection, realization.

contact, n. touching, tangency, impact, contiguity.

contagious, adj. communicable, infectious. Antonym: incommunicable.

contain, v. comprise, embody, include, hold, restrain.

container, n. receptacle, bin, box.

contaminate, v. corrupt, pollute, defile, infect, taint, vitiate, debase.

contamination, n. corruption, pollution, defilement, taint.

contemporaneous, adj. contemporary, synchronal.

contemporary, adj. modern, up-to-date, fashionable.

contempt, n. disdain, scorn, derision, detestation.

contemptible, adj. despicable, abject.

contemptuous, adj. disdainful, scornful, insolent, cynical.

contend, v. struggle, wrestle, combat, dispute, argue.

content, v. satisfy, gratify.

contented, adj. content, satisfied.

contention, n. controversy, dissension, quarrel.

contentious, adj. litigious, quarrelsome; dissentious.

contest, n. rivalry, match, tourney, competition; dispute, controversy, dissension.

continual, adj. ceaseless, incessant, constant.

continuance, n. endurance, persistence, constancy.

continuation, n. protraction, continuance, perpetuation.

continued, adj. prolonged, extended; serial.

continuous, adj. ceaseless, uninterrupted, unceasing, continual, constant. Antonyms: intermittent, occasional.

contraband, adj. prohibited, forbidden, unlawful.

contract, v. reduce, narrow; incur, acquire; agree; shrivel, shrink; syncopate.

contract, n. agreement, compact, pact, treaty, convention, stipulation.

contracting, adj. astringent.

contradict, v. gainsay, controvert, dispute.

contradiction, n. gainsaying, opposition, antagonism.

contradictory, adj. inconsistent, irreconcilable, opposing, contradicting.

contrary, adj. opposite, adverse, counter, opposed; repugnant, incompatible, contradictory, retroactive.

contrast, n. comparison; opposition, unlikeness.

contravene, v. thwart, oppose, counteract, transgress.

contravention, n. opposition, counteraction, violation.

contrite, adj. penitent, repentant. Antonym: impenitent.

contrition, n. penitence, remorse, self-reproach.

contrivance, n. contriving, devising; device, scheme.

contrive, v. devise, concoct, invent, scheme, plan.

control, v. restrain, regulate, govern, manage, repress, direct, bridle.

control, n. restraint, repression, hindrance; domination, regulation, governance. Antonyms: unrestraint, abandon.

controller, n. governor, regulator, ruler.

controversial, adj. disputatious, provocative, debatable, contentious.

controversy, n. dispute, contention, disputation.

convene, v. assemble, convoke, gather.

convenient, adj. handy, advantageous; seasonable, timely, suitable.

convent, n. nunnery, monastery, cloister, abbey.

convention, n. custom, usage; assembly congress, diet.

conversation, n. colloquy, parley, chat, conference, interview.

conversational, adj. colloquial.

converse, v. talk, chat, commune, parley, gab, chew the fat.

conversion, n. transmutation, transformation; regeneration; appropriation, application.

convert, v. transform; regenerate; appropriate.

convex, adj. protuberant, bulging, Antonym: concave.

convexity, n. protuberance. Antonym: concavity.

conveyance, n. carriage, transmission; transfer.

convict, n. felon, prisoner, criminal, culprit.

convincing, adj. persuasive.

convivial, adj. festive, social.

convocation, n. convention, congress, diet, council.

convoy, n. protection, escort; guard, escort.

convulsion, n. spasm, paroxysm; agitation, upheaval.

cook, n. chef.

cooking, n. cuisine.

cool, v. chill, refrigerate.

cool, adj. deliberate, self-possessed, unexcited, dispassionate, indifferent, nonchalant, unconcerned, composed.

cooler, n. refrigerator.

coolness, n. dispassion, nonchalance.

coop, n. pen, cote, mew, hutch.

coop, v. confine, shut up, imprison, encage.

cooperate, v. concur, unite, work together.

cooperating, adj. cooperative, auxiliary.

cooperation, n. concurrence, working together; collusion; synergy. Antonym: antagonism.

copier, n. copyist, transcriber; imitator. Antonym: originator.

copious, adj. plentiful, abundant, overflowing, ample.

copse, n. thicket, brushwood.

copy, n. transcript, reproduction, transcription, replica, facsimile, duplicate, counterpart.

copy, v. transcribe, reproduce, trace, duplicate; imitate, follow.

copyist, n. transcriber, copier; imitator.

coquette, n. flirt.

cord, n. string, twine.

cordial, adj. hearty, sincere, affectionate; invigorating.

cordiality, n. sincerity, heartiness, ardor.

cork, n. stopper, stopple.

corn, n. maize; callus.

corner, n. angle, crook, bend, cusp, bight, coin, nook, recess, niche.

corner, v. trap, surround.

corporal, adj. bodily, material.

correct, adj. accurate, right, exact, precise. Antonym: wrong.

correct, v. rectify, amend, emend, right; reprove, modify.

correctible, adj. rectifiable.

correction, n. rectification, amendment.

corrective, adj. rectifying, reformatory.

correctness, n. accuracy, exactness, precision.

correspond, v. accord, comport, tally, correlate.

correspondence, n. adaptation, agreement, congruity, homology.

corrode, v. erode, canker; consume, wear away.

corrosion, n. erosion.

corrosive, adj. erosive, eroding, corroding; vexing.

corrupt, adj. spoiled, tainted, addled, rotten, decaying; depraved, dissolute.

corrupt, v. rot, spoil, deprave, pervert, debase, demoralize, defile, infect.

corruption, n. putrefaction, decay; pollution; improbity, depravity, dishonesty, bribery.

cortege, n. procession.

cost, n. charge, expense, price, outlay; detriment.

costly, adj. expensive, dear, high-priced.

coterie, n. clique, set.

cottage, n. cabin, lodge, bungalow, chalet, croft, shack, shanty.

couch, n. lounge, sofa, settee, divan.

council, n. cabinet; assembly.

counsel, n. consultation; prudence, deliberation, forethought; advice, admonition.

counsel, v. advise, admonish.

counselor, n. adviser, mentor, monitor, lawyer, attorney.

count, v. enumerate, number; esteem, consider, reckon.

count, n. numbering, total.

countenance, n. face, visage, features; support, good will.

counter, adj. contrary, opposite.

counteract, v. defeat, frustrate, neutralize.

counteraction, n. frustration, contravention.

counterbalance, v. counterpoise, countervail, balance.

counterfeit, adj. false, fraudulent, fictitious, sham.

countermand, v. revoke, cancel, recall.

counterpoint, n. polyphony.

count out, v. exclude.

countrified, adj. rustic, rural.

country, n. region, territory; nation; rural parts, farming region.

countryman, n. compatriot, fellow-citizen; farmer, granger, husbandman, rustic.

county, n. shire.

couple, n. two, pair, brace, span, team.

couple, v. join, link, connect.

courage, n. intrepidity, heroism, bravery, gallantry, hardihood, fortitude, valor. Antonyms: cowardice, fear.

courageous, adj. intrepid, brave, heroic, gallant, hardy, bold, fearless, valiant.

courier, n. messenger, runner.

course, n. progress, passage; direction, bearing; bout; procedure; sequence.

court, n. tribunal, judicatory, judicature, judiciary, forum, mall; courtyard, cortile.

court, v. woo, spark; solicit, seek, allure, invite.

courteous, adj. deferential, polite, debonair, gracious, urbane, civil, respectful.

courtesy, n. politeness, urbanity, civility, favor.

courtly, adj. elegant, polite.

cove, n. bay, recess, inlet.

covenant, n. compact, agreement, pact.

cover, v. overspread, overlay, thatch, hide, conceal, comprise, embrace, embody.

cover, n. lid, covering, case, canopy, awning, tilt, roof, casing.

covered, adj. covert, screened, protected, hidden.

covering, n. cover, sheath.

covert, adj. secret, hidden, disguised, stealthy.

cow, v. overawe, daunt, scare.

coward, n. craven, poltroon.

cowardice, n. pusillanimity, timidity.

cowardly, adj. craven, dastardly, recreant, timorous.

cowboy, n. cattle herder, drover, herdsman.

cower, v. crouch, squat.

cowlike, adj. bovine.

coworker, n. colleague, collaborator, associate.

coxcomb, n. fop, dandy, dude.

coy, adj. shy, modest, retiring.

cozy, adj. snug; talkative.

crack, n. chink, crevice, cranny, rift, rent, cleft; rupture, flaw.

crack, v. break, chop, split.

craft, n. dexterity, skill; trade; guild; cunning.

craftiness, n. artfulness, craft, cunning.

craftsman, n. artificer, mechanic, skilled workman.

crafty, adj. shrewd, artful, wily, tricky, cunning, sly, deceitful. Antonyms: guileless, artless.

cragged, adj. jagged, broken.

cram, v. compress, crowd, press, squeeze.

cramp, v. restrain, confine, hinder, restrict, obstruct.

cranium, n. skull.

crank, n. winch, turning-handle; bend, turn, twist.

cranky, adj. crotchety, capricious, unreasonable, cross, perverse, unsteady.

cranny, n. crevice, chink.

crash, n. ruin, smash, failure.

crass, adj. coarse, unrefined.

crave, v. long for, yearn for, hanker after; beseech, entreat.

craven, adj. cowardly.

craving, n. longing, yearning, hankering, hungering; entreaty.

crawler, n. creeper, reptile.

craze, v. madden, distract.

cream, n. best part, elite, finest, best.

crease, n. ruck, wrinkle.

creation, n. origination, making, invention.

creative, adj. imaginative, original, inventive, artistic.

creature, n. being, beast, individual.

credence, n. belief, credit.

credit, n. belief, faith, confidence; esteem, honor; prestige; trust. Antonyms: discredit, unbelief.

credulous, adj. unsuspecting, gullible.

creek, n. brook, streamlet, waterway.

creep, v. sneak, slink, steal, slither.

crest, n. tuft; helmet; top, ridge, crown; device.

crestfallen, adj. dejected, discouraged, downcast.

crevice, n. cleft, rent, cranny, crack.

crew, n. assemblage, gang, mob, band, crowd.

crib, n. manger, rack; bin, bunker, box.

crime, n. felony, outrage, enormity; offense, misdemeanor, dereliction, malefaction.

criminal, adj. felonious.

criminal, n. felon, culprit.

crimp, v. curl, crisp, frizz.

cringe, v. truckle, fawn, crouch.

cringing, adj. truckling, servile, slavish, fawning.

crinkle, v. curl, wrinkle.

crinkly, adj. wavy, wrinkly.

crisis, n. critical juncture; emergency, strait.

crisp, adj. brittle, friable, short; crackling, lively.

critic, n. censor, reviewer, judge, inspector; carper.

critical, adj. discriminating; carping, censorious, captious, caviling; crucial, decisive.

criticism, n. critique, censure, stricture, cavil.

croak, v. forebode, decry.

croaker, n. grumbler, alarmist, pessimist.

crock, n. jar, pot.

crony, n. bosom friend, intimate, chum, best pal.

crook, n. bend, turn, curve, curvature; crosier; artifice, trick, subterfuge.

crook, v. bend, curve.

crooked, adj. twisted, bent, devious, deformed, tortuous, winding, flexuous, curved.

crookedness, n. tortuousness, sinuosity, curvature, deformity, wryness.

crop, n. harvest, fruit, product.

crop, v. clip, lop, cut off; gather, reap, harvest; browse.

cross, n. crucifix, rood.

cross, n. hybrid, mongrel.

cross, adj. athwart, transverse, intersecting; adverse, contrary; petulant, cynical.

cross, v. intersect; traverse; run counter to, thwart, frustrate, foil.

crossbeam, n. girder, stringer.

crosscut, v. intersect.

cross-examination, n. inquisition.

crossing, n. hybridization.

crossing, n. intersection, cancellation; traversing; junction; crosswalk; frustration, interference.

crossness, n. petulance, cynicism, crankiness, irritability, ill-nature.

crosswise, adv. across, transversely.

crotchet, n. whim, fancy, caprice.

crotchety, adj. irritable, grumpy, difficult, crusty, touchy, bad-tempered.

crouch, v. squat, couch, stoop; cringe, fawn.

crowd, n. concourse, crush, multitude, number, mass, horde, host, troop.

crowded, adj. congested, dense, compact, mobbed.

crowding, n. congestion.

crown, n. diadem, coronet, corona; tiara; wreath, garland, laurel; royalty.

crowning, n. coronation.

crucial, adj. vital, key, necessary, critical. Antonym: trivial.

crude, adj. undeveloped, uncouth, inartistic.

cruel, adj. pitiless, merciless, inhuman, unmerciful, relentless, ruthless, brutal.

cruelty, n. inhumanity, implacability, severity.

crumble, v. disintegrate, decay.

crumbly, adj. friable.

crumple, v. rumple, wrinkle, crush together.

crush, v. overpower, vanquish, quell, subdue, conquer, suppress; squeeze, press.

crush, n. compression; pressure, crowd.

crushing, adj. overwhelming.

crusty, adj. cross, irritable, touchy, cranky, surly; crispy, brittle.

crux, n. root, bottom, heart, core, nitty-gritty.

cry, v. weep, sob, wail, bawl, squall, whimper, blubber, bewail; shout, yell.

cry, n. exclamation, acclamation, outcry, clamor, scream, shriek, howl, yell.

cryptic, adj. hidden, secret, occult.

cuddle, v. nestle, snuggle.

cudgel, n. club, bludgeon.

cue, n. catchword; hint, suggestion.

cuff, n. box, slap, buffet.

cuff, v. box, slap, smite, strike.

cull, n. cully, dupe, gull.

culprit, n. offender, delinquent, criminal, sinner.

cultivate, v. till.

culture, n. cultivation, tillage; refinement, education.

cultured, adj. refined, educated.

cumbersome, adj. burdensome, troublesome, unwieldy.

cunning, adj. artful, crafty, sly, wily, arch, designing, deceitful; curious; skillful.

cunning, n. craft, deceit, craftiness, subtlety, wiliness.

cup, n. mug, beaker, tankard.

cupboard, n. locker, buffet, pantry.

cupidity, n. covetousness, greed, avarice.

cupola, n. dome.

curative, adj. remedial.

curator, n. custodian, keeper, trustee.

curb, v. check, restrain, control.

curdle, v. coagulate, thicken.

curdled, adj. coagulated, thickened.

cure, n. spiritual charge, curacy; medical treatment, therapy; antidote, remedy.

cure, v. heal, remedy.

cure-all, n. panacea.

curiosity, n. inquisitiveness; freak, rarity.

curious, adj. inquisitive; strange, rare, unusual.

curl, n. ringlet, kink.

curl, v. crisp, crimp; writhe, wreathe, twist, wind.

current, adj. present, instant; circulating.

curse, n. denunciation, anathema, ban, execration, imprecation, fulmination.

curse, v. execrate, fulminate, condemn.

cursed, adj. accursed, abominable.

curtail, v. shorten, reduce.

curtain, n. hanging, drapery, valance.

curvature, n. curve, flexure, sinuosity.

curve, v. bend, crook, turn, inflect, deviate, wind.

cushion, n. pad, bolster, pillow; pouf.

custodian, n. curator, guardian, keeper.

custody, n. safe-keeping, care; imprisonment.

custom, n. usage, practice; patronage; impost, duty.

customary, adj. usual, wonted, habitual, conventional.

customer, n. patron.

cut, v. gash, slash, hew, crop, reap, mow, lop, prune, clip.

cut, n. incision, gash, slash, slit, wound; slight; sarcasm; notch.

cut down, v. fell; retrench, curtail, reduce.

cute, adj. attractive, cunning.

cut off, v. interrupt, stop.

cut out, v. exscind, excise, remove; supplant; exclude.

cutting, adj. incisive, sharp, keen; penetrating, biting; sarcastic, caustic.

cutting, n. incision, felling, cleavage, curtailment, dissection, slashing.

cut up, v. play pranks, play tricks, cut capers, misbehave.

D

dabble, v. experiment, play at.

dagger, n. stiletto, dirk.

daily, adj. diurnal, quotidian.

dainty, adj. fastidious, squeamish, finical; delicate.

dale, n. glen, dell, dingle.

dalliance, n. delay, procrastination.

dally, v. dawdle, trifle; delay.

dam, n. barrier, weir.

dam, v. restrain, obstruct.

damage, v. injure, hurt, harm, scathe, deface, impair.

damage, n. injury, detriment, impairment, harm, hurt.

damn, v. condemn, curse, reprobate, denounce.

damnable, adj. accursed, atrocious, execrable.

damnation, n. condemnation, reprobation, perdition.

damning, adj. condemnatory, damnatory.

damp, adj. moist, wet, humid.

dampen, v. moisten, damp; check, repress, restrain.

damper, n. check, setback, wet blanket, discouragement.

dampness, n. moisture, humidity.

dance, n. ballet, cotillion, waltz, reel, fandango, polka, two-step, minuet.

dandified, adj. foppish.

dandy, adj. fine, great, good.

dandy, n. fop, dude. Antonym: sloven.

danger, n. jeopardy, hazard, peril, insecurity, risk, exposure. Antonyms: safety, immunity, security, shelter, protection.

dangerous, adj. perilous, hazardous, risky, unsafe, critical, imminent. Antonym: safe.

dapper, adj. spruce, trim, spry.
dappled, adj. spotted, mottled.
dare, v. venture, presume; defy, challenge.
daredevil, adj. reckless, rash, inconsiderate.
dark, adj. sunless, dusky, murky, dingy, shadowy; brunette.
darken, v. shade, obscure, shadow, becloud; perplex, confuse; tarnish, discolor.
darkness, n. obscurity, shadow, dimness, gloom, nighttime.
dart, v. hurl, launch; spring, dodge, bolt.
dash, v. hurry, rush, run, sprint, scurry, dart; smash, shatter, hurl, fling.
dashing, adj. spirited, bold, brilliant, suave, urbane.
dastard, n. coward, craven.
daub, v. smear, besmear, soil.
daunt, v. cow, intimidate, frighten, alarm.
dauntless, adj. intrepid, daring, fearless.
dawn, n. daybreak, sunrise, morning.
daydream, n. reverie, fantasy, fancy.
dazzle, v. daze, blind; bewilder, awe, astonish.
dazzling, adj. brilliant, intense, glaring, awesome.
dead, adj. lifeless, inanimate, defunct, extinct; inert, obtuse, impassive; numb.
deaden, v. blunt, benumb, hebetate, moderate; devitalize, subdue.
deadly, adj. fatal, mortal, lethal.
deal, v. distribute, apportion, dispense, allot; trade, traffic.
dealer, n. trader, dispenser, retailer, shopkeeper, merchant, vendor, tradesman.
dealing, n. distribution, apportionment; traffic, barter, business.
dear, adj. costly, expensive, high-priced; beloved, darling. Antonyms: cheap, inexpensive.
dearth, n. scarcity, lack, deficiency, paucity, want. Antonym: plenty.
death, n. decease, demise, dissolution, dying, mortality, expiration, mort.
debar, v. preclude, exclude.
debase, v. degrade, deteriorate, abase, corrupt, alloy, humiliate.
debasement, n. degradation, abasement, deterioration.
debatable, adj. contestable, disputable. Antonyms: incontestable, indisputable.
debate, v. argue, discuss, contend, controvert.
debate, n. discussion, argument, dispute, controversy, forensic.
debauch, v. vitiate, deprave, corrupt.
debauchery, n. abandon, drunkenness, lechery. Antonyms: temperance, moderation.
debauched, adj. dissolute, dissipated, corrupt.
debauchee, n. libertine, lecher, rake, drunkard.
debauchery, n. lechery, libertinism, sensuality.
debonair, adj. suave, courteous, urbane, gracious.
debt, n. liability, due, obligation, debit. Antonym: asset.

decadent, adj. deteriorating.

decay, v. decline, retrograde; rot, decompose, putrefy.

deceit, n. deception, imposition, trickery, artifice, delusion, guile, duplicity.

deceive, v. delude, beguile, mislead, gull, impose upon, circumvent.

decency, n. propriety, seemliness, decorum.

decent, adj. suitable, modest, seemly.

deception, n. imposition, craft, duplicity, deceit, fallacy, ruse, imposture. Antonyms: guilelessness, candor, disillusionment, fair dealing.

deceptive, adj. delusive, deceitful, specious, sophistical. Antonyms: guileless, candid, sincere, open.

decide, v. determine, settle, conclude, resolve.

decided, adj. unequivocal, determined, pronounced, unwavering, positive.

decision, n. determination, settlement, conclusion, verdict, inference; firmness, resolution, constancy. Antonyms: indecision, irresolution.

decisive, adj. conclusive, final, summary.

deck, v. bedeck, array.

declaration, n. assertion, affirmation, predication.

declare, v. affirm, assert, state, predicate.

decline, v. lean, incline, bend; languish, sink, diminish, decrease; deviate.

decline, n. deterioration, diminution, degeneracy, declination, decay. Antonyms: progress, advancement.

decorate, v. embellish, adorn, beautify, ornament, garnish, trim, bedeck.

decorated, adj. embellished, ornate, trimmed. Antonym: plain.

decorative, adj. ornamental, embellished.

decoy, v. entice, lure, allure, entrap.

decrease, n. decrement, diminution, reduction, decline, abatement.

decrease, v. diminish, reduce, dwindle, subside, abate.

decree, n. edict, fiat, mandate,

decree, v. enact, ordain, enjoin.

decrial, n. condemnation, disparagement, detraction, belittling.

decry, v. disparage, belittle.

dedicate, v. consecrate.

dedication, n. consecration.

deduct, v. subtract, rebate.

deduction, n. subtraction, discount; inference, conclusion, illation.

deed, n. exploit, act, feat, perpetration, performance.

deep, adj. profound, intricate, inexplicable, unfathomable, recondite, abstruse; sagacious, cunning. Antonyms: superficial, shallow.

deepen, v. intensify.

deer, n. buck, doe, roe, stag.

deface, v. mar, disfigure.

defacement, n. disfigurement, marring.

defamation, n. calumny, libel, lampoon.

defamatory, adj. slanderous, libelous, vituperative.

defame, v. calumniate, malign, vilify, lampoon, slander.

defeat, n. repulse, overthrow, foil, rout, frustration.

defeat, v. conquer, vanquish, repulse, discomfit, checkmate, outwit, balk, frustrate.

defect, n. blemish, flaw, imperfection, failing, shortcoming, infirmity.

defend, v. guard, protect, shield, secure, screen, shelter, fortify, preserve.

defender, n. defendant, vindicator, advocate, champion, upholder, guardian.

defense, n. protection, defending, maintenance, protection, bulwark, fortification, shield. Antonyms: betrayal, exposure, surrender.

defiance, n. challenge, provocation; opposition, contempt, mutiny, rebellion.

defiant, adj. disobedient, rebellious, refractory, mutinous. Antonyms: obedient, submissive.

deficiency, n. inadequacy, insufficiency, shortage.

deficient, adj. defective, imperfect, scanty, inadequate.

defile, v. contaminate, pollute, soil, vitiate, taint, corrupt, sully.

definite, adj. positive, specific, explicit, specified, precise. Antonym: indefinite.

deformed, adj. misshapen, disfigured.

deformity, n. malformation, disfigurement, distortion.

defraud, v. cheat, deceive, swindle, con.

deft, adj. dexterous, expert, skillful, clever.

defy, v. challenge, dare; spurn, scorn.

degeneracy, n. decline, retrogression.

degenerate, v. deteriorate, decline.

degradation, n. abasement, disgrace, humiliation.

degrade, v. abase, disgrace, pervert, dishonor.

deify, v. apotheosize, glorify, exalt.

deign, v. condescend.

delay, n. deferring, procrastination, postponement, respite, reprieve. Antonyms: dispatch, promptness, haste.

delegate, v. depute, commission.

deleterious, adj. hurtful, pernicious.

deliberate, adj. intentional. Antonyms: accidental, unpremeditated.

delicacy, n. daintiness, fineness, refinement, discrimination; daintiness. Antonym: coarseness.

delicate, adj. graceful, fine, minute, slender; refined, sensitive, dainty; critical.

delicious, adj. luscious, palatable, savory, yummy, mouth-watering, delightful. Antonyms: unpalatable, distasteful, fulsome.

delightful, adj. charming, enchanting, rapturous, ravishing, delectable, delicious, enjoyable.

delirious, adj. irrational. Antonyms: rational, lucid, sane.

deliverance, n. rescue, salvation,

redemption.
delivery, n. rescue, release, liberation, extrication; surrender, transfer.
delusion, n. illusion, deception, hallucination, ruse. Antonyms: disillusionment, reality, fact.
demand, n. exaction, requirement, order.
demeanor, n. deportment, carriage, bearing.
demerit, n. fault, misconduct.
demon, n. devil, fiend.
demoralize, v. deprave, corrupt.
demure, adj. sedate, staid.
den, n. cavern, cave, retreat.
denial, n. negation, rejection, disclaimer, refusal, renunciation. Antonyms: affirmation, acceptance.
denote, v. signify, imply.
denunciation, n. condemnation, accusation, malediction.
denunciatory, adj. condemnatory.
deny, v. gainsay, contradict; disown, renounce.
department, n. division, section, part, category; district, precinct, branch; station.
departure, n. deviation; withdrawal.
depend, v. lean, rely, trust.
dependable, adj. trustworthy, reliable. Antonym: untrustworthy.
dependant, n. retainer, minion, feudatory, adherent; consequence.
dependence, n. suspension, dependency; reliance, trust.
dependent, adj. needy, reliant. Antonym: independent.
depict, v. portray, describe.

depiction, n. portrayal, description.
deplore, v. lament, regret.
deportment, n. behavior, demeanor.
depository, n. storehouse, magazine, depot, warehouse.
depot, n. depository; station.
depredation, n. pillage, sacking, spoliation, plunder.
depressed, adj. dejected.
depression, n. cavity, hollow, concavity; dejection, discouragement, despondency.
deprive, v. dispossess, strip.
depth, n. profundity; extent, intensity; deep; astuteness, discernment.
derelict, adj. abandoned, forsaken; lost, adrift; careless, negligent, remiss.
deride, v. ridicule, mock, taunt, jeer.
derision, n. ridicule, jeering.
derogatory, adj. disparaging.
descent, n. fall, drop, decline, dive, tumble, plunge; ancestry, parentage, origin.
describe, v. delineate, depict.
description, n. delineation, depiction, portrayal.
desecrate, v. profane, pollute.
desecration, n. profanation.
desert, v. forsake, abandon, leave, run away from, leave in the lurch.
deserted, adj. forsaken, desolate, derelict.
deserter, n. renegade, turncoat, delinquent, backslider, rat, traitor.
desertion, n. abandonment.
deserve, v. merit.

deserved, adj. merited, earned.
deserving, adj. meritorious, worthy. Antonym: undeserving.
design, n. sketch, outline, plan; scheme, intention, purpose, project, intent.
designing, n. artful, wily, crafty, subtle, politic.
desire, n. longing, craving, will, aspiration, hankering, cupidity, impulse. Antonyms: apathy, aversion.
desire, v. want, crave, long for, lust, covet, yearn, aspire, request.
desolate, adj. dreary, waste; broken-hearted, solitary.
despair, n. hopelessness, desperation.
desperate, adj. irretrievable, hopeless, incurable, remediless; frantic; outrageous, monstrous.
desperation, n. despair, hopelessness.
despicable, adj. contemptible.
despise, v. hate, loathe, scorn. Antonym: admire.
despondency, n. melancholy, depression.
despondent, adj. disheartened, discouraged, dejected.
despot, n. tyrant, autocrat.
despotic, adj. autocratic, tyrannical, absolute.
despotism, n. absolutism, tyranny.
destine, v. doom, preordain, appoint.
destiny, n. fate, doom, lot.
destitute, adj. devoid, deficient, lacking; needy.
destroy, v. annihilate, undo, demolish, raze, desolate, sack, dismantle. Antonyms: conserve,

preserve, spare.
destroyer, n. iconoclast, vandal, destructionist.
destruction, n. annihilation, demolition, ruin, perdition, havoc, vandalism, desolation. Antonyms: conservation, preservation.
destructive, adj. ruinous, internecine, pernicious.
desultory, adj. fitful, irregular, unsystematic.
detach, v. disconnect, disjoin, disunite, isolate.
detachment, n. disconnection, separation, isolation.
detail, v. particularize.
detention, n. restraint, custody, arrest.
deter, v. hinder, prevent, restrain.
deteriorate, v. decline, degenerate; corrupt, debase.
detest, v. loathe, despise, abhor, hate, execrate.
detestation, n. abomination, loathing, antipathy.
deuced, adj. devilish, excessive, extreme.
devastate, v. desolate, sack, ravage, plunder.
devastation, n. desolation, sacking, ravage, havoc.
develop, v. mature, evolve; unfold, disentangle, unravel. Antonyms: atrophy, blast, blight.
development, n. progression, evolution.
deviate, v. swerve, deflect, digress, stray, wander. Antonym: continue.
deviation, n. swerving, digression.
device, n. invention, expedient, wile, artifice, trickery; symbol,

legend.

devil, n. Satan, Lucifer, demon, fiend.

devilish, adj. demoniac, diabolical, fiendish, infernal.

devil-may-care, adj. reckless, defiant.

devious, adj. wandering, circuitous, winding, tortuous; sinful.

devise, v. contrive, invent, scheme, concoct, bequeath.

devotion, n. consecration, dedication; zeal, allegiance, love; worship, adoration.

devour, v. consume, eat, gobble up, gulp.

devout, adj. pious, reverent, devotional, godly, holy, religious. Antonyms: irreverent, impious, unholy.

dexterity, n. expertness, skill, aptitude, readiness.

dexterous, adj. expert, skillful.

dialogue, n. colloquy, duologue, interlocutory.

diatribe, n. harangue, tirade, rant, invective.

dice, v. chop, cube.

dicker, v. trade, barter, negotiate, exchange.

dictate, n. command, admonition, impulse.

dictator, n. despot, autocrat.

dictatorial, adj. tyrannical, despotic, autocratic, dogmatic, overbearing.

dido, n. trick, antic, caper.

die, v. expire, perish; wither, fade, vanish, recede, subside.

differ, v. be unlike; disagree. Antonyms: agree, concur.

difference, n. dissimilarity, unlikeness, variation, discrepancy, disparity, dissimilitude. Antonyms: uniformity, agreement, correspondence.

different, adj. dissimilar, unlike, contrary, opposite, variant, manifold, diverse. Antonyms: similar, like, same.

differentiate, v. discriminate.

difficult, adj. complicated, intricate, hard; perverse, exacting. Antonyms: light, easy.

difficulty, n. obstacle, impediment, obstruction; hardness; controversy, disagreement. Antonyms: ease, facility, release.

diffidence, n. timidity.

diffident, adj. bashful, timid.

diffuse, adj. copious, full.

dig, v. delve, excavate; thrust, poke, jab; exhume.

dig, n. thrust, punch, poke.

digest, v. systematize, classify.

digest, n. summary, code, system.

dignified, adj. stately, majestic, imposing.

dignify, v. exalt, grace, honor, elevate.

dignity, n. exaltation, eminence; stateliness; honor.

digress, v. deviate, depart.

digression, n. deviation, divergence; episode.

dike, n. levee.

dilapidated, adj. ramshackle.

dilate, v. expand, distend.

dilation, n. expansion, distention.

dilemma, n. predicament, difficulty, strait. Antonyms: extrication, release.

diligence, n. assiduity, sed-

ulousness, perseverance.
diligent, adj. sedulous, assiduous, persevering. Antonym: lazy.
dillydally, v. dawdle, fritter, loiter.
dilute, v. attenuate, thin, weaken.
dim, adj. obscure, indistinct, faint, blurred. Antonyms: bright, vivid.
diminish, v. decrease, reduce, lessen, curtail.
diminution, n. reduction, decrease, decrement.
din, n. clamor, noise, racket, clangor.
dint, n. indentation, dent.
dip, v. plunge, immerse, douse, dive.
direct, adj. straight, undeviating. Antonyms: indirect, round-about.
direction, n. guidance, government, administration, superintendence, oversight; instruction.
directly, adv. Straight, unswervingly; completely; clearly, openly, frankly.
dirt, n. earth, soil; filth, muck, ground.
dirty, adj. defiled, unclean, nasty, filthy, soiled, begrimed, uncleanly, loathsome.
dirty, v. soil, befoul, begrime, sully, tarnish, defile.
disable, v. incapacitate, disqualify.
disadvantage, n. detriment, hindrance, drawback.
disagree, v. be at variance, differ, dissent, contradict, quarrel, contend.
disagreeable, adj. unpleasant, distasteful, offensive, contrary.
disagreeing, adj. incompatible.
disagreement, n. difference; quarrel, bickering, dispute, squabble,

controversy.
disappear, v. vanish, recede, be lost to view.
disappearance, n. vanishing, evanescence.
disappoint, v. dissatisfy, frustrate, balk, foil, defeat.
disapproval, n. disapprobation, dislike.
disaster, n. calamity, mishap, casualty.
disastrous, adj. calamitous, deplorable, unfortunate.
disband, v. demobilize, disorganize.
discern, v. perceive, discriminate.
discernible, adj. perceptible, visible, discoverable, apparent, manifest.
discerning, adj. acute, sharpsighted, shrewd.
discernment, n. insight, penetration, judgment.
discharge, v. absolve, acquit, release, exonerate, free; dismiss, remove. Antonyms: retain, hold.
discharge, n. firing, burst, volley; release; fulfillment, performance.
discharged, adj. dismissed, acquitted; emeritus.
disciple, n. adherent, follower.
disciplinarian, n. martinet.
discipline, n. correction, chastisement, submission, regulation. Antonyms: laxity, unrestraint.
disclaim, v. disown, deny, denounce.
discomfiture, n. disconcertion, confusion, frustration, defeat.
discommode, v. inconvenience, trouble.
discomposure, n. agitation, per-

turbation, confusion.

discommode, v. inconvenience, trouble.

discomposure, n. agitation, confusion.

disconnect, v. detach, dissever, disjoin.

disconnected, adj. detached, separate, isolated.

disconnection, n. detachment, disunion, incoherence.

disconsolate, adj. inconsolable.

discontent, n. dissatisfaction.

discontented, adj. dissatisfied, restless, disgruntled.

discord, n. dissonance, disharmony, variance. Antonyms: harmony, agreement, consonance.

discordant, adj. inharmonious, dissonant, jarring, strident; at variance, contradictory.

discount, n. deduction, allowance, rebate.

discourage, v. dishearten, dispirit, depress, dampen, unnerve, oppose.

discouragement, n. depression, dejection; opposition, intimidation, determent, damper, difficulty.

discouraging, adj. depressing, disheartening, dissuasive.

discourse, n. dissertation, address, oration, harangue, speech.

discourteous, adj. uncivil, rude, disrespectful, abrupt, unmannerly.

discourtesy, n. rudeness, incivility, impoliteness.

discover, v. ascertain, detect, descry, discern, disclose.

discovery, n. ascertainment, unearthing, disclosure.

discredit, n. disesteem, disrepute.

discreet, adj. tactful, judicious, prudent, wary.

discretion, n. prudence, circumspection, wariness; choice, liberty. Antonyms: indiscretion, imprudence, constraint.

discretional, adj. optional, discretionary, elective. Antonym: compulsory.

discriminating, adj. distinguishing, discerning.

discrimination, n. difference, distinction, discernment.

discuss, v. debate, argue, canvass, agitate, deliberate.

discussion, n. debate, argument, canvass, agitation, consideration.

disdain, n. scorn, contempt.

disdainful, adj. contemptuous, scornful, supercilious.

disease, n. ailment, disorder, malady, complaint, affection, distemper; plague. Antonyms: health, vigor.

disengage, v. extricate, disembarrass, disentangle, detach, dissociate.

disfavor, n. disapproval.

disfigure, v. deface, mar.

disfigurement, n. disfiguration, defacement; blemish.

disgrace, n. reproach, discredit, dishonor, shame, infamy, disrepute, scandal.

disgrace, v. dishonor, humiliate, degrade, discredit, tarnish.

disgraceful, adj. ignominious, shameful, dishonorable, scandalous, disreputable.

disgruntled, adj. dissatisfied.
disguise, v. mask, dissemble, cloak, masquerade.
disguise, n. mask, blind, cloak.
disguised, adj. veiled, masked, incognito.
disgust, n. aversion, repulsion.
disgust, v. revolt, offend.
disgusting, adj. revolting, loathsome, repulsive, nauseating, sickening, repugnant.
disheveled, adj. disarranged, disorderly, frowzy.
dishonest, adj. unscrupulous, deceitful.
dishonesty, n. improbity, fraudulence, cheating.
dishonor, n. disrepute, discredit.
dishonorable, adj. discreditable, disgraceful.
disillusion, v. disenchant, let down.
disinterested, adj. impartial, indifferent, neutral, unselfish.
disjoint, v. dislocate, disarticulate.
disjointed, adj. incoherent, desultory, loose.
dislike, v. disapprove, abhor, detest.
dislike, n. aversion, disapproval, hatred.
disloyal, adj. perfidious, unfaithful, false, treasonable, traitorous.
disloyalty, n. perfidy, unfaithfulness, treason, faithlessness.
dismal, adj. dreary, gloomy, cheerless, joyless, somber.
dismantle, v. raze, demolish.
dismay, n. consternation.
dismiss, v. discharge, fire, banish.
dismissal, n. discharge, removal.
disobedience, n. contumacy, defiance, noncompliance, insub-ordination.
disobedient, adj. contumacious, undutiful, defiant, remiss, derelict.
disobey, v. transgress, violate, disregard, defy, infringe.
disorder, n. confusion, disarray, disarrangement, disorganization, chaos, litter, disturbance.
disorder, v. disarrange, confuse, jumble, disorganize, derange, discompose.
disordered, adj. deranged, confused, jumbled.
disorderly, adj. immethodical, confused; chaotic, lawless.
disorganization, n. disorder, demobilization, dissolution.
disorganize, v. dissolve, disband, disorder, disarrange.
disown, v. repudiate, deny, disclaim, disavow, reject.
disowning, n. denial, disclaimer, disavow, renounce.
disparage, v. belittle, decry, depreciate. Antonyms: laud, commend, praise.
disparagement, n. detraction, decrial, defamation, dispraise.
disparaging, adj. derogatory, unfavorable, insulting.
dispatch, n. haste, speed, expedition; message.
dispense, v. deal out, apportion, distribute; execute.
disperse, v. dissipate, dispel, scatter.
displace, v. remove, disarrange; supplant.
display, n. exhibition, parade, show.
display, v. exhibit, evince, expose, parade, flourish.

displease, v. offend, anger.
displeasure, n. disapprobation, dislike, disapproval, resentment, dissatisfaction.
disposed, adj. inclined, minded, willing.
disposition, n. temperament, mood, nature; willingness, readiness, inclination. Antonyms: indisposition, unwillingness.
dispossess, v. dislodge, oust, eject, remove.
dispossession, n. dislodgment, ejection, ousting, divestiture, ouster.
disproof, n. confutation.
disprove, v. confute, refute.
disputable, adj. controvertible. Antonyms: indisputable, incontrovertible.
disputatious, adj. contentious, polemical, quarrelsome.
dispute, v. contend, argue, controvert, wrangle, bicker, squabble.
dispute, n. quarrel, controversy, argument, debate, squabble, contention.
disregard, n. indifference, slight, neglect.
disregard, v. ignore, slight, overlook.
disrepute, n. disesteem, disgrace.
disrespect, n. discourtesy, disesteem, rudeness, irreverence.
disrespectful, adj. discourteous, uncivil, rude, irreverent, insolent, saucy.
dissatisfaction, n. discontent, disapproval, displeasure.
dissatisfied, adj. discontented, displeased, restless, impatient.

dissection, n. anatomy; analysis, examination.
dissent, n. dissension, disagreement, variance; nonconformity.
dissenter, n. nonconformist, sectary, dissident, separatist.
dissertation, n. discourse, thesis, exposition, tract.
dissipated, adj. profligate, dissolute, fast.
dissipation, n. dispersion, scattering; dissoluteness.
dissolute, adj. debauched, dissipated, abandoned.
dissolution, n. dissolving, analysis; solution; decomposition, resolution.
dissolvable, adj. dissoluble, soluble, fusible.
dissolve, v. melt, liquefy, macerate, fuse, disorganize, disband, disperse; disunite.
distance, v. outstrip, outdo, surpass.
distant, adj. remote, far-off, reserved, cold.
distaste, n. aversion, dislike, revulsion. Antonyms: taste, liking, relish.
distasteful, adj. unpleasant, offensive, repugnant, unpalatable, unsavory.
distill, v. trickle, drop, drip.
distillation, n. trickling; rectification.
distinction, n. discrimination; eminence, celebrity, renown, fame, repute. Antonym: obscurity.
distinctive, adj. discriminative, individual, unique.
distinguish, v. characterize; dis-

criminate, discern, recognize.

distinguished, adj. marked, special; eminent, illustrious, famous, renowned, noted. Antonyms: undistinguished, obscure, humble.

distinguishing, adj. distinctive, peculiar, characteristic.

distort, v. deform, twist; falsify.

distortion, n. misrepresentation, alteration, falsehood.

distracted, adj. frantic, frenzied, raving; preoccupied, unfocused; sidetracked. Antonyms: calm; focused.

distraction, n. diversion, amusement; confusion, bewilderment; commotion, despair.

distress, n. anguish, torture, sorrow, grief; misery, affliction, adversity, disaster.

distress, v. pain, grieve, afflict, wound.

distribute, v. apportion, allot, deal out, dispense; classify.

distribution, n. apportionment, allotment, dispensing, division; disposition, grouping.

district, n. region, precinct, circuit, locality, ward.

distrust, n. doubt, suspicion.

distrustful, adj. suspicious.

disturb, v. perturb, annoy, agitate, disarrange, derange, unsettle.

ditch, n. trench, moat, channel.

dive, v. plunge.

divergence, n. radiation; disagreement, variance.

divergent, adj. diverging; variant, different.

diverse, adj. varied, sundry, different, heterogeneous, diversified.

diversion, n. turning aside; amusement, sport, recreation.

diversity, n. difference, dissimilarity; variety.

divide, v. sunder, split, cleave, disunite, part, separate, sever, detach.

divine, adj. Godlike; religious, holy; heavenly, angelic, seraphic, transcendent.

divine, v. foresee, foreknow, surmise, forebode, foretell.

divisible, adj. separable, dividable.

division, n. separation, partition, dimidiation; section, part, portion, category, group.

dizziness, n. vertigo.

dizzy, adj. vertiginous, giddy, woozy, lightheaded; silly, scatterbrained, flighty.

do, v. effect, accomplish, produce, achieve, consummate, perform; perpetrate, commit.

docile, adj. tractable, teachable, gentle, submissive.

dock, v. curtail; deduct from.

dock, n. wharf, pier, jetty.

dockhand, n. stevedore.

doctor, n. physician, medical practitioner; homeopath; intern; extern.

doctor, v. repair, treat, falsify, adulterate.

doctrine, n. tenet, dogma, belief, principle.

doddering, adj. shaking, trembling, infirm.

dodge, v. duck, evade, parry; shift, evade, parry.

dodger, n. prevaricator; handbill, circular.

dog, n. canine; pup, puppy, whelp; cur, mongrel.

dog, v. follow, worry, hound.

dogged, adj. stubborn, obstinate, mulish, headstrong.

doggish, adj. surly, sullen, cynical, morose.

dogma, n. doctrine, tenet.

dogmatic, adj. positive, magisterial, dictatorial, imperious, overbearing.

doings, n. actions, proceedings, deeds, acts, performances.

dole, n. pittance, alms; distribution, share, portion; grief, sorrow.

doleful, adj. sorrowful, plaintive, piteous, lugubrious.

domain, n. dominion, sovereignty; realm, territory; province, department.

dome, n. cupola.

domestic, adj. home, household, family; tame.

dominant, adj. predominant, prevailing, paramount.

dominate, v. predominate, sway, rule, govern, control.

domineer, v. tyrannize, lord it; swagger.

dominion, n. sovereignty, sway, supremacy; realm.

donation, n. gift, present.

doom, n. judgment; destiny.

door, n. entrance, portal, gate; postern.

doorkeeper, n. porter, concierge.

doorsill, n. threshold.

dormancy, n. abeyance, inactivity, lethargy.

dormant, adj. quiescent, latent, inert, inactive, torpid.

dose, n. draught, potion.

dot, n. period, point; speck.

doting, adj. fond, loving, devoted, adoring.

double, adj. twofold, duplex.

double, v. duplicate, multiply.

double, n. duplicate, counterpart.

double-dealing, n. duplicity, trickery.

doubling, n. duplication, reduplication; fold, double.

doubt, v. waver, hesitate, question; distrust, suspect. Antonyms: believe, trust, rely upon.

doubtful, adj. unsettled, undetermined, unsure, dubious, precarious; questionable, involved. Antonyms: certain, implicit, sure.

doughty, adj. redoubtable, valiant, bold, fearless.

dour, adj. hard, obstinate.

douse, v. duck, immerse, dip, plunge, souse, submerge.

dowdy, adj. drab, plain, frumpy, dated.

down, adv. downward, below.

down, v. overthrow, subdue.

down, adj. descending, sloping.

downcast, adj. despondent, dejected, gloomy.

downfall, n. descent, reverse, humiliation.

downhearted, adj. dejected, despondent.

downhill, n. descent, declivity, slope.

downright, adj. blunt, direct, positive, absolute, unmixed, straightforward.

draft, n. drawing, draught; bill of exchange; sketch, current of air.

drag, v. haul, tug, pull; break.

drag, n. dragging; dragnet; harrow; skid; obstacle.

drain, n. channel, gutter, trench, ditch.

drain, v. empty, exhaust.

draw, v. haul, drag, tug, tow; attract; entice, allure, induce. Antonyms: repel, repulse, reject, alienate.

drawback, n. disadvantage, hindrance, imperfection; rebate, discount.

draw back, v. retract; shrink, recoil, withdraw, wince.

drawer, n. till.

drawing, n. traction, pulling; graphics, delineation; sketch, diagram, picture.

dread, n. apprehension, fear.

dread, v. fear, apprehend.

dreadful, adj. fearful, formidable, awful.

dream, n. vision; illusion, wild conceit, reverie, fantasy. Antonyms: fact, actuality, reality.

dreamer, n. visionary, enthusiast.

dreamy, adj. visionary, unreal. Antonyms: practical, real.

dreary, adj. dismal, drear, lonesome, wearisome, dull.

dregs, n. refuse, sediment; riffraff.

dress, n. gown, frock, robe.

dress, v. clothe, deck, apparel, adjust, align. Antonyms: undress, disrobe.

dressmaker, n. modiste, millinery.

dribble, v. drip, trickle.

drift, n. course, direction, bearing, tendency, aim, intention, design, meaning.

drill, v. perforate, pierce; train, exercise.

drink, v. quaff, sip, imbibe; tipple,

guzzle, booze; absorb.

drink, n. beverage, potation; draught, drench.

drinkable, adj. potable. Antonym: undrinkable.

drinking, n. potation; tippling, guzzling. Antonyms: temperance, abstinence.

drip, v. drop, trickle.

dripping, n. trickling.

drive, v. impel, force, compel; propel, send; rush, press; conduct.

drive away, v. dispel, disperse.

drive back, v. repulse, repel.

drivel, n. driveling; nonsense.

drivel, v. drool.

driver, n. chauffeur, coachman, charioteer.

driving, adj. violent, forcible; impelling, impulsive.

driving, n. guiding by reins; propulsion, compulsion.

droll, adj. ludicrous, comical, facetious, funny.

drollery, n. pleasantry, facetiousness.

drone, n. sluggard, idler.

drool, v. drivel, slaver.

droop, v. languish, faint, grow faint, sink; bend, drop, hang; crouch; fade, wilt.

drop, n. globule, minim, blob; descent, fall.

drop, v. distill, dribble, trickle; drip; fall; lower, sink, depress.

dropping, n. distillation, trickling, dribbling, falling.

dross, n. refuse, scum, dregs, waste.

drought, n. aridity, dryness; scarcity, dearth.

drove, n. herd, flock; crown.

drown, v. overwhelm, submerge, flood, inundate.

drowsiness, n. sleepiness.

drowsy, adj. sleepy.

drudge, n. menial, hack, slave, scullion.

druggist, n. pharmacist, apothecary.

drunk, adj. intoxicated, drunken, tipsy, boozy. Antonym: sober.

drunkard, n. inebriate, toper, tippler, carouser, winebibber, sot, debauchee. Antonyms: abstainer, ascetic, teetotaler.

drunken, adj. intoxicated, drunk; maudlin, mellow, groggy.

drunkenness, n. intoxication, inebriety, inebriation, debauch; excitement, frenzy. Antonyms: sobriety, temperance.

dry, adj. desiccated, dried, evaporated; anhydrous; barren, uninteresting, vapid, prosaic.

dry, v. evaporate, desiccate, insolate, torrefy.

drying, n. desiccation, evaporation, torrefaction.

dryness, n. aridity, desiccation, drought.

dubious, adj. undetermined, undecided, doubtful; questionable, vague.

duck, v. souse, dip, plunge, immerse; dive; dodge, cringe.

duck, n. drake; teal.

duct, n. tube, canal, pipe.

dude, n. dandy, fop, coxcomb, swell, exquisite.

dudgeon, n. resentment, anger.

duds, n. frippery, clothes, effects, things.

due, adj. payable, unpaid; appropriate, becoming, proper, regular, appointed; owing.

due, n. debt; duty, right.

dugout, n. excavation.

dull, adj. unintelligent, obtuse, stolid, inapt, blockish, sluggish; apathetic, unfeeling.

dull, v. blunt, rebate, benumb, stupefy, deaden; tarnish, obscure, dim.

dumb, adj. mute, speechless.

dumfound, v. astound, amaze, astonish.

dunce, n. dullard, numskull, witling, blockhead, coot, ninny, oaf, nincompoop.

dupe, n. gull, sucker, victim, fool.

dupe, v. trick, fool, con, deceive.

duplicate, n. double, copy, counterpart, facsimile.

dusk, n. twilight, evening.

dutiful, adj. obedient, duteous, submissive, deferential.

duty, n. responsibility, incumbency, accountability; service, business, work, function.

dweller, n. denizen, resident, inhabitant.

dwelling, n. residence, domicile, house, abode.

dwindle, v. decrease, diminish, shrink.

dwindling, n. decrease, diminution, shrinkage.

dye, v. color, stain, tinge.

E

eager, adj. ardent, avid, zealous, intent, impatient, athirst, impassioned. Antonyms: indifferent, apathetic, dispassionate, unconcerned, unmoved, stolid.

ear, n. spike; auricle.

earlier, adj. antecedent, previous, prior. Antonym: later.

early, adj. seasonable, timely, premature, beforehand.

earnest, adj. unfeigned, ardent, sincere, impassioned, intent.

earnest, n. sincerity, seriousness, good faith; pledge, token.

earth, n. world, terra firma, globe; land, soil, ground.

earthenware, n. crockery, pottery, stoneware, porcelain.

earthly, adj. worldly, carnal, terrestrial; temporal.

earthwork, n. fortification.

earthy, adj. terrestrial, terrene, earthly; unsophisticated.

ease, n. facility, easiness; repose, comfort, contentment, peace, serenity. Antonyms: constraint, discomfort, uneasiness.

ease, v. facilitate, mitigate, appease, allay, soothe, alleviate, release, relax.

easiness, n. ease, facility.

easy, adj. facile, slight; comfortable, untroubled, quiet, tranquil.

easy-going, adj. mild-tempered, laid-back, even-tempered, carefree.

eat, v. feed, devour; bolt, gulp, gorge; consume, corrode, erode. Antonyms: abstain, fast, diet, starve, famish.

eating, n. corrosion, erosion.

ebb, v. recede, diminish, return, retire; decline, wane, decay.

eccentric, adj. whimsical, erratic, strange, irregular, odd.

eccentricity, n. whimsicality, oddness, freakishness, irregularity.

echo, n. reverberation.

echo, v. resound, reverberate.

eclipse, n. occultation; obscuration, extinction, concealment.

eclipse, v. obscure, outshine, surpass, outrival.

economical, adj. frugal, saving, thrifty, provident. Antonym: extravagant.

economize, v. save, retrench.

economy, n. thrift, frugality, thriftiness, retrenchment; management, system.

eddy, n. vortex, whirlpool.

edge, n. verge, brink, border, margin, rim, sharpness, intensity.

edge, v. sharpen, fringe, border, rim; hitch along.

edgy, adj. touchy, sharp, irritable, excitable.

edible, adj. eatable, comestible. Antonym: inedible.

edict, n. mandate, decree, manifesto, ordinance.

educate, v. teach, instruct, school, nurture, edify.

educated, adj. learned, versed, erudite, scholarly, enlightened, schooled, literate.

education, n. culture, learning, schooling, tuition, scholarship, enlightenment, literacy.

efface, v. expunge, obliterate, erase, eradicate.

effect, n. result, outcome, issue; validity, force; execution, performance.

effect, v. effectuate, accomplish,

realize, achieve, consummate, compass.

effective, adj. effectual, efficient, cogent, productive.

effectual, adj. efficacious, effective, availing, successful. Antonym: ineffectual.

effervescence, n. ebullition.

effete, adj. exhausted, unfruitful, wasted, barren.

efficacious, adj. potent, effectual, effective.

efficacy, n. usefulness, effectiveness, productiveness. Antonyms: inefficacy, impotency.

efficient, adj. competent, capable, proficient, potent.

effort, n. attempt, endeavor, trial, essay, strain, struggle.

egg, n. ovum, germ, cell; spawn.

egg, v. urge on, instigate.

egg-shaped, adj. oval, ovoid.

egotism, n. self-conceit, vanity.

egotistical, adj. conceited, vain, self-important, opinionated.

eightfold, adj. octuple.

eight-sided, adj. octagonal, octahedral, octangular.

eject, v. void, disharge; oust, evict, dislodge.

ejection, n. voiding, disharge; ousting.

elastic, adj. resilient, springy, ductile, rebounding.

elasticity, n. resiliency, springiness, stretch, ductility.

elated, adj. ebullient, ecstatic, exhilarated, overjoyed, jubilant.

electric, adj. stimulating, inspiriting, magnetic.

elegance, n. beauty, grace, richness, sumptuousness.

elegant, adj. courtly, sumptuous, luxurious, rich.

element, n. constituent, ingredient.

elemental, adj. rudimental, elementary.

elementary, adj. rudimental, elemental, constituent, primary; simple.

elevate, v. lift, raise; promote, advance; ennoble.

elevation, n. promotion, exaltation, dignity, advancement; eminence, hill.

elf, n. sprite, fairy, imp, gnome.

elfish, n. mischievous, impish, prankish.

embankment, n. levee, dike.

embarrass, v. disconcert, discompose, mortify, abash, pose, perplex.

embarrassment, n. discomposure, chagrin, mortification, disconcertion.

embellish, v. decorate, beautify, garnish, ornament.

embellishment, n. adornment, decoration, beautification; ornament, garnish, trimming.

embezzle, v. peculate, defalcate.

embezzlement, n. peculation.

embezzler, n. defalcator.

emigrate, v. migrate.

emigration, n. migration, exodus.

eminent, adj. distinguished, renowned, illustrious, famous.

emphasis, n. accentuation.

emphasize, v. accentuate.

empire, n. sovereignty, sway, dominion, domain, kingdom.

emptiness, n. vacancy, inanition;

hollowness, mockery; space, vacuum, void; triviality.

empty, adj. depleted, vacant, inane; unoccupied, void, unfilled, blank.

empty, v. deplete, exhaust, unburden, evacuate; disembogue, deflate.

enchant, v. bewitch, charm, enrapture, transport, delight.

enchantment, n. charm, witchery, glamour; sorcery, witchcraft, spell. Antonyms: disenchantment, disillusionment.

enchantress, n. siren, charmer, sorceress.

encircle, v. environ, surround, gird, enfold.

encounter, n. meeting, collision; battle, conflict, attack.

encourage, v. reassure, inspirit, stimulate, rally, countenance, incite.

encouragement, n. incentive, stimulus, fomentation, patronage.

encouraging, adj. reassuring, inspiriting, assuring.

encroach, v. trespass, entrench, infringe, invade.

encroachment, n. trespass, intrusion invasion.

end, n. termination, terminal, extremity, limit; close, finale, finis.

end, v. terminate, conclude, discontinue, close.

endanger, v. imperil.

ending, n. termination, conclusion.

endless, adj. interminable, limitless, boundless; continuous, uninterrupted, continual.

endowment, n. donation, bounty, bequest, talent, faculty, dower.

endurable, adj. sufferable, tolerable. Antonym: unendurable.

endurance, n. permanence, continuance, persistence, continuation; sufferance, patience.

endure, v. suffer, experience, undergo; stand, brook; submit to; sustain. Antonyms: succumb, falter, yield.

enduring, adj. lasting, durable, permanent, imperishable.

enemy, n. foe, adversary, opponent, rival, hostile.

energetic, adj. forcible, potent, cogent, active, strenuous.

energizing, adj. potent, vitalizing, invigorating.

energy, n. power, force, vigor, zeal, strength.

engage, v. pledge, bind, commit; betroth, plight; engross, busy, occupy.

engagement, n. betrothal, affiance; contract, pledge, promise; encounter, combat.

engine, n. locomotive.

engrave, v. chisel, carve, cut; imprint, infix, impress.

engraving, n. carving; print, plate.

enjoyment, n. pleasure, delight, delectation, felicity.

enlarge, v. magnify, amplify, expand, develop, increase, extend; dilate, descant.

enlargement, n. augmentation, extension, expansion, dilation, growth, increase.

enmity, n. hostility, unfriendliness, opposition, antagonism, malignity, hatred.

enormity, n. atrocity, heinousness, flagrancy.

enormous, adj. colossal, gigantic, mammoth, huge; atrocious, flagrant, flagitious.

enough, n. sufficiency, plenty, abundance, adequacy. Antonyms: deficiency, surplus.

enrich, v. fertilize; embellish, adorn, beautify.

enrichment, n. fertilization; endowment; embellishment, decoration.

enroll, v. enlist, register, list, record.

enrollment, n. registration, enlistment, register, record, roster.

enslave, v. enthrall, overcome.

enslavement, n. enthrallment, subjection, bondage, slavery.

entangle, v. interweave, complicate, tangle, snarl; ensnare, puzzle, involve.

entanglement, n. complication, intricacy, snarl, tangle, embarrassment.

enter, v. penetrate, pierce, perforate; embark in, enlist in; insert.

enterprise, n. project, undertaking; activity.

enterprising, adj. active, stirring, energetic.

entertain, v. divert, amuse, please, junket, cheer; harbor, hold, lodge.

entertaining, adj. diverting, amusing, interesting.

entertainment, n. diversion, amusement, recreation, pastime, play; banquet, junket.

enthusiasm, n. eagerness, intensity, ardor, fervency, verve, unction. Antonyms: indifference, wariness, caution, calmness.

enthusiast, n. zealot, fanatic, devotee.

enthusiastic, adj. eager, zealous, fanatical, fervent.

entice, v. seduce, allure, persuade, tempt.

enticement, n. seduction, allurement, temptation, decoy.

enticing, adj. seductive, alluring, tempting.

entire, adj. complete, undivided.

entirety, n. completeness, integrity, totality.

entrance, n. ingress, access; entry, portal, inlet, gate.

entrap, v. ensnare, entangle, decoy, entice.

entry, n. entrance, access; hall, vestibule; minute, record.

envelop, v. surround, enwrap, enclose, encircle, encompass.

envelope, n. wrapper, enclosure, capsule, case.

enveloping, adj. surrounding, enfolding, encircling.

environment, n. conditions.

epicure, n. gourmand, gourmet; sensualist; sybarite.

epicurean, adj. sensual, voluptuous, luxurious.

epicurism, n. hedonism, sensuality, gastronomy.

epitome, n. compendium, abstract, digest.

equal, adj. coordinate, tantamount, equivalent, identical, commensurate, adequate.

equal, n. peer, mate, compeer, match. Antonyms: inferior, subordinate.

equality, n. coordination, uniformity, parity, agreement.

equilibrium, n. equipoise.

equip, v. accouter, furnish, fit out, gird.

equipage, n. equipment; carriage, turnout; suite, train.

equipment, n. apparatus, accouterments, rigging, gear.

equipoise, n. equilibrium.

equivalent, adj. tantamount, equal; interchangeable.

eradicate, v. remove, cleanse, expunge, erase; extirpate, annihilate, destroy.

eradication, n. extirpation.

erase, v. expunge, rub out, efface, obliterate, delete.

erasure, n. expunging.

erect, v. build, raise.

erect, adj. upright, vertical, raised; undaunted, bold, undismayed. Antonyms: horizontal, inverted, oblique.

erosion, n. corrosion, eroding.

err, v. misjudge, mistake, blunder; deviate, sin.

errand, n. mission, commission.

erratic, adj. nomadic, wandering; eccentric.

erring, adj. sinful, fallible, weak. Antonyms: impeccable, inerrable.

erroneous, adj. false, incorrect, untrue, mistaken.

error, n. mistake, inaccuracy, blunder, falsity.

erudition, n. learning, scholarship.

eruption, n. outburst, outbreak; exanthema, rash.

escort, n. guard, convoy, usher.

especial, adj. special, particular, specific.

essay, n. dissertation, article, thesis; attempt, effort, trial.

essential, adj. indispensable, necessary, requisite. Antonyms: nonessential, superfluous.

establish, v. found, organize, institute; verify, ratify.

establishment, n. organization, founding, verification.

esteem, v. respect, value, honor, revere; rate, reckon.

esteem, n. respect, honor, regard; opinion, judgment. Antonyms: disesteem, aversion, antipathy.

estimable, adj. computable, calculable; worthy, excellent. Antonyms: inestimable, incalculable.

estimate, v. appraise, value, rate, prize; calculate.

estimation, n. esteem, respect, honor; appraisement, estimate.

estrange, v. alienate, disaffect.

estranged, adj. alienate.

estrangement, n. alienation, disaffection.

eternal, adj. self-existent, infinite; endless.

eulogize, v. laud, praise, extol.

eulogy, n. encomium, panegyric, laudation, praise.

evade, v. shun, avoid; elude, parry, foil, baffle; prevaricate, dodge, quibble.

evaporate, v. vaporize, evanesce.

evaporation, n. vaporization, evanescence; exhalation.

evasion, n. evading, eluding, escape; baffling, foiling; prevarication, sophistry.

evasive, adj. equivocal, indefinite, elusive.

even, adj. plane, level, flush, flat, smooth; uniform.

evening, n. dusk, twilight, nightfall, eventide.

evenness, n. uniformity, smoothness, equableness.

event, n. occurrence, affair, incident, happening; result, outcome.

everlasting, adj. continual, perpetual, interminable, eternal, endless, never-ending.

everyday, adj. commonplace, common, customary.

evident, adj. manifest, obvious, clear, patent.

evil, adj. sinful, immoral, unrighteous, vicious.

evil, n. wickedness, depravity, sin.

evildoer, n. sinner, culprit, offender.

evil-minded, adj. malicious, wicked, depraved.

evolution, n. development, evolvement, unfolding.

exact, adj. precise, accurate, true, undeviating; methodical, rigid, severe, rigorous.

exact, v. demand, extort.

exacting, adj. severe, harsh, oppressive.

exaction, n. extortion, oppression.

exactness, n. precision. accuracy, strictness, scrupulousness.

exaggerate, v. overstate.

exalt, v. elevate; dignify, ennoble; magnify, apotheosize.

exaltation, n. elevation, loftiness, apotheosis.

exalted, adj. sublime, elevated, lofty, grand, dignified.

examination, n. inquiry, autopsy, scrutiny, inspection, audit, inquest, inquisition.

examine, v. inspect, scrutinize, question, audit, heckle, review, search, probe.

examiner, n. inspector, inquirer, questioner, auditor, reviewer, inquisitor.

example, n. sample, specimen, exemplification; model, pattern, prototype, copy.

exasperate, v. provoke, irritate, incense, anger; aggravate, embitter.

exceed, v. surpass, transcend; excel, outdo; preponderate.

exceeding, adj. surpassing.

excel, v. outrival, outstrip, surpass, eclipse, outdo, exceed.

excellence, n. preeminence, superiority, eminence; integrity, probity, goodness, worth.

excellent, adj. estimable, meritorious, good, worthy, choice.

excess, n. superabundance, superfluity, redundancy; surplus, residue.

excessive, adj. superfluous, exuberant, disproportionate; outrageous, unreasonable, exorbitant.

exchange, v. trade, barter, traffic, commute, interchange, bandy, permute.

exchange, n. traffic, trade, barter, commutation, interchange, reciprocity.

excitable, adj. susceptible, sensitive, emotional, impressible, mobile; irritable. Antonyms: unexcitable, imperturbable, calm.

excite, v. stimulate, arouse, inflame, incite, provoke; perturb, agitate.

excitement, n. perturbation, agitation, commotion, inquietude, tumult, turmoil. Antonyms: imperturbation, calmness, serenity.

exciting, adj. stirring, rousing, stimulating.

exclaim, v. blurt, cry, shout.

exclamation, n. ejaculation, outcry; interjection.

exclude, v. debar, preclude; except, omit; eject.

exclusion, n. debarment, preclusion; exception, ejection, expulsion.

excusable, adj. venial, pardonable, justifiable. Antonym: inexcusable.

excuse, v. absolve, forgive, pardon, exonerate, justify, acquit, release.

excuse, n. justification, apology, plea, palliation, pardon; evasion, makeshift.

execute, v. effectuate, perform, accomplish, consummate, achieve.

execution, n. performance, consummation, perpetration.

exercise, n. performance, application, practice, employment, use; activity; training.

exercise, v. employ, apply, busy, exert; practice, discipline, drill, train.

exertion, n. effort, struggle, attempt.

exhaust, v. drain, deplete; prostrate, enervate.

exhaustion, n. depletion, draining; lassitude, collapse, weariness.

exhibit, v. display, show.

exhibition, n. display, show.

exile, n. banishment, proscription.

exile, v. banish, expatriate.

exorbitant, adj. unreasonable, inordinate, excessive.

expand, v. dilate, distend, enlarge.

expansion, n. dilation, distension.

expatiate, v. descant.

expect, v. anticipate.

expel, v. eject, drive out; ostracize, banish, exile; excommunicate; discharge.

expelling, n. expulsion, ejection, dismissal; exile, ostracism.

expend, v. disburse.

expenditure, n. disbursement.

expense, n. outlay, cost, charge.

expensive, adj. costly, dear, high-priced. Antonym: inexpensive.

experienced, adj. practiced, veteran. Antonym: inexperienced.

experiment, n. test, trial.

experimental, adj. empirical, tentative.

expert, adj. skilled, proficient, adroit. Antonym: inexpert.

expert, n. adept, master, connoisseur. Antonyms: tyro, bungler.

explain, v. expound, elucidate, unfold.

explainable, adj. explicable, solvable. Antonym: unexplainable.

explanation, n. elucidation, explication; solution, deduction.

explanatory, adj. expository, elucidative, interpretative.

explode, v. burst; detonate.

exploitation, n. utilization.

explosion, n. detonation; bursting; outburst.

expose, v. exhibit, show, display;

uncover, unveil. Antonyms: conceal, suppress, dissemble, hide.

exposition, n. display, exposure; commentary; fair.

expostulate, v. remonstrate.

expostulation, n. remonstration.

exposure, n. exposing, disclosure, divulgement, revelation; subjection, jeopardy.

express, adj. definite, specific. Antonyms: vague, tacit, implied, indefinite.

express, v. say, utter; represent, indicate, denote, mean.

expression, n. assertion, statement, declaration; indication; phrase, term, word.

expulsion, n. expelling, ejection, debarment.

exquisite, adj. beautiful, rare, choice; fastidious; keen, acute, poignant.

extend, v. lengthen, protract; jut, project; enlarge.

extension, n. enlargement, expansion, projection.

extent, n. magnitude, size, volume; reach.

exterminate, v. eradicate, extirpate.

extermination, n. eradication, uprooting.

external, adj. outward, exterior, extrinsic.

extol, v. eulogize, praise, exalt.

extortion, n. exaction, overcharge, rapacity.

extortionate, adj. oppressive, exacting.

extra, adj. supplemental, additional, supernumerary.

extract, n. essence, quintessence; excerpt, quotation, citation.

extraordinary, adj. uncommon, unusual, remarkable, phenomenal.

extravagance, n. improvidence, prodigality, waste, preposterousness. Antonyms: economy, thrift, frugality.

extravagant, adj. wasteful, unthrifty, prodigal, lavish; wild, preposterous. Antonym: thrifty.

extreme, adj. outermost, utmost, farthest; last, final; ultra, radical, fanatical.

extreme, n. extremity, acme.

extremist, n. radical.

exuberance, n. superabundance, rampancy, excess, luxuriance.

exuberant, adj. overflowing, copious, excessive, wanton, rank, luxuriant.

exultant, adj. triumphant, jubilant, joyous.

eyesore, n. blemish, defect.

F

fable, n. apologue; fiction, fabrication, myth.

fabulous, adj. fictitious, feigned, unverified; inordinate.

face, n. countenance, visage, features; front, exterior; obverse; facet.

face, v. confront, meet; bully, bluff; plane, dress.

facsimile, n. duplicate, copy, likeness, counterpart.

fact, n. reality, actuality.

faction, n. dissension, sedition, rebellion, division.

factious, adj. turbulent, rebellious, refractory, insubordinate.

factor, n. broker, middleman, commission, merchant, agent; element.

factory, n. manufactory, shop, plant, mill.

facts, n. data.

faculty, n. endowment, capability, talent, ability, knack, gift; dexterity.

fade, v. decay, decline, droop, evanesce, disappear.

fading, adj. waning, evanescent, declining, vanishing.

fail, v. default, lack; deteriorate, decline, disappoint, desert; miscarry, foil.

failing, n. shortcoming, deficiency, imperfection, fault, defect, fallibility, decline, deterioration.

failure, n. failing, shortcoming, lack; omission, pretermission, default, nonperformance, neglect.

faint, adj. weak, exhausted, feeble; indistinct, dim, faded, dull.

faint, v. swoon.

fainthearted, adj. timorous, diffident, fearful.

faintheartedness, n. timidity, diffidence.

fair, adj. impartial, equitable, unbiased, just, honorable, ingenuous; average, tolerable.

fair, adv. clear, openly, honestly, favorably, impartially.

fair, n. bazaar; exposition.

fairly, adv. impartially, equitably, openly, favorably.

fair play, n. justice, equity.

fairy, n. fay, elf, pixy, sprite, sylph.

faith, n. credence, belief, trust, dependence, credit, confidence; tenet, creed. Antonyms: doubt, incredulity, unbelief.

faithful, adj. true, constant, staunch, unwavering, devoted; trustworthy, reliable, exact.

faithfulness, n. constancy, devotion, loyalty, fidelity, fealty, allegiance; exactness, accuracy.

faithless, adj. unbelieving, skeptical, incredulous, doubting, disloyal, false.

faithlessness, n. unbelief, incredulity, doubt; disloyalty.

fake, n. trick, swindle, imposture, fraud, imposition; humbug.

fake, v. cheat, swindle, defraud, manipulate fraudulently.

faker, n. trickster, swindler.

fall, v. descend, drop, gravitate; collapse, founder, slump, tumble, topple.

fall, n. descent, collapse, tumble, drop; decrease, decline, slump; cadence.

fallacious, adj. sophistical, misleading, illusive.

fallacy, n. deception, delusion; sophism, sophistry.

fall away, v. emaciate; renounce, rebel; backslide; decline.

fall back, v. recede, retreat, retire, withdraw.

fallen, adj. dropped, prostrate, degraded, debased.

fallible, adj. erring; imperfect; frail. Antonym: perfect.

falling away, v. emaciation, pining; desertion, revolt; apostasy, defection, decline, declension.

falling back, v. recession, retreat, retirement, withdrawal.

falling down, v. prostration, collapse.

falling off, v. dropping; withdrawal, separation, detachment; defection; depreciation.

falling short, n. deficiency, inadequacy, deficit, shortcoming.

falling star, n. meteor.

falling to pieces, v. disintegration, dilapidation.

fall off, v. drop; withdraw, separate; apostatize, depreciate, deteriorate.

fallow, adj. uncultivated, untilled; dormant.

fall short, v. be deficient, be inadequate.

fall to pieces, v. disintegrate.

false, adj. spurious, forged, counterfeit, sham, unauthentic, bogus, feigned, fallacious.

falsehood, n. inveracity, untruthfulness; lie, fiction, untruth, fabrication, canard.

falsification, n. forgery, counterfeiting, n. falsifying; distortion.

falsify, v. misstate, garble, misrepresent, distort, pervert, fake; refute, disprove.

falter, v. hesitate, tremble, waver, vacillate.

faltering, adj. wavering.

faltering, n. hesitation, wavering, vacillation.

fame, n. celebrity, note, eminence, renown, glory, repute. Antonyms: obscurity, oblivion.

familiar, adj. intimate, close, cordial, near, friendly; informal, unconstrained, easy. Antonyms: unfamiliar, shy, distant.

familiarity, n. intimacy, conver-

sance; informality, freedom, disrespect. Antonyms: unfamiliarity, strangeness.

family, n. household; genealogy, lineage, ancestry.

famous, adj. renowned, famed, noted, eminent, distinguished. Antonyms: obscure, inglorious, unknown.

fan, v. winnow; cool, ventilate; stimulate, rouse, provoke, encourage.

fanatic, n. extremist, zealot.

fanatical, adj. fanatic, rabid, overzealous.

fancied, adj. imaginary.

fanciful, adj. whimsical, visionary, unpractical; fantastic, illusory, bizarre, erratic.

fancy, n. imagination, conception, conceit, idea, impression, opinion, notion; caprice.

fancy, adj. ornate, elaborate; fanciful, fabulous.

fancy, v. believe, imagine, conjecture, conceive; like.

fandangle, adj. fantastic, highfalutin'.

fan-shaped, adj. plicate, flagellate.

fantastic, adj. fanciful; unreal, spectral, illusive; whimsical, erratic; grotesque, odd, baroque, bizarre.

far, adj. distant, remote; alienated, estranged.

farce, n. burlesque, caricature, sham, take-off.

farcical, adj. burlesque, ludicrous, absurd.

farewell, n. adieu, leave-taking, good-bye, valedictory, parting.

far-fetched, adj. forced, strained, unlikely, implausible, improbable.

farm, n. grange; plantation; croft; hacienda.

farmer, n. agriculturist, granger.

farming, n. agriculture, husbandry.

far-off, adj. remote, distant.

fascinate, v. bewitch, enchant, charm, captivate, enamor, infatuate, entrance, enrapture.

fascination, n. enchantment, witchcraft, sorcery, magic, captivation, charm. Antonym: disenchantment.

fashion, n. vogue, style.

fast, adj. immovable, firm, rigid; strong, invincible, fortified; steadfast, faithful.

fast, adv. swiftly, rapidly, quickly, posthaste, speedily; fixedly, firmly.

fasten, v. secure, fix, lock, find, tie, attach, rivet, cement.

fastidious, adj. critical, punctilious. Antonyms: careless, slovenly.

fastness, n. fixedness, immovability, firmness, security; fortress, stronghold, swiftness.

fat, adj. fleshy, plump, obese, portly, burly, pampered, gross, stout.

fatal, adj. mortal, deadly.

fatality, n. destiny; mortality; calamity.

fate, n. destiny, lot, doom; chance, fortune; karma; kismet.

fated, adj. destined, doomed, predestined.

fateful, adj. ominous.

father, n. pater familias, procreator, sire, founder, originator, author.

father, v. beget, engender.

fatherhood, n. paternity.

fatherly, adj. paternal.

fatigue, n. weariness, languor, exhaustion.

fatigue, v. weary, tire, exhaust, bore.

fatness, n. corpulency, obesity, plumpness, fleshiness, stoutness, pudginess; fertility.

fatty, adj. greasy, unctuous.

fault, n. defect, imperfection, failing, shortcoming, flaw; dereliction, offense, lapse. Antonyms: merit, perfection, beauty.

fault-finder, n. critic, grumbler, censurer, censor.

fault-finding, adj. captious, critical, dissatisfied, grumbling, discontented, carping.

faultiness, n. defectiveness, imperfection, peccability.

faultless, adj. perfect, blameless, impeccable.

faulty, adj. imperfect, defective; erring.

faun, n. satyr, sylvan.

favor, n. countenance, regard, good-will, kindness; support, promotion, befriending. Antonyms: disfavor, opposition.

favor, v. support, countenance, encourage.

favorable, adj. propitious, conducive, beneficial, partial. Antonyms: unfavorable, unpropitious.

favoring, adj. partial, approving.

favoritism, n. partiality, bias. Antonym: impartiality.

fawn, v. truckle, curry favor, court.

fawner, n. bootlicker, footlicker.

fawning, adj. obsequious, servile.

fear, n. apprehension, anxiety,

solicitude, alarm, dread, panic, dismay, terror.

fear, v. apprehend, dread, be afraid of; reverence, stand in awe of.

fearful, adj. apprehensive, alarmed, afraid, frightened; timid, faint-hearted, cowardly, craven.

fearless, adj. intrepid, courageous, bold, undaunted, unafraid, unflinching.

feasibility, n. practicability.

feasible, adj. practicable.

feast, n. banquet, repast, regale, junket.

feast, v. banquet, junket; delight, gratify.

feat, n. exploit, stunt, act, deed.

feather, n. plume, quill.

feature, n. aspect, appearance; lineament; trait, characteristic, peculiarity.

federation, n. confederation, league, union.

fee, n. retainer, tip, honorarium, perquisite.

feeble, adj. infirm, doddering.

feed, v. bait, regale.

feed, n. provender, fodder.

feel, v. touch, handle; grope, grabble; experience, suffer.

feeler, n. antenna, tentacle, horn.

feeling, adj. susceptible, sensitive, sympathetic. Antonyms: insentient, unfeeling, stoic.

feeling, n. sensibility, sensation; emotion. Antonyms: insensibility, numbness.

feign, v. pretend, dissemble, affect, assume.

feigned, adj. pretended, simulate,

counterfeit, assumed. Antonyms: real, sincere, unfeigned.

feigning, n. simulation, dissembling.

feint, n. pretense, blind.

felicitate, v. congratulate.

fellow-countryman, n. compatriot.

fellowship, n. companionship, communion, converse.

felon, n. criminal, convict.

felonious, adj. heinous, atrocious, flagitious, infamous.

female, adj. feminine.

fence, n. barrier, stockade, hurdle, defense, enclosure, hedge.

fend, v. ward off, avoid.

fender, n. protection, defense, screen, guard.

ferment, v. stir up.

fern, n. brake, maiden hair, Venus hair, polypody.

ferocious, adj. rapacious, ravenous, savage.

ferocity, n. rapacity, fierceness.

fertile, adj. fruitful, fecund. Antonyms: infertile, barren.

fertility, n. fruitfulness, fecundity, richness. Antonyms: infertility, barrenness.

fertilizer, n. manure, phosphate of lime, compost.

fervency, n. ardor.

festival, n. fete, banquet, feast, holiday.

festive, adj. festal, convivial.

festoon, n. garland.

fetid, adj. malodorous, stinking.

fetter, n. shackle, bond, hamper, restraint.

fetter, v. shackle, manacle, hamper; restrain, impede.

feverish, adj. febrile.

fiat, n. order, decree, mandate, edict.

fib, n. falsehood, untruth.

fiber, n. staple, thread.

fickle, adj. vacillating, volatile, irresolute, fitful, unstable, variable, wavering. Antonyms: constant, steadfast.

fickleness, n. vacillation, irresolution, volatility.

fiddler, n. violinist.

fidelity, n. loyalty, fealty, faithfulness; truth. Antonym: infidelity.

fidget, v. squirm, fiddle, jiggle, be uneasy.

field, n. meadow, lea; campaign, croft; scope, range, room, province.

fiend, n. demon, brute, beast.

fiendish, adj. diabolical, infernal.

fierce, adj. violent, unrestrained, furious, impetuous, passionate, fiery. Antonyms: tame, gentle, docile.

fiery, adj. igneous; vehement, impetuous, passionate, irritable.

fight, n. combat, battle, engagement, struggle, fray, scrimmage; pugnacity.

fight, v. battle, combat, militate, cope with.

fighter, n. warrior, champion, combatant, gladiator.

figment, n. fabrication.

figurative, adj. typical, representative; metaphorical.

figure, n. shape, form, outline, image, statue, bust, likeness; numeral, digit.

figure, v. compute, cipher; contrive, scheme, plan; typify, repre-sent.

figure of speech, n. trope, metaphor.

file, n. line, row; rasp.

fill, n. sufficiency, plenty.

fill, v. satisfy, cloy, sate, glut, stuff; occupy, replenish; expand.

fill out, v. extend, inflate, complete, amplify.

filter, v. strain, clarify, percolate, exude, ooze, transude.

filtering, n. filtration; exudation, infiltration.

filth, n. squalor, foulness, corruption, muck, dirt.

filthy, adj. nasty, dirty, squalid, foul; obscene, indecent, lewd.

finally, adv. ultimately, eventually.

find fault, v. object, disapprove, demur, except, criticize, repine, complain.

finding, n. discovery; verdict.

finding out, n. detection, discovery.

find out, v. discover, detect, solve.

fine, n. penalty.

fine, adj. refined, nice, exquisite, excellent, elegant, admirable, choice, select. Antonyms: coarse, crude, stout, crass, thick.

finery, n. ornaments, decorations, clothes.

finesse, n. artifice, maneuvering, ruses.

finger, v. touch, handle; strum; name, inform on.

finicky, adj. finical, fastidious, dainty.

finish, v. complete, elaborate, conclude.

finish, n. completion.

fire, v. ignite, kindle; dismiss; inflame, irritate, excite; animate.

fire, n. combustion, ignition, burning; conflagration, holocaust; flame, blaze.

firebug, n. arsonist, incendiary.

firedog, n. andiron.

fireman, n. fire-tender, stoker.

fireproof, adj. incombustible.

fireside, n. hearth, ingleside.

firm, adj. fast, immovable, secure; compact, solid, dense; fixed, resolute. Antonyms: flaccid, soft, irresolute, yielding, facile.

first, adj. earliest; foremost, leading, chief, premier; primary, primordial, primitive.

first-rate, adj. excellent, first-class.

fish eggs, n. spawn, roe.

fishing, n. angling, trawling, trolling, whiffing, fishing.

fishy, adj. fishlike; extravagant, exaggerated.

fisticuffs, n. boxing, pugilism.

fit, n. spasm, paroxysm, convulsion; access, outburst, attack; humor, whim.

fit, adj. meet, becoming, suitable, proper, congruous, expedient, apposite, qualified.

fit, v. adapt, qualify, prepare, equip, shape, adjust.

fitful, adj. variable, capricious, unstable, inconstant, changeable.

fitness, n. becomingness, appropriateness, competency, congruity, eligibility; health, robustness, vigor.

fitting, adj. suitable, proper, fit.

fivefold, adj. quintuple.

five-sided, adj. pentagonal, pentahedral.

five years, n. quinquennium, lustrum.

fix, v. mend, repair, restore, adjust; rivet, fasten; settle, implant, define.

fix, n. dilemma, predicament, plight, quandary. Antonym: extrication.

fixed, adj. immovable, stable, firm, unchangeable, steadfast.

fixings, n. embellishments, trimmings.

fizzle, n. failure, fiasco.

flabbergast, v. astonish, amaze, surprise.

flabbiness, n. flaccidity, limpness.

flabby, adj. yielding, limp, soft. Antonyms: firm, stiff, rigid.

flag, n. colors, standard, banner, pennant, ensign, streamer; iris.

flagrant, adj. glowing, flaming, ardent; heinous, wicked.

flake, n. film, flock, scale.

flame, n. blaze, fire; love.

flaming, adj. blazing, afire, flagrant; dazzling, brilliant; ardent.

flare, v. flicker, flutter; dazzle, blaze, glare.

flare, n. glare, flicker.

flare-up, n. passion, anger.

flash, n. gleam, glare; instant, moment.

flash, v. glitter, gleam, sparkle, glisten.

flashy, adj. dazzling; gaudy, tawdry, showy.

flat, adj. level, even, plane, smooth; prone; stale, vapid, tasteless. Antonyms: convex, concave, undulating, projecting.

flatter, v. blandish, cajole, wheedle.

flatterer, n. wheedler, toady, flunky, sycophant.

flattering, adj. wheedling, adulatory, alluring, obsequious.

flattery, n. adulation, wheedling, flummery, cajolery.

flaunting, adj. ostentatious, showy.

flavor, n. savor, taste, relish, zest, gusto.

flavorful, adj. tasty, appetizing, savory.

flavorless, adj. insipid, vapid, unpalatable.

flaw, n. defect, fault, blemish.

flawed, adj. defective, faulty.

flawless, adj. faultless, perfect.

fleece, v. plunder, swindle, despoil.

fleet, n. squadron, navy, armada.

fleeting, adj. impermanent, transitory, ephemeral, fugitive, temporary.

fleshiness, n. corpulence, obesity, plumpness.

fleshly, adj. carnal, sensual.

fleshy, adj. corpulent, fat, obese, plump.

flexibility, n. pliability, suppleness, ductility.

flexible, adj. pliable, supple, pliant, lithe, limber; compliant. Antonyms: inflexible, incompliant.

flight, n. flying; exodus, hegira; fleeing.

flighty, adj. volatile, mercurial, giddy, fickle.

flimflam, n. trick, deception.

flimsy, adj. superficial, weak, feeble, shallow.

flinch, v. shrink, wince, recoil, withdraw.

flinty, adj. pitiless, obdurate, steely, impenetrable, unyielding.

flippant, adj. voluble, glib, fluent; pert, forward.

flirt, n. coquette,

flirtation, n. coquetry.

flirtatious, adj. coquettish.

float, n. raft; buoy.

flock, n. covey, herd, bevy, drove, pack, lot, brood.

flood, v. inundate, deluge.

floor, v. prostrate, fell, overthrow; embarrass.

florid, adj. flushed.

flounce, n. ruffle, furbelow.

flourish, v. thrive; wave.

flourish, n. embellishment; curlicue; fanfare, call; parade, show, display; waving.

flout, v. mock, jeer, sneer.

flow, v. circulate; proceed, issue. Antonyms: stagnate, ebb.

flower, n. blossom, bloom.

flowery, adj. florid, ornate.

flowing, adj. running, gliding, cursive. Antonym: stagnant.

fluctuate, v. vacillate, waver. Antonyms: continue, persist, adhere, abide, remain.

fluctuation, n. vacillation, oscillation, instability.

fluent, adj. flowing, gliding.

fluid, n. liquid, liquor.

flunk, v. fail, back out.

flunky, n. lackey, gofer.

flurried, adj. agitated, excited, perturbed.

flurry, n. squall, breeze, wind; agitation, commotion.

flush, n. flush, flow; thrill; redness.

flush, adj. liberal, prodigal, free; even, plane.

fluster, v. perturb, discompose,

disconcert.

fluster, n. perturbation, discompose, confusion.

flutter, v. tremble, palpitate; hover; fluctuate.

flutter, n. tremor, agitation, palpitation; confusion, disorder, commotion.

fly, v. wing, soar, flit, hover; decamp, flee.

flying, n. aviation, flight.

foam, n. froth, spume, lather.

foamy, adj. frothy, spumy.

foe, n. antagonist, enemy.

fog, n. haze, mist, vapor.

fog, v. befog, obscure, confuse.

foggy, adj. misty, hazy, vaporous; beclouded, confused.

foil, v. baffle, frustrate.

foist, v. interpolate.

fold, n. doubling, plait; sheeppen, embrace.

fold, v. double; embrace, clasp.

foliage, n. leafage, leaves.

folks, n. people, persons.

follow, v. succeed, chase, pursue, tag; result, flow, ensue, issue; pursue, practice, engage in; track.

follower, n. pursuer; attendant, retainer, disciple, advocate, adherent, imitator.

following, n. pursuance, pursuit; sequence, succession; adherents, retinue; vocation, trade, business.

following, adj. succeeding, ensuing, consecutive.

folly, n. foolishness, fatuity, absurdity.

foment, v. encourage, stimulate, fuel.

fond, adj. indulgent, doting; affectionate, loving; baseless, vain.

fondle, v. caress, pet, cosset, humor.

fondness, n. indulgence, doting; affection, love; partiality, liking, propensity, appetite.

food, n. aliment, nutriment, pabulum, nutrition, fare, diet, bread, meat.

fool, n. idiot, imbecile; simpleton, dunce, blockhead, ninny.

fool, v. dupe, gull, delude, deceive, trick, beguile, victimize.

fooling, n. foolishness, folly.

foolhardy, adj. daredevil, reckless.

foolish, adj. idiotic, senseless, irrational, silly, imbecile, witless, insensate, half-witted.

foolishness, n. idiocy, fatuity, silliness, irrationality, imprudence, folly, absurdity.

foot, n. paw; hoof; base, bottom.

footboy, n. page, lackey.

footing, n. foothold; rank, status, grade, amount, total; tread, step.

footprint, n. footmark, track.

footstep, n. footmark, footprint, track, trace; football, tread, step.

fop, n. coxcomb, dude, dandy, exquisite, blade. Antonyms: sloven, guy.

foppish, adj. dandified, finical, fashion-conscious. Antonyms: slovenly, seedy.

forbear, v. refrain, stop, pause, withhold; endure.

forbearance, n. withholding; long-suffering, patience, toleration.

forbearing, adj. long-suffering, patient, tolerant, lenient.

forbears, n. ancestors.

forbid, v. prohibit, interdict, inhibit, restrain, preclude, proscribe.
forbidden, adj. prohibited, proscribed, contraband, illicit, taboo.
forbidding, adj. repellent, repulsive, offensive, odious.
forbidding, n. prohibition, interdiction, restraint, taboo.
force, v. compel, coerce, constrain, oblige, make; impel, obtrude, extort. Antonyms: induce, seduce, persuade.
force, n. strength, energy, power, vigor, might, potency, validity, efficacy.
forced, adj. involuntary, compulsory, strained. Antonyms: spontaneous, voluntary.
forcible, adj. energetic, potent, effective, coercive, drastic, vigorous.
forcing, n. compelling, compulsion, coercion, extortion, constraint. Antonyms: discretion, option, election.
forebode, v. portend, presage, augur, betoken.
foreboding, n. premonition, presentiment, prescience.
forecast, n. predetermination, premeditation.
forefather, n. ancestor, progenitor, forbear.
forego, v. quit, relinquish, surrender, yield, do without.
foregoer, n. predecessor, forefather; forerunner, herald, precursor, harbinger.
foregoing, adj. previous, anterior, preceding, fore, prior, aforesaid.
foreign, adj. alien, extraneous, exotic; remote, adventitious.
foreigner, n. alien, emigrant, immigrant. Antonyms: native, indigence.
foreknowledge, n. prescience.
foreordain, v. preordain, predestinate, foredoom, predetermine.
forerun, v. precede, herald.
forerunner, n. precursor, harbinger, herald.
foreshadow, v. presage, augur, foretell, prefigure.
foresight, n. prescience, foreknowledge.
forest, n. wood, woodland, timberland, woods, wildwood.
forestall, v. anticipate; preoccupy.
foretell, v. predict, prophesy, augur, portend, forebode, divine, presage.
foretelling, adj. prophetic, portentous, predictive.
foretelling, n. prediction, prophecy, prognostication, presage, foreboding, divination.
forever, adv. eternally, continually, perpetually.
forewarning, n. premonition.
forfeit, n. forfeiture, penalty, fine, loss.
forger, n. fabricator, falsifier.
forgery, n. counterfeiting, falsification, counterfeit.
forgetfulness, n. amnesty, amnesia, oblivion.
forgivable, adj. pardonable, venial.
forgive, v. pardon, excuse, absolve, condone, connive.
forgiveness, n. pardon, remission, absolution, acquittal.
forgiving, adj. compassionate, indulgent, placable. Antonym: un-

forgiving.

forgo, v. omit, relinquish.

fork, v. ramify, branch.

forlorn, adj. deserted, disconsolate.

form, n. shape, structure, figure, formation, cast; formula, ritual; formality.

form, v. shape, fashion.

formal, adj. ceremonial, express, explicit, prim, ceremonious.

formality, n. ceremoniousness, precision, ceremony.

formative, adj. plastic, creative.

former, adj. antecedent, preceding, prior, bygone.

formerly, adv. heretofore.

formless, adj. shapeless, amorphous.

formula, n. ritual, ceremony; rule, recipe.

formulary, n. ritual, ceremonial, rule.

forsake, v. quit, abandon, leave; renounce, reject, relinquish.

forsaken, adj. abandoned, deserted, derelict.

forsaking, n. desertion.

fort, n. fortress, fortification, fastness, stronghold, redoubt.

forthwith, adv. immediately, directly.

fortunate, adj. lucky, favored; favorable. Antonym: unfortunate.

fortuneteller, n. chiromancer, palmist.

fortunetelling, n. chiromancy, palmistry.

forum, n. tribunal.

forward, adj. anterior, fore; presumptuous, impertinent, intrusive; premature.

forward, v. advance, promote, accelerate, further; transmit, send, ship.

forwarding, n. transmission.

fossilize, v. petrify, lapidify.

fossilized, adj. petrified; antiquated.

foster, v. nourish, nurse, support; promote.

foul, adj. filthy, squalid, dirty; abusive, obscene, vituperative, vulgar; detestable.

foul, v. defile, soil, dirty.

foul-mouthed, adj. scurrilous, abusive; profane, obscene.

found, v. establish, plant; cast, form.

foundation, n. substructure, base; founding; endowment.

founder, n. establisher, institutor, planter originator.

founder, v. fall, stumble; fail.

fount, n. spring,

fountain, n. fount, spring; source, fountainhead.

fourth, n. quarter.

foxy, adj. cunning, sly, wily.

fracas, n. brawl, uproar, disturbance, quarrel.

fractious, adj. unruly, perverse, irritable, ugly.

fracture, n. rupture, breach.

fragile, adj. brittle, frangible, frail.

fragility, n. brittleness, frailty.

fragment, n. remnant, chip, scrap, piece, flitter.

fragmentary, adj. disconnected, fractional.

fragrance, n. perfume, aroma, redolence. Antonym: stench.

fragrant, adj. sweet-smelling, redolent. aromatic, balmy.

frail, adj. fragile, brittle; feeble, weak, infirm.

frailty, n. fragility, brittleness; imperfection, fault.

frame, v. devise, plan, contrive; invent, fabricate; adjust, fit.

framework, n. frame, skeleton.

frank, adj. candid, outspoken, ingenuous.

frankness, n. candor, unreserve.

frantic, adj. distracted, frenzied, crazed.

fraternal, adj. brotherly.

fraternity, n. brotherhood.

fraud, n. imposture, deceit, duplicity, imposition, wile, circumvention, hypocrisy.

fraudulent, adj. deceptive, wily, crafty, surreptitious.

fraught, adj. laden, freighted, charged.

fray, n. fight, battle, combat, affray; fret.

frazzle, v. fray, tatter; exhaust.

freakish, adj. whimsical, capricious, fanciful, crotchety.

free, v. liberate, disenthrall, deliver, release, disengage, exonerate, extricate, disentangle.

free, adj. exempt, immune, unrestrained; liberated, freed, released, delivered; unreserved. Antonyms: subject, reserved, formal, coercive, restrained, bound.

free and easy, adj. informal, unceremonious, unrestrained.

freebooter, n. buccaneer, pillager, pirate.

freedom, n. exemption, immunity; liberty, independence, autonomy; privileges, immunities. Antonyms: subjection, liability, heteronomy, reserve, constraint, repression.

freeing, n. emancipation, liberation, release, enfranchisement, extrication, discharge, exoneration.

freely, adv. bounteously, readily, abundantly, voluntarily, copiously, unreservedly.

freethinker, n. infidel, skeptic.

freeze, v. congeal.

freight, n. cargo, lading.

frenzied, adj. distracted, frantic.

frenzy, n. distraction, rage.

frequent, adj. recurrent, everyday, normal, numerous.

frequent, v. visit, patronize, haunt.

freshen, v. refresh, revive.

fret, v. chafe, abrade, fray; gnaw, corrode; ruffle, agitate; worry, tease, irritate, fume, rankle.

fretful, adj. irritable, petulant, peevish, captious.

friction, n. abrasion, attrition, rubbing; clashing.

friend, n. wellwisher, intimate, chum, associate; patron, adherent, supporter; ally; Quaker.

friendliness, n. comity, amity, good will.

friendly, adj. amicable, favorable, kind; fraternal, neighborly, cordial; favorable, salutary. Antonym: unfriendly.

friendship, n. amity, intimacy, friendliness. Antonyms: enmity, estrangement, disaffection, hostility.

fright, n. alarm, fear, terror, dismay.

frighten, v. terrify, alarm, scare, intimidate, dismay, daunt, appall.
frightful, adj. terrible, dreadful, hideous, fearful, gruesome, grim, dire, awful, horrible.
frill, n. ruffle, gathering.
fringe, n. edging, margin, confine, border.
frisk, v. frolic, gambol.
frisky, adj. frolicsome, sportive, playful.
frivolous, adj. trivial, trifling, petty.
frolic, v. play, skip, leap, gambol, cavort, frisk.
frolicsome, adj. playful, prankish, frisky.
front, n. facade; obverse, face.
frost, n. rime, hoarfrost; unsociability.
frosting, n. icing.
frosty, adj. cold, icy; distant, aloof.
froth, n. spume, foam.
frothy, adj. foamy, soapy, lathered, bubbly.
froward, adj. refractory, unyielding, insubmissive, stubborn, disobedient.
frown, n. scowl, lower.
frowning, adj. scowling, lowering, stern.
frugal, adj. economical, saving, sparing, thrifty.
frugality, n. economy, thriftiness, thrift.
fruitful, adj. prolific, productive, fertile, bountiful.
fruitless, adj. unproductive, futile, ineffective.
frustrate, v. baffle, defeat, foil, balk, circumvent, nullify.
frustration, n. defeat, disap-

pointment, balking, foiling.
fugitive, n. runaway, escapee, deserter, renegade.
fulfill, v. accomplish, complete, realize; satisfy, fill, answer, meet; discharge.
fulfillment, n. consummation, fruition, realization; discharge, performance.
full, adj. filled up, replete; copious, ample, bountiful, abundant, liberal.
fulsome, adj. offensive, nauseous, disgusting, gross, immoderate.
fume, n. exhalation, reek, smoke, steam, vapor.
fume, v. smoke, reek; storm, rage.
fun, n. merriment, mirth, gaiety, frolic, jest, divertissement, amusement, relaxation.
function, n. duty, province, office, business, part; discharge, performance, execution.
fundamental, adj. basal, elementary, original, essential.
fundamentally, adv. primarily, essentially, radically.
funny, adj. comic, comical, amusing, laughable, witty, ludicrous, burlesque, absurd, humorous.
furbish, v. polish, scour, clean.
furious, adj. infuriated, angry, raging, violent, turbulent.
furnish, v. supply, provide, bestow, purvey, cater.
furniture, n. goods, movables.
furthermore, adv. moreover.
fury, n. wrath, rage, indignation, frenzy; termagant, shrew, vixen; agitation, excitement.
fuse, v. melt, liquefy, dissolve, smelt; commingle, blend, intermix.

fusion, n. melting, fluidity; intermingling, coalition, blending.

fuss, n. ado, bustle, to-do agitation, excitement.

fuss, v. pother, fume, fret; disturb, annoy, bother.

fussy, adj. fidgety, finical, scrupulous, overnice.

futile, adj. vain, bootless, unavailing, abortive.

fuzz, n. down, lint, fluff.

fuzzy, adj. downy, fluffy, furry.

G

gabble, n. gibberish, babble, prate, chatter.

gabble, v. gibber, jabber, babble, prate, chatter.

gag, v. silence, muzzle, muffle, hush.

gag, n. muffler, silencer.

gaiety, n. merriment, mirth, hilarity, sportiveness, joviality, elation.

gain, n. increase, profit, advantage, increment, acquisition, accretion, store; lucre.

gain, v. get, acquire, achieve, win, obtain, attain; persuade.

gainsay, v. contradict, dispute, deny, controvert.

gale, n. wind, tempest; excitement, confusion.

gall, n. bile; bitterness, rancor.

gall, n. impudence, audacity, insolence.

gall, v. chafe, fret; vex, annoy.

gallant, adj. polite, deferential, courtly.

gallant, n. spark, beau, philanderer; lover, seducer.

gallantry, n. chivalry, bravery;
heroism; politeness; intrigue.

gallery, n. balcony; corridor, passage, museum.

galoot, n. rowdy, blusterer.

gambler, n. gamester, card-sharp, blackleg, punter.

gambol, v. caper, frolic, play, sport, curvet.

game, n. play, amusement, pastime, fun, sport; context; prey; scheme, plan.

game, adj. plucky, resolute, courageous, unflinching, undaunted.

gang, n. band, crew, company, group, crowd, set, party, number.

gap, n. hiatus, rift, rent, chasm.

gape, v. yawn; gaze, stare.

garbage, n. trash, refuse, swill, waste.

garble, v. pervert, distort, falsify, misstate, wrench.

gardener, n. horticulturist.

gardening, n. horticulture.

garland, n. wreath, chaplet, bays, laurel; rosary.

garnish, v. embellish, beautify, decorate, trim.

gaseous, adj. aeriform, gassy, gasiform; tenuous, thin.

gash, v. slash, incise.

gash, n. incision, slash.

gassy, adj. gaseous, aeriform; boastful, vaporous.

gate, n. entrance, portal; wicket; turnstile, postern; tollgate; sluice gate; staunch.

gather, v. congregate, assemble, convene, muster, collect; harvest, pick, glean.

gather, n. pucker, plait, ruffle.

gathering, n. collection, crowd, assembly, congregation, concourse, muster, party, company.

gaudy, adj. showy, flashy, ostentatious, garish.

gaunt, adj. emaciated, pinched, meager, lean.

gawk, v. gape, stare, gaze.

gay, adj. merry, sportive, lively, exhilarating, jolly, blithe, airy, convivial.

gear, n. rigging, tackle, mechanism; accouterments.

gem, n. jewel.

general, adj. indefinite, vague, ill-defined; prevalent, extensive; usual, common, regular. Antonyms: specific, definite.

generality, n. bulk, common run, mass, main body; universality.

generalship, n. strategy.

generate, v. procreate, beget, reproduce, originate, produce.

generation, n. procreation, reproduction, begetting; origination, formation.

generative, adj. generating, procreative, genial.

generosity, n. magnanimity, nobleness; liberality, bounty, beneficence, lavishness.

generous, adj. magnanimous, noble, high-minded, ingenuous; munificent, bountiful, liberal, lavish. Antonyms: illiberal, stingy, scant, miserly.

genial, adj. generative, procreative; cheerful, pleasant, cordial, friendly.

gentle, adj. well-born, genteel, high-born; docile, tame, subdued; mild, quiet. Antonyms: drastic, vicious, brusque, harsh, rough,

severe, rigorous.

gentlemanly, adj. courteous, deferential, polite, urbane, gallant.

genuine, adj. authentic, veritable, sterling, unmixed, real, pure; sincere, unaffected. Antonyms: spurious, counterfeit, false, adulterated.

germ, n. origin, first principle; embryo, bud, seed.

germane, adj. related, allied, akin, relevant.

gesture, n. gesticulation, gesturing.

gesture, v. gesticulate.

get, v. procure, obtain, acquire, secure, gain, achieve, attain, realize.

getting, n. acquisition, obtaining, receiving, procurement.

ghastly, adj. cadaverous, ghostly, pallid, pale, horrible, repulsive.

ghost, n. shade, phantom, apparition, specter, spook, revenant, sprite.

ghostly, adj. spiritual; spectral.

giant, n. colossus, monster, Hercules, Goliath, Titan, Cyclops, ogre.

gibberish, n. jargon, jabber, gabbling, babble.

gibe, v. scoff, flout, jeer, sneer, deride.

gibe, n. ridicule, sneer, sarcasm.

giddy, adj. fickle, mercurial, volatile, flighty, unstable, thoughtless; light-headed, dizzy.

gift, n. gratuity, present, largess, offering, grant, donation, bounty, bequest.

gifted, adj. talented.

gigantic, adj. enormous, colossal,

vast, prodigious, titanic, gargantuan.

giggle, n. snicker, snigger.

gingerly, adv. carefully, cautiously, timidly.

gird, v. encircle, engird, surround prepare.

girdle, n. sash, belt, band.

girl, n. maiden, maid, lass, lassie, damsel, miss, nymph, female.

gist, n. core, substance, pith.

give, v. confer, bestow, accord, grant, donate, contribute, impart. Antonyms: withhold, refuse.

given, adj. granted, assumed; disposed, inclined; stated.

giver, n. donor.

give up, v. surrender, disgorge; yield, cease, desist, quit, relinquish, waive. Antonyms: resist, withstand, continue, persist.

give way, v. withdraw, retire, recede; yield.

giving, n. conferring, bestowal, granting.

glad, adj. pleased, delighted, happy, joyous, joyful, gratified, merry, elated. Antonyms: sad, sorrowful.

gladden, v. cheer, delight, please, exhilarate, gratify, elate.

gladness, n. delight, pleasure, elation, jubilation, rejoicing.

glamour, n. charm, witchery, magic, spell; illusion, glitter, glory. Antonyms: disillusionment, disenchantment.

glance, n. glimpse; gleam, flash.

glare, v. glitter, glisten, dazzle; frown.

glaring, adj. dazzling, intense, brilliant; flagrant, notorious.

glass, n. tumbler, goblet, bumper, beaker; decanter; carafe; mirror, telescope, binocular.

glasses, n. spectacles, eyeglasses, pince-nez, goggles.

glassy, adj. vitreous, transparent, crystal.

gleam, v. glimmer, glitter, radiate, beam, sparkle.

gleam, n. beam, ray, glimmer, glance, flash; splendor, sparkle.

glee, n. merriment, joy, mirth.

gleeful, adj. merry, gay, mirthful.

glib, adj. smooth slippery; fluent, voluble, bland.

glimmering, n. glimmer, glimpse.

glimpse, n. glance; flash; inkling.

glisten, v. sparkle, shine, gleam, flash, glitter, glister.

glister, v. sparkle, glisten, glitter.

glitter, n. brilliancy, shine, gleam.

glitter, v. sparkle, gleam, glisten.

glittering, adj. sparkling, glistening, glistering, bright, tinsel.

globe, n. sphere, ball, orb.

gloom, n. gloominess, shadow; melancholy, dejection.

gloomy, adj. dark, dismal, obscure, dim, shaded, overcast, lurid.

glorious, adj. magnificent, grand, splendid, admirable, excellent; hilarious, elated.

glory, n. fame, renown, honor, celebrity; magnificence, splendor; pride. Antonyms: ignominy, dishonor, obscurity, shame.

glory, v. exult, boast, vaunt.

gloss, n. luster, polish, sheen, glaze, enamel; show, commentary, note, comment.

gloss, v. annotate, illustrate; glaze, polish; extenuate.

glossy, adj. shining, sleek, lustrous, polished, glazed; specious.

glowing, adj. ardent, warm, flushed; luminous.

glum, adj. moody, sullen, morose, sour.

glut, v. satiate, sate, cloy; overfeed, overstock.

glut, n. superfluity, overstock, excess.

glutton, n. gormandizer, gourmand; wolverine.

gluttony, adj. voracity, greed, excess.

go, v. operate, pass, move, advance, repair, hark, stir, resort.

goad, v. urge, incite, prod, spur, instigate.

goal, n. end, aim.

goblin, n. gnome, specter.

go-between, n. middleman, agent, broker, procurer, factor, arbitrator, referee, advocate.

go beyond, v. surpass, transcend, exceed, overstep.

god, n. deity, divinity, idol.

godless, adj. irreligious, impious.

godlike, adj. divine.

godlessness, n. irreligion, impiety, atheism, ungodliness.

godly, adj. devout, religious, pious.

godmother, n. sponsor.

going, v. traveling, leaving, exiting, departing.

gold, n. aurum; bullion.

good, adj. virtuous, worthy, moral, exemplary, conscientious, sterling, saintly, altruistic.

good, n. welfare, benefit, advantage, utility, interest; virtue, worth.

good-bye, n. farewell, adieu.

good humor, n. amiability, affability.

good-looking, adj. comely, handsome, pretty, personable.

good-natured, adj. amiable, affable, indulgent, genial.

goods, n. chattel, effects, possessions; merchandise, wares.

goose, n. simpleton, gull, dupe.

gore, v. stab, pierce, penetrate.

gorge, n. gully, defile, ravine.

gorge, v. bolt, gulp, eat greedily; glut, stuff.

gorgeous, adj. magnificent, elegant, grand, splendid.

gossip, n. tattler, tale-bearer.

govern, v. direct, control, regulate, command, reign, restrain, bridle, guide.

governable, adj. manageable, obedient.

government, n. governance, sway, dominion, command, regency, regulation. Antonyms: anarchy, license.

governor, n. chief magistrate, executive.

gown, n. dress; robe; wrapper.

grab, v. seize, snatch, clutch.

grace, n. compassion, lenity, mercy, love, comeliness; refinement, elegance, polish.

grace, v. adorn, beautify, embellish; dignify, exalt.

graceful, adj. elegant, easy, willowy, courtly, polished. Antonyms: ungraceful, clumsy, awkward.

gracious, adj. merciful, lenient, compassionate, benign, tender; graceful.

graduate, n. alumnus.

grain, n. kernel, seed; cereals; granule, pellet; fiber, texture; disposition, humor, temper; particle.

grand, adj. august, imposing, sublime, stately, splendid, lofty, glorious, superb.

grandeur, n. splendor, magnificence, elegance, majesty.

grandiose, adj. impressing, imposing; declamatory, grandiloquent.

grant, v. convey, transfer, cede; give, bestow, allot, deign; admit.

grant, n. conveyance, transfer, cession; concession; gift.

grapple, v. seize, attack, clutch, struggle, contend.

grasp, v. seize, clutch, clinch, clasp, gripe; wrestle; comprehend.

grasp, n. seizure, apprehension, gripe, grip; hold, possession; understanding.

grasping, adj. avaricious, covetous.

grass, n. herbage, pasture; sward, sod, lawn, esplanade.

grateful, adj. thankful. Antonym: ungrateful.

gratification, n. satisfaction, indulgence, enjoyment, pleasure.

gratify, v. satisfy, indulge, content, delight, humor. Antonyms: deny, mortify.

grating, adj. harsh, jarring, rasping.

gratitude, n. thankfulness. Antonym: ingratitude.

gratuitous, adj. spontaneous, free, voluntary; uncalled for, unwarranted.

grave, adj. important, momentous, serious; sober, solemn, demure, sedate.

grave, n. tomb, sepulcher, ossuary, crypt, mausoleum.

gravel, n. pebbles, grit, shingle; arena; pebble, calculus.

graver, n. engraver, sculptor; burin.

gray, adj. hoary; slate, drab.

grease, n. lubricant, fat.

grease, v. lubricate.

greasy, adj. sebaceous, oily, oleaginous, fatty.

great, adj. immense, enormous, prodigious, gigantic; numerous; superior, excellent.

greatest, adj. supreme, superlative, utmost.

greediness, n. avarice, voracity, covetousness, rapacity, insatiableness, cupidity.

greedy, adj. avaricious, grasping; sordid, covetous; insatiable, ravenous, gluttonous; insatiate.

green, adj. verdant, emerald; awkward, unskilled; fresh. Antonyms: sear, parched, seasoned, ripe, veteran.

greenhorn, n. tyro, novice, gull, dupe, yahoo.

greenhouse, n. conservatory.

greenness, n. verdure; rawness, immaturity; inexperience, gullibility.

greet, v. address, salute, hail.

greeting, n. salutation, salute.

grief, n. anguish, sorrow, heartbreak, regret, remorse, misery, woe, tribulation.

grievance, n. wrong, injustice, resentment, trouble.

grieve, v. mourn, regret, lament, rue, weep, sorrow, bewail, deplore.

grievous, adj. afflictive, distressing, deplorable.

grill, n. gridiron, broiler.

grimy, adj. begrimed.

grind, v. crush, powder, pulverize, comminute, bruise; harass, persecute.

grind, n. grinding, pulverization; drudgery; dig.

grinding, n. pulverization, crushing.

grip, n. clutch, grasp; valise, satchel.

grip, v. seize, clutch, grasp.

grit, n. firmness, resolution, courage, fortitude, spirit.

gritty, adj. sandy; unyielding, plucky, spirited.

groan, v. moan, whimper.

groom, n. valet; hostler, stableman; bridegroom.

groove, n. rut, channel, furrow; rabbet, fluting.

groove, v. channel, furrow; chamfer.

grooved, adj. channeled, chamfered, fluted, striated.

gross, n. aggregate.

grotesque, adj. fantastic, bizarre, outlandish.

grouchy, adj. unamiable, sullen, surly, morose, cross, cranky.

ground, n. soil, earth, dirt, clod, loam, mould, clay, land.

groundless, adj. unfounded, chimerical, baseless.

grounds, n. settlings, sediment.

groundwork, n. foundation, basis.

group, n. cluster, crowd.

grovel, v. crawl, sneak, cringe.

groveling, adj. debased, abject, servile.

grow, v. increase, extend, augment, wax, accrue, develop, expand, flourish. Antonyms: wane, atrophy, blast, stunt, stagnate.

grower, n. cultivator.

growing, adj. developing, waxing.

growl, n. grumble, snarl.

growler, n. grumbler, snarler; cynic, pessimist.

growth, n. growing, development, accretion, extension, augmentation, enlargement. Antonyms: atrophy, decrease, blasting.

grub, v. drudge, slave, moil; root out, uproot.

grub, n. caterpillar, larva; food, meal.

grudge, n. ill-will, hatred, rancor, enmity, envy.

grudge, v. begrudge, resent.

grudgingly, adv. unwillingly, reluctantly, sullenly, resentfully.

gruff, adj. ungracious, surly, rude, impolite, stern.

grumble, v. murmur, repine, complain, croak.

grumbler, n. complainer, croaker, fault-finder.

grumpy, adj. surly, disgruntled, grouchy, sullen.

guarantee, n. warranty, security.

guard, v. protect, defend, shield, shelter, fortify. Antonym: expose.

guard, n. guardsman, watch, sentinel, patrol, sentry, picket; convoy, escort.

guarded, adj. cautious, wary, careful, reserved.

guardian, n. defender, guard, saint, keeper, protector, defense.

Antonyms: ward, protégé.
guardian, adj. tutelary, protecting.
guardianship, n. protection, care, watch.
guess, v. conjecture, speculate, surmise; think, suppose, presume, believe, opine.
guess, n. conjecture, surmise, speculation.
guesswork, n. conjecture.
guide, v. pilot, steer, direct.
guide, n. conductor, pilot, mentor, monitor; key.
guild, n. society, fraternity, corporation.
guile, n. subtlety, cunning, deceit, artifice.
guileful, adj. deceitful, crafty, artful, wily, subtle.
guilt, n. criminality, guiltiness, complicity, crime; wrong, offense. Antonyms: innocence, inculpability.
guiltless, adj. inculpable, blameless.
guilty, adj. culpable, punishable, criminal, sinful.
gulch, n. gully, ravine.
gulf, n. abyss, chasm; vortex, rapids; bay.
gull, n. cheat, swindle, humbug, fraud; dupe, gudgeon; mew.
gullet, n. esophagus.
gullible, adj. trusting, credulous.
gully, n. gulch, ravine, gorge.
gummy, adj. viscous, adhesive.
gun, n. firearm, weapon, rifle, shotgun, pistol, revolver, cannon.
guns, n. artillery, ordnance, cannon.
gush, v. rush, pour, stream.
gushing, adj. rushing, pouring;

effusive, demonstrative, sentimental.
gusto, n. enjoyment, appreciation.
gutter, n. trough; conduit, channel, drain.
guy, v. steady, guide, shore, stay.
gymnastics, n. athletics.
gypsy, n. nomad, vagabond.

H

habit, n. wont, custom, practice, usage, addiction, way.
habitual, adj. wonted, customary, regular.
habituate, v. accustom, addict, inure. Antonyms: disaccustom, wean.
hag, n. crone, virago, termagant, fury, beldame.
haggard, adj. gaunt, emaciated.
haggle, v. hack, hackle; chaffer.
hail, v. accost, salute, address.
hair, n. bristle; lock, tress; coiffure; forelock.
hairsplitting, adj. subtle, fine.
hairy, adj. hirsute, shaggy, bristly.
half, adv. partially, imperfectly.
half, n. moiety.
half-hearted, adj. indifferent, lukewarm, perfunctory.
halfway, adv. in the middle, imperfectly, partially
halfway, adj. intermediate, midway.
hall, n. auditorium, lyceum; vestibule, entry, court; corridor, passage, lobby.
hallow, v. consecrate, venerate, reverence, sanctify, bless.
hallowed, adj. holy, sacred, consecrated, dedicated, blessed,

sanctified.

hallucination, n. aberration, fallacy, self-deception, delusion, phantasm, illusion.

halo, n. nimbus, glory, aureole.

halve, v. bisect, dimidiate.

halving, n. bisection, dichotomy, dimidiation.

hammer, n. maul, mallet, gavel.

hammer, v. beat, forge, pound, strike.

hamper, v. fetter, shackle, impede, restrain, hinder, encumber, embarrass.

hamper, n. hanaper; shackle, fetter, restraint.

handbag, n. purse, pocketbook, satchel, reticule.

handbook, n. manual, guidebook, hornbook, enchiridion, manual.

handcuff, n. manacle, fetter, shackle.

handle, n. bail; hilt, haft.

handy, adj. dexterous, adroit, ready; convenient.

hang, v. suspend; dangle; droop, drop; append, attach.

hang, n. connection, arrangement, plan.

hanging, adj. suspended, pendent, pendulous, dangling.

hanging, n. suspension; drapery, valance, tapestry, dorsal, lambrequin.

hanging on, n. persistence, tenacity, importunity.

hanker, v. long for, yearn, crave, covet, lust.

hankering, n. longing, craving.

haphazard, n. chance, accident.

happen, v. occur, befall, betide;

supervene, intervene.

happiness, n. felicity, blessedness, delight, gladness, pleasure, bliss, rapture. Antonyms: sorrow, grief.

happy, adj. joyous, light-hearted, gay, blissful, glad, delighted, elated, merry. Antonym: unhappy.

happy-go-lucky, adj. improvident, easy-going, unthrifty.

harangue, n. declamation, ranting, screed.

harangue, v. declaim, spout, rant.

harass, v. fatigue, tire, weary; annoy, vex, torment, perplex, distress.

harbinger, n. forerunner, precursor, herald.

harbor, n. refuge, shelter, retreat; port, haven.

hard, adj. firm, solid, compact, impenetrable, unyielding, rigid, dense, insoluble.

harden, v. indurate, solidify; petrify, ossify, sear; inure, season, steel.

hardened, adj. callous, ossified, obdurate, incorrigible, inveterate, case-hardened.

hard-headed, adj. shrewd, astute.

hard-hearted, adj. unsympathetic, inexorable, unsparing, obdurate.

hardness, n. compactness, solidity, firmness.

hardship, n. privation, adversity, reverse, disaster.

hardy, adj. courageous, intrepid, brave; hearty, robust.

hare-brained, adj. heedless, reckless, rash, giddy.

harm, v. injure, hurt, damage, impair, mar, deface, abuse.

harm, n. injury, damage, scathe, mischief, misfortune.

harmful, adj. injurious, detrimental, baneful, prejudicial, ruinous.

harmless, adj. innocuous; inoffensive, peaceable.

harmonious, adj. symmetrical, consistent, conformable; consonant, melodious; amicable. Antonyms: inharmonious, discordant, incompatible.

harmonize, v. agree, chime, tally, accord, adjust.

harmony, n. concord, agreement, consonance, chime, unison; concordance, congruity, consistency.

harness, n. armor, array, gearing, tackling, gear; caparison.

harness, v. equip, array, caparison.

harp, n. lyre.

harsh, adj. inharmonious, rough, disagreeable, unpleasant; dissonant, discordant, austere, morose.

harum-scarum, adj. wild, giddy, volatile, hare-brained.

harvest, n. ingathering; crop, produce, fruit.

hash, n. ragout, potpourri, olio.

haste, n. celerity, swiftness, dispatch, speed; hurry, urgency. Antonyms: slowness, dilatoriness.

hasten, v. accelerate, expedite, quicken, urge; hurry.

hastiness, n. haste, precipitancy, precipitance.

hasty, adj. swift, rapid, quick, fast; rash, eager; hurried; superficial.

hatch, v. breed, incubate; concoct, brew, scheme.

hate, v. dislike, detest, abhor, despise, loathe.

hateful, adj. execrable, odious, detestable, abominable, malicious.

hatred, n. hate, aversion, animosity, malignity, spite, feud, malice, grudge.

haughtiness, n. arrogance, hauteur, disdain.

haughty, adj. arrogant, disdainful, magisterial, lordly.

haunt, n. hangout, meeting place.

haunt, v. frequent, revisit.

hauteur, n. arrogance, superciliousness, haughtiness.

haven, n. harbor, port, retreat, refuge, shelter.

havoc, n. destruction, waste, ruin, demolition, wreck.

hawk, n. falcon; kestrel.

haystack, n. rick.

hazard, n. chance, casualty; risk, random, danger, venture. Antonyms: safety, security, certainty.

hazard, v. venture, risk, jeopardy.

hazardous, adj. perilous, precarious, risky, unsafe.

haze, n. obscurity, dimness, fog, mist.

hazy, adj. foggy, misty, obscure.

head, n. chief, leader, commander, director; crisis, culmination; ear, spike.

head, adj. principal, chief, leading, cardinal, main, premier.

heading, n. title, caption.

headland, n. cape, foreland.

headlong, adv. headforemost; precipitately, rashly; helter-skelter, confusedly.

headstrong, adj. willful, perverse,

stubborn, froward.

heal, v. cure, repair.

healing, adj. curative, sanative, remedial, lenitive, medicinal, hygienist, sanitary.

healthful, adj. healthy; wholesome.

healthy, adj. hale, well, hearty; salubrious, salutary. Antonyms: unhealthy, ill, silky, delicate, diseased.

heap, n. pile, mass, accumulation, lot, stack.

heap, v. amass, accumulate, pile, stack.

hearing, n. audition, listening; audience; earshot, sound, hearing distance.

hearsay, n. rumor, report, gossip, bruit.

heart, n. conscience, character; essence, core, pith, kernel, marrow.

heart-broken, adj. disconsolate, inconsolable.

heartless, adj. cruel, pitiless.

hearty, adj. cordial, heartfelt, sincere; healthy, robust; nourishing.

heat, n. vehemence, fire, ardor, impetuosity, fervor, zeal, intensity; warmth.

heathen, n. pagan, idolater.

heaven, n. Paradise, Eden, Olympus, Nirvana.

heavenly, adj. celestial, supernal; divine, ravishing, sublime.

heaviness, n. weight, ponderousness, gravity.

heavy, adj. weighty, massive; burdensome, oppressive, onerous; soggy, unleavened.

hector, v. torment, tease, plague, bully.

heed, v. mind, regard, consider, notice.

heed, n. regard, attention, notice.

heedful, adj. attentive, circumspect, cautious, vigilant. Antonyms: inattentive, unmindful, careless, heedless.

height, n. altitude, loftiness; elevation; stature, eminence; summit, apex, culmination.

heinous, adj. atrocious, flagrant, monstrous.

heir, n. inheritor; scion; coheir.

hell, n. inferno, infernal regions, Hades.

hellish, adj. infernal, malignant, fiendish, atrocious.

helm, n. rudder, tiller, wheel; steersman, pilot; command, control.

help, v. abet, assist, befriend, aid, cooperate, second, subsidize.

help, n. aid, assistance, succor, support, facilitation, subsidy, cooperation.

helper, n. assistant, ally, supporter, helpmeet, coadjutor, confederate, deputy, aider.

helpful, adj. assistant, conducive, useful, salutary.

helping, adj. assisting, auxiliary.

helter-skelter, adv. irregularly, disorderly, headlong.

herald, n. messenger, precursor.

herald, v. proclaim, announce, foretell.

herd, n. drove; rabble, mob.

herdsman, n. ranch man, cowboy.

hereditary, adj. ancestral, patrimonial, inheritable.

heritage, n. inheritance, patrimony; possession.

hermit, n. recluse, anchorite, eremite.

heroic, adj. valiant, bold, daring, brave.

heroism, n. courage, valor, prowess, bravery.

hesitancy, n. indecision, vacillation, irresolution.

hesitate, v. doubt, falter, waver, scruple, demur, deliberate.

hesitation, n. indecision, doubt, reluctance, wavering.

hidden, adj. covert, latent; recondite, abstruse.

hide, v. veil, cloak, conceal, dissemble, secrete, mask; lurk.

hideous, adj. horrible, grim, grisly, repulsive, ugly, ghastly.

hiding, n. concealment, secretion.

high, adj. lofty, tall, elevated.

high and mighty, adj. arrogant, overbearing, lordly.

highest, adj. loftiest, superlative, meridian, supreme.

highfaluting, adj. bombastic, pretentious, grandiose.

highflying, adj. aspiring, presumptuous.

highhanded, adj. overbearing, arbitrary, despotic.

high jinks, n. revelry, carousal, wild sport.

highland, n. plateau.

high-minded, adj. magnanimous, honorable, noble. Antonyms: mean, base, low, servile, abject.

high-mindedness, n. magnanimity.

high-toned, adj. shrill, acute; honorable; fashionable.

highwayman, n. bandit, desperado, outlaw.

hill, n. mound, eminence, knoll; mount, rise, tor, prominence.

hilly, adj. undulating, uneven.

hinder, v. retard, obstruct, hamper, impede, thwart.

hindrance, n. hindering; obstacle, obstruction, restraint, encumbrance, check.

hint, v. intimate, suggest, imply, refer.

hint, n. allusion, suggestion, intimation, inkling.

hip, adj. trendy, fashionable, stylish, in vogue, modish.

hire, n. salary, wages, pay, stipend, compensation.

hire, v. engage; let, lease.

hireling, adj. mercenary, venal.

hiss, n. sibilate

hissing, n. derision, heckling, mocking; Antonym: applause.

history, n. annals, chronicle, record, account; autobiography.

hit, v. smite, buffet, strike.

hitch, n. catch, impediment, obstacle, contretemps.

hitch, v. hook, yoke, unite.

hoard, v. garner, amass, save.

hoard, n. store, supply, stock.

hoarse, adj. harsh, discordant, husky, raucous.

hobo, n. tramp, vagrant, bum.

hodgepodge, n. medley, farrago, potpourri.

hog, n. swine, porker; boar; sow

hoggish, adj. swinish, gluttonous.

hoity-toity, adj. flighty, giddy, frivolous; arrogant, self-important.

hold, v. sustain, restrain, retain, withhold, arrest; contain; clutch, grasp.

holder, n. tenant, occupier.

hold in, v. restrain, curb, check, repress, retain.

holding, n. restraint, retention, checking, detention; tenure, incumbency. Antonyms: incontinence, release.

hole, n. cavity, excavation, pit, perforation, rent, opening. Antonyms: imperforation, closure.

holiday, n. festival.

holiness, n. sanctity, piety, godliness.

hollow, adj. excavated; cavernous, vacant, void, empty; concave. Antonyms: convex, protuberant.

hollow, v. scoop, excavate, concave.

holy, adj. sacred, consecrated, hallowed, saintly, godly, pious.

homage, n. deference, obeisance, reverence, honor; fidelity; adoration.

home, n. domicile, residence, dwelling-place, abode, hearth; habitat, seat; asylum.

homely, adj. plain, uncomely; inelegant, rude.

homesickness, n. nostalgia.

honest, adj. honorable, reputable; upright, sincere, ingenuous.

honesty, n. uprightness, probity, integrity, candor, sincerity.

honey-tongued, adj. persuasive, seductive.

honor, n. respect, esteem, veneration, reverence, homage; probity. Antonyms: dishonor, disesteem, improbity, disrepute.

honor, v. esteem, respect, revere, venerate; dignify, exalt.

honorable, adj. upright, honest, reputable, magnanimous.

honors, n. titles, dignities, privileges.

hoodlum, n. rowdy, tough, vandal, thug, lout.

hoodwink, v. deceive, impose upon, delude, dupe, overreach.

hook, n. hasp, clasp, catch; crook.

hook, v. fasten, catch, secure; entrap, ensnare.

hoot, v. shout, deride, denounce.

hop, v. spring, jump, skip, bound, leap, caper, gambol, dance.

hope, n. optimism, anticipation. Antonyms: despair, desperation, pessimism.

hopeful, adj. expectant, promising.

hopeless, adj. despairing, desperate, unpromising.

horde, n. troop, gang, throng, multitude.

horn, n. trumpet, bugle, cornet, shofar.

horrible, adj. dreadful, terrible, shocking, grim, ghastly, revolting, appalling.

horrid, adj. offensive, detestable.

horror, n. abhorrence, dread, detestation.

horror-stricken, adj. horror-struck, horrified, appalled.

horse, n. equine, stallion, stud, sire; mare; colt, foal, filly; pony.

horseman, n. jockey; equestrian; cavalier.

hospital, n. infirmary, asylum, retreat.

host, n. entertainer; landlord; multitude, horde; army, legion.

hostile, adj. antagonistic, inimical, repugnant.

hostility, n. enmity, animosity, opposition, warfare.

hostler, n. groom.

hot, adj. torrid, sultry, fiery, scorching, grilling, tropical; vehement, passionate.

hot-blooded, adj. ardent, irritable, excitable.

hotel, n. hostelry, inn, tavern.

hound, v. importune, harass.

house, n. dwelling, residence, abode; mansion, palace; tenement; chateau.

house, v. shelter, protect, harbor; abide, dwell.

hovel, n. hut, shanty, shack, cabin, den, dugout.

howl, v. yowl, roar, ululate, yawl.

hub, n. nave; protuberance.

hubbub, n. tumult, uproar, din, clamor, racket, commotion.

huckster, n. peddler, hawker, cadger.

huff, n. petulance, tiff, pet.

huffy, adj. petulant, touchy.

hug, n. embrace, cuddle.

hug, v. embrace, clasp, squeeze.

huge, adj. mammoth, colossal, vast.

hullabaloo, n. uproar, vociferation, din, clamor, tumult.

hum, n. drone, murmur, buzz; croon.

humble, adj. lowly, meek, modest, unpretentious.

humble, v. humiliate, debase, abase.

humbug, n. imposition, hoax, deception, imposture, quackery; imposter, deceiver, cheat.

humbug, v. deceive, impose on.

humdrum, adj. monotonous, tedious, prosy, tiresome.

humiliate, v. humble, mortify, abash, disgrace.

humiliation, n. abasement, mortification, degradation; humbleness, meekness.

humility, n. meekness; lowliness, diffidence, modesty.

humor, n. disposition, temper, mood; jocularity, pleasantry, wit, satire.

humor, v. indulge, please, gratify.

humorist, n. wag, droll, wit.

humorous, adj. facetious, droll, comical, waggish.

hump, n. protuberance, hunch.

hungry, adj. voracious, ravenous, eager; starved, infertile, barren.

hunt, v. chase, pursue, follow; search, seek, rummage, ferret; poach.

hunt, n. chase, pursuit, search, hunting.

hunter, n. huntsman, sportsman, Nimrod; seeker, pursuer.

hurly-burly, n. tumult, bustle, turmoil, commotion.

hurrah, n. cheer, huzzah.

hurricane, n. cyclone, tornado.

hurried, adj. cursory, hasty.

hurry, n. haste, speed dispatch, expedition.

hurry, v. hasten, impel; expedite, accelerate, speed.

hurt, v. damage, wound, impair, harm, injure, offend.

hurt, n. injury, wound, detriment, harm.

husband, n. spouse, benedict. Antonym: bachelor.

hush, v. silence, still, repress; appease.

husk, n. hull, rind, shell.

husky, adj. dry, raucous, harsh, guttural, hoarse.

hut, n. hovel, shack, shed.

hypocrisy, n. dissimulation, Pharisaism, insincerity, double standards, duplicity.

hypocrite, n. dissembler, charlatan, fraud.

hypocritical, adj. pharisaical, dissembling, sanctimonious. Antonyms: sincere, unfeigned, ingenuous.

I

icy, adj. glacial; slippery.

idea, n. conception, notion, opinion, fancy, impression; intention.

ideal, adj. faultless, consummate.

idiocy, n. imbecility, foolishness, fatuity, senselessness.

idiot, n. imbecile.

idle, adj. leisure, vain, futile; indolent, inactive, lazy.

idleness, n. indolence, sloth, laziness; vanity.

idler, n. sluggard, drone, loafer.

idol, n. image, effigy.

idolize, v. deify, worship, adore.

ignoble, adj. humble, untitled; base.

ignominious, adj. dishonorable, shameful, disreputable.

ignominy, n. disgrace, dishonor, reproach, shame, humiliation.

ignoramus, n. dunce, illiterate, wiseacre, dullard.

ignorance, n. illiteracy, unen-

lightenment.

ignorant, adj. illiterate; unaware, unlearned, unlettered, nascent; Antonyms: educated, instructed, schooled, trained, learned.

ignorantly, adv. unknowingly, inadvertently, unwittingly.

ignore, v. disregard, slight, connive.

ill, adj. ailing, sick, unwell; evil, adverse, bad.

ill at ease, adj. uneasy, uncomfortable, on edge, tense.

illegal, adj. illicit, contraband, illegitimate.

illegality, n. unlawfulness, illegitimacy.

illegitimate, adj. illegal, illicit; spurious.

illiberal, adj. ungenerous, stingy; narrow-minded, bigoted.

illiberality, n. parsimony, narrow-mindedness, intolerance.

illicit, adj. prohibited, unlawful.

illness, n. malady, sickness.

illogical, adj. fallacious, sophistic.

illusion, n. mockery hallucination, phantasm, delusion.

illusive, adj. delusive, illusory, mocking.

illustrate, v. elucidate, picture, demonstrate.

illustration, n. elucidation; comparison, example, simile.

ill-will, n. malice, resentment, grudge, rancor, antipathy, hatred.

image, n. statue; effigy, figure; idol.

imaginary, adj. fancied, visionary, chimerical, illusive.

imagination, n. fancy, conception,

notion, conceit, figment.

imagine, v. conceive, fancy; think, suppose, opine.

imbecile, n. idiot, fool.

Imitate, v. copy, ape, counterfeit; personate, mimic, simulate; parody, caricature.

imitation, n. copy, counterfeit; mimicry, impersonation; parody, travesty, burlesque.

imitative, adj. apish, copying, mimicking, mimetic.

imitator, n. copyist, follower, mimic, mime, ape, echo.

immanence, n. inherence, indwelling.

immanent, adj. inherent, indwelling.

immature, adj. undeveloped, embryonic, crude, unripe, premature.

immediately, adv. instantly, forthwith, directly, straightway, at once, now, instant. Antonyms: hereafter, by and by, after a while.

immense, adj. vast, infinite, illimitable.

immerse, v. submerge, plunge into, dip, immerge, douse.

immersion, n. submersion, immersing; engrossment.

immoderate, adj. excessive, exorbitant, inordinate, intemperate.

immodest, adj. indecorous, indelicate, shameless; lewd, unchaste.

immoral, adj. licentious, dissolute, vicious, profligate, loose, illicit.

immorality, n. vice, depravity, profligacy.

immovable, adj. fast, permanent, impassive, firm.

impact, n. collision, forcible contact.

impart, v. communicate; imbue, instill, lend.

impartial, adj. equitable, fair, disinterested, unbiased.

impartiality, n. fairness, equity, justice.

impassable, adj. impenetrable, pathless.

impatient, adj. restless, restive, fretful, eager.

impede, v. retard, obstruct, block, delay.

impediment, n. obstacle, barrier, stumbling block.

impending, adj. imminent, threatening.

impenetrable, adj. impervious.

impenitence, n. obduracy.

impenitent, adj. unrepentant, obdurate, recusant.

imperative, adj. binding, compulsory, obligatory, imperious.

imperfect, adj. defective, faulty, deficient, abortive, fallible, frail.

imperfection, n. detect, blemish, shortcoming, infirmity, deformity, vice, frailty, fallibility.

imperious, adj. despotic. magisterial, domineering, tyrannical, imperative.

imperishable, adj. permanent, enduring.

impersonate, v. personate: personify.

impersonator, n. mimic, mime, actor

impertinent, adj. irrelevant, inapplicable, impudent.

impervious, adj. impermeable, solid.

impetus, n. momentum, force, impulse.

implacable, adj. unappeasable, vindictive, pitiless.

implant, v. instill, inculcate.

implied, adj. tacit, inferential.

implore, v. beseech, supplicate, entreat, beg, plead.

impolite, adj. discourteous, inurbane, rude, uncivil, disrespectful, saucy, insolent, impertinent.

impoliteness, n. discourtesy, inurbanity, incivility, insolence.

importance, n. moment, materiality, consequence; self-importance.

important, adj. momentous, material, essential; pompous.

imposing, adj. impressive, stately, august.

impossibility, n. impracticability.

impossible, adj. impracticable, unfeasible.

impostor, n. pretender, cheat, mountebank, quack.

Imposture, n. fraud, imposition, deception.

impracticability, n. unfeasibility.

impracticable, adj. impossible.

imprison, v. incarcerate, immure, jail.

imprisonment, n. incarceration, durance, duress, confinement, commitment.

impromptu, adj. improvised, offhand.

improper, adj. indecorous, unseemly, indecent, inappropriate, wrong.

impropriety, n. unsuitableness, unfitness, indecency.

improve, v. amend, ameliorate, rectify, better, mend; utilize, use; gain, get better.

improvement, n. betterment, amelioration; utilization.

impudence, n. insolence, impertinence, rudeness,

impudent, adj. insolent impertinent, flippant, pert, brazen, saucy.

impulse, n. motive, incentive: impulsion, impetus.

impulsive, adj. passionate, capricious, hasty; impellent, propulsive.

impure, adj. tainted, defiled, contaminated, polluted, vitiated, infected; adulterated, alloyed.

impurity, n. defilement, contamination, taint, pollution: adulteration, alloy, sophistication.

inability, n. incompetence, impotence, incapability, incompetency, inefficiency, disability.

inaccuracy, n. inexactness. incorrectness, impropriety.

inaccurate, adj. incorrect, inexact, erroneous, faulty, wrong.

inaction, n. inactivity, inertness, stagnation, idleness.

inactive, adj. inert, motionless, sedentary, dormant, inoperative, sluggish, stagnant, dilatory.

inactivity, n. inaction, passivity, inertia, lethargy, dormancy, stagnation, torpor.

inadequate, adj. insufficient, deficient; defective, incomplete, imperfect.

inappropriate, adj. unsuitable, unbecoming, inapplicable.

inapt, adj. irrelevant, unsuitable, inept, inapplicable.

inattention, n. inadvertence, abstraction, heedlessness, disregard, neglect, remissness.

inattentive, adj. heedless, absentminded, inadvertent, unmindful, careless.

inborn, adj. congenital, inherent, innate, instinctive, ingenerate.

incapable, adj. incompetent, disqualified, unfit, insusceptible.

incarnation, n. embodiment, manifestation, avatar; personification.

incautious, adj. unwary, inconsiderate, indiscreet, thoughtless.

incentive, n. motive, spur, incitement, stimulus, inducement, provocation.

incivility, n. discourtesy, rudeness, inurbanity, disrespect.

inclination, n. leaning, slant; tendency, propensity, proneness, penchant, predilection.

incline, n. slant, slope, ascent, descent, grade.

incline, v. lean, tend, dispose.

include, v. comprise, comprehend, consist of, embrace; incorporate, involve, rope in. Antonym: exclude.

inclusion, n. comprisal.

income, n. revenue, proceeds; tontine, annuity.

incomparable, adj. peerless, matchless, transcendent, inimitable, unrivalled, unapproachable.

incompetent, adj. inefficient, unqualified, incapable; inadequate; unfit, unsuited.

incomplete, adj. unfinished, defective, imperfect, deficient, partial, inchoate.

incomprehensible, adj. inconceivable, abstruse, unfathomable.

inconsiderate, adj. thoughtless, heedless, inattentive, careless.

inconsistency, n. discordance, incoherence, contrariety, incompatibility.

inconsistent, adj. disagreeing, incoherent, contradictory, discrepant, incompatible.

Inconstancy, n. fickleness, variableness, instability.

inconstant, adj. fickle, changeable, volatile, flighty, mercurial, variable.

inconvenient, adj. tiresome, inopportune, difficult, problematic, awkward; embarrassing, undesirable, untoward.

incorrect, adj. inaccurate: erroneous, inexact, wrong; ungrammatical.

incorrectness, n. inaccuracy, inexactness, error; impropriety.

increase, v. augment, advance, enlarge; multiply, be prolific.

increase, n. augmentation, accretion, increment, accession, amplification, addition,

incumbent, adj. obligatory, imposed, binding.

incurable, adj. irremediable, immedicable; irreparable.

indebtedness, n. obligation; debts, liabilities.

indecency, n. immodesty, indelicacy, shamelessness, obscenity, ribaldry, lewdness.

indecent, adj. immodest, obscene, indelicate, shameless, ribald, lewd, unchaste.

indecision, n. vacillation, indetermination, irresolution, wavering, inconstancy.

indecisive, adj. inconclusive, vacillating, hesitating, irresolute, wavering.

indefatigable, adj. untiring, persistent, unremitting sedulous, unflagging.

indefinite, adj. vague, indeterminate, equivocal, ambiguous, inexplicit, inexact.

indelicacy, n. tactlessness, tastelessness, coarseness, indecency, impropriety, rudeness, indecorum, immodesty.

indelicate, adj. unrefined, indecorous, immodest, unchaste, rude, vulgar.

indemnity, n. security, insurance; restitution, reimbursement, indemnification.

indentation, n. bruise, notch, depression, indenture, jag.

independence, n. freedom, self-government, liberty, autonomy; opulence, affluence.

independent, adj. self-governing, exclusive, irrespective; affluent.

indicate, v. designate, betoken, signify.

indication, n. designation, signifying; symptom, evidence, sign, token, manifestation.

indictment, n. accusation, charge, arraignment, crimination.

indifference, n. apathy, coolness, negligence, unconcern, nonchalance, insouciance; mediocrity.

indifferent, adj. disinterested, unconcerned, nonchalant, perfunctory, apathetic, neutral, impartial.

indirect, adj. roundabout, circuitous, tortuous.

indiscreet, adj. unwise, imprudent.

indiscretion, n. folly, imprudence; misstep, lapse.

indisposed, adj. averse, disinclined, unwilling, loath, reluctant; sick, ill, unwell.

indisposition, n. disinclination, averseness, reluctance, unwillingness.

indisputable, adj. undeniable, incontestable, indubitable, incontrovertible.

indocile, adj. intractable, refractory, unruly.

indolence, n. idleness, laziness, sloth, inactivity, faineance.

indolent, adj. lazy, slothful, supine, dronish, listless.

inducement, n. incentive, incitement, motive, stimulus.

indulge, v. satisfy, gratify, luxuriate; humor, pamper, coddle, spoil; grant. Antonyms: mortify, deny, suppress, restrain.

indulgence, n. humoring, pampering, gratification; kindness, favor. Antonyms: denial, restraint.

indulgent, adj. forbearing, kind, lenient, lax, merciful.

industrious, adj. assiduous, diligent, sedulous, persistent, hardworking. Antonyms: idle, indolent, inactive, lazy.

industry, n. assiduity, diligence, activity; labor, work, exertion, efforts.

indwelling, n. immanence, inherence.

indwelling, adj. inherent.

ineffective, adj. ineffectual, unavailing, inefficacious.

inefficient, adj. ineffective, inefficacious; slack, remiss, incompetent.

inelastic, adj. inductile, inextensible, rigid.

inelasticity, n. inductility, inextensibility, rigidity.

ineligible, adj. disqualified.

inequality, n. disparity, disproportion, unevenness, irregularity; unfairness, injustice.

inexcusable, adj. unpardonable, indefensible, unjustifiable, unwarrantable.

inexhaustible, adj. exhaustless.

inexorable, adj. unyielding, relentless, implacable, unmovable, unrelenting.

inexperienced, adj. untrained, unpracticed, undisciplined, raw, unskilled.

inexpert, adj. maladroit, unskillful, bungling.

inexpressible, adj. ineffable, unspeakable, unutterable.

infallibility, n. inerrability.

infallible, adj. inerrable, unerring, sure, certain, undeniable.

infamous, adj. disreputable, ignominious, scandalous, odious, heinous.

infamy, n. disgrace, ignominy, odium, obloquy, opprobrium.

infancy, n. babyhood; minority, nonage, pupilage.

infant, n. baby; minor. infantile paralysis, poliomyelitis.

infatuate, v. enamor, charm. Antonyms: repel, disgust, disillusion.

infection, n. contagion, contamination, vitiation, pollution.

infectious, adj. contagious, pestiferous, epidemic, vitiating.

infer, v. deduce, imply, gather.

inference, n. deduction, conclusion, illation, corollary.

inferior, adj. poorer, lower, subordinate, menial, minor, mediocre, subaltern.

inferior, n. subordinate. Antonyms: peer, equal, superior.

inferiority, n. subordination, mediocrity, deficiency. Antonym: superiority.

infidel, n. free-thinker, atheist, unbeliever, skeptic.

infirmity, n. weakness, malady, ailment, sickness.

inflammable, adj. combustible; irascible, irritable, excitable.

inflate, v. expand, enlarge, distend.

inflated, adj. distended; blown up; bombastic, pompous, grandiloquent, declamatory.

inflation, n. distention, expansion.

inflection, n. modulation, accent.

Inflexibility, n. rigidity, stiffness; firmness, pertinacity, obstinacy, steadfastness.

inflexible, adj. unyielding, rigid; immovable, resolute, steadfast.

influence, n. sway, control; persuasion, authority, ascendency, prestige.

influence, v. move, persuade, induce, sway, control, prevail upon, actuate, impel.

informal, adj. unceremonious, unconventional, easy, natural, unconstrained.

information, n. knowledge, intelligence, instruction, data, facts, evidence.

infringe, v. violate, transgress; encroach, trespass, entrench.

infringement, n. transgression, violation, breach. encroachment, trespass, entrenchment.

ingenious, adj. inventive, resourceful.

ingratitude, n. thanklessness, ungratefulness. Antonym: gratitude.

ingredient, n. constituent, element, component, part.

inhabitant, n. dweller, denizen, resident, citizen. Antonyms: sojourner, pilgrim, visitor.

inherent, adj. innate, adhering, inexistent, inborn, inalienable, inheritable.

inheritance, n. heritage, patrimony, legacy.

inhuman, adj. savage, barbarous, fiendish, brutal, cruel.

inhumanity, n. cruelty, brutality, barbarity, mercilessness.

injure, v. damage, harm, hurt, impair, disfigure, maim, mar, wound.

injurious, adj. hurtful, harmful, detrimental, pernicious, deleterious, baneful, maleficent.

injury, n. damage, detriment, harm, hurt, wound, impairment, mutilation.

injustice, n. inequity, unfairness; grievance.

inkling, n. hint, intimation, allusion.

inlet, n. entrance, ingress; bay, recess, estuary, cove, firth, bayou.

inmate, n. occupant; prisoner, convict.

inn, n. lodging house, tavern, hotel; cabaret, caravansary.

innate, adj. inborn, inherent, native.

inner, adj. internal, interior; obscure.

innocence, n. blamelessness, guilelessness, guiltlessness, impeccability.

innocent, adj. blameless, guileless, guiltless, impeccable, inoffensive, sinless, artless.

inquiring, adj. curious, inquisitive.

inquiry, n. question, query, interrogation; research, investigation.

inquisitive, adj. inquiring, curious, intrusive, prying, meddlesome. Antonyms: indifferent, unconcerned, disinterested.

insatiable, adj. unappeasable; voracious, rapacious, omnivorous.

inscrutable, adj. incomprehensible, inexplicable, unsearchable.

insecure, adj. risky, unsafe, precarious, rickety, unstable, dangerous.

insecurity, n. risk, instability, precariousness.

insensibility, n. unconsciousness, torpor, coma, narcosis, lethargy.

insensible, adj. unfeeling, numb, insensate, torpid, unsusceptible, unconscious.

inseparable, adj. indivisible, indissoluble.

insert, v. interpolate, intercalate, interject.

insertion, n. interjection, interpolation, intercalation.

inside, adj. internal, inner, interior.

insight, n. discernment.

insignificance, n. unimportance,

pettiness, immateriality, triviality, inanity.

insignificant, n. meaningless; unimportant, immaterial, petty, trivial, paltry.

insincere, adj. disingenuous, dissembling, false, hypocritical, affected, deceitful.

insincerity, n. duplicity, disingenuousness, hypocrisy.

insinuation, n. innuendo, intimation; ingratiation.

insist, v. persist, press, urge, contend.

insistence, n. persistence, pertinacity, importunity, contention, instance.

insistent, adj. persistent, importunate, insisting.

insolence, n. impudence, contumely, impertinence, effrontery, disrespect.

insolent, adj. impudent, contumelious, overbearing, disrespectful.

insoluble, adj. indissoluble; unexplainable, unsolvable, inexplicable.

inspect, v. examine.

inspiration, n. motivation, stimulation, muse; idea, insight, flash, revelation.

inspiring, adj. elevating, promethean, stirring, rousing, moving, stimulating.

install, v. instate, induct.

installation, n. induction.

instance, n. persistency, request, solicitation, urgency; example, case, illustration.

instantly, adv. immediately, forthwith, at once, urgently, persis-tently.

instruct, v. teach, indoctrinate, edify, enlighten, coach.

instruction, n. nurture, tuition, teaching, information, indoctrination, education, admonition,

instructive, adj. edifying, didactic, informative, educational, useful, helpful, enlightening.

instructor, n. teacher, preceptor, tutor, master, coach, mentor, counselor, monitor, trainer.

instrument, n. tool, utensil, implement; agent, means, medium.

insufferable, adj. intolerable, unendurable; detestable, offensive.

insufficiency, n. deficiency, inadequacy.

insufficient, adj. inadequate, deficient, incommensurate, lacking.

insult, n. indignity, affront.

insult, v. offend, affront, flout.

insulting, adj. offensive, contemptuous, scurrilous.

insurance, n. assurance, indemnity.

insure, v. assure, indemnify; underwrite.

insurgency, n. revolt, rebellion, mutiny.

insurgent, adj. rebellious, mutinous, insurrectionary. Antonym: content.

insurgent, n. rebel, mutineer, insurrectionist, revolutionary, guerrilla.

intelligence, n. knowledge, discernment, insight, acumen.

intelligent, adj. clever, discerning, astute, bright, knowing, apt, sensible.

intemperance, n. excess, immoderation, debauchery.

intemperate, adj. immoderate, excessive, unrestrained.

intend, v. design, purpose, propose, contemplate; plan.

intense, adj. extreme, excruciating.

intensify, v. aggravate, exacerbate, heighten.

intention, n. design, plan, purpose, aim.

intentional, adj. deliberate, premeditated. Antonyms: unintentional, inadvertent, accidental.

intercede, v. mediate, interpose, propitiate.

intercessor, n. mediator, interceder, propitiator.

interchange, n. reciprocation, reciprocity; alternation; junction, crossroads.

interest, n. concern; share, portion, part, participation. Antonyms: boredom, ennui, indifference, unconcern.

interested, adj. concerned; prejudiced, partial. Antonyms: disinterested, unconcerned, bored.

interfere, v. clash, conflict; intermeddle, interpose, intervene.

interference, n. clashing, collision; intermeddling, interposition, intervention.

interloper, n. intruder, interferer.

intermediate, adj. intervening, interlocutory; middle, midway, inbetween, transitional, halfway.

intermittent, adj. remittent, periodical, recurrent.

internal, adj. inward, interior, inside, inner; inherent.

interpret, v. construe, translate, render.

interpretation, n. understanding, explanation, reading, construal, elucidation, analysis, rendering, rendition, translation.

interval, n. interstice; interim, meantime.

intervening, adj. intermediate, overriding, overruling, dominant.

intervention, n. interference, interposition; mediation, intercession.

intolerable, adj. insufferable, unendurable, unbearable, excruciating.

intolerance, n. bigotry, dogmatism.

intolerant, adj. bigoted, prejudiced, narrow-minded.

intricacy, n. complication, entanglement, complexity.

intricate, adj. complicated, entangled, involved, complex, elaborate, convoluted.

intrigue, n. conspiracy, machination, cabal, plot; amour, liaison.

intrigue, v. plot, scheme, machinate, cabal.

intriguer, n. machinator, plotter, schemer.

intriguing, adj. scheming, wily.

intrinsic, adj. inherent, innate, real, genuine. Antonym: extrinsic.

introduction, n. preface, proem, prelude, prologue, foreword, preamble.

introductory, adj. preliminary, prefatory.

intrude, v. infringe, invade, encroach, obtrude, interlope.

intrusion, n. encroachment, ob-

trusion, infringement, interloping.
intrusive, adj. obtrusive. Antonym: retiring.
invade, v. infringe, encroach, trespass, entrench.
invalid, adj. null, void; baseless, unfounded.
invalidate, v. annul, abrogate, cancel, quash, nullify.
invalidation, n. nullification, abrogation, annulment.
invasion, n. foray, raid, aggression; violation, infringement, encroachment, entrenchment.
inveigle, v. wheedle, seduce.
inveiglement, n. wheedling, seduction.
investigate, v. probe, sift, examine.
investigation, n. examination, inquiry, research.
invidious, adj. objectionable, offensive.
invincible, adj. indomitable, unconquerable.
invisible, adj. imperceptible, microscopic.
invitation, n. bidding, call, summons.
invite, v. bid, ask, summon; allure, induce, entice.
invocation, n. prayer, supplication.
involuntary, adj. uncontrollable, instinctive, forced.
iota, n. scintilla, tittle, atom, mite, jot, whit, bit, particle.
iridescent, adj. prismatic, nacreous.
iron, v. smooth; mangle.
irons, n. fetters, chains, handcuffs, shackles, manacles.
irrecoverable, adj. irretrievable.
irregular, adj. abnormal, anomalous, exceptional, unusual, baroque, aberrant.
irregularity, n. abnormality, asymmetry, anomaly, aberration, intermittency.
irreligious, adj. ungodly, impious, godless, sacrilegious, blasphemous, profane.
irresolute, adj. wavering: vacillating, inconstant, fickle.
irresolution, n. indecision, vacillation, inconstancy, fickleness.
irresponsible, adj. unaccountable, unanswerable, unreliable,
irritable, adj. irascible, fretful, spleeny, choleric, petulant, fiery, captious.
irritate, v. intensify, stimulate: provoke, vex, annoy, offend, chafe.
island, n. isle, ait, islet; atoll.
isolate, v. insulate, segregate, dissociate, detach, separate.
isolated, adj. insulated, separate, solitary, segregated.
isolation, n. insulation, segregation; loneliness, solitude.
issue, v. gush; sally forth, debouch; proceed, emanate, ensue, follow, result.
jab, n. thrust, punch, dig.
jabber, n. gibberish, chatter, gabble, babble.
jaded, adj. world-weary, worn-out, fed-up, bored, cynical, exhausted. Antonym: fresh.
jag, n. notch, cleft, barb, protuberance. v. notch.
jagged, adj. cleft, jaggy, notched, serrated, erose, sharp.
jail, n. prison, lockup, calaboose, workhouse.

jailbird, n. prisoner, convict, inmate, detainee.

jailer, n. warden, turnkey, sheriff.

jam, n. preserve, conserve; crowd, throng, crush.

jam, v. squeeze, crowd, press, wedge in, bruise.

jamboree, n. carousal, revelry, carouse, spree.

jangle, n. clashing, clang, discord, dissonance; wrangling, quarrel, dispute.

jangle, v. clash, clang; quarrel, wrangle, dispute, altercate.

jangling, adj. discordant, dissonant, clashing, inharmonious.

jar, n. crock, pot, container.

jar, v. jolt, jounce, shock, discompose, unsettle; grate, irritate, irk.

jargon, n. gibberish, drivel, babble, gabble, twaddle, bosh, slang.

jaundiced, adj. prejudiced, biased, warped.

jaunty, adj. jolly, dashing, cheerful, spry, lively, brisk, merry, sprightly, self-confident.

jealous, adj. suspicious, distrustful.

jealousy, n. suspicion, distrust.

jeer, v. mock, deride, ridicule, taunt, jibe.

jeering, n. mockery, derision, ridicule, scoffing, sneer, taunt.

jellylike, adj. gelatinous, colloid.

jeopardize, v. imperil, risk, expose, endanger, hazard.

jeopardy, n. danger, peril, hazard, exposure.

jerky, adj. abrupt, unconnected.

jest, n. joke, witticism, quip.

jester, n. joker, wag; buffoon, merry-andrew, clown, harlequin, zany.

jesting, n. joking, raillery, banter, persiflage, facetiousness.

jesting, adj. waggish, jocular, facetious, sportive.

jet, v. spurt, spout, gush; protrude, project.

jet, n. spouting, spurt, gush.

jewel, n. gem, brilliant.

jewelry, n. jewels; gems.

Jezebel, n. virago, she-devil, fury, Gorgon, termagant.

jibe, v. agree, harmonize, fit.

jiffy, n. moment, instant, second, trice.

jingle, n. tinkling, jingling, tintinnabulation; rhyme.

jingle, v. tinkle.

job, n. task; situation, position.

jog, n. shake, jolt, shove: hitch, break.

jog, n. push, shake, jostle; suggest to, notify, remind.

join, v. connect, couple, unite, combine, associate, add, append. Antonyms: disjoin, disconnect.

joiner, n. link, coupling, bond; woodworker, carpenter.

joint, adj. combined, joined, united.

jointed, adj. articulated, hinged; knotted, gnarled.

joke, n. jest, witticism, jocosity, sally, quip, quirk.

joke, v. rally, banter, jest.

joking, n. jesting, rallying, banter.

jolly, adj. jovial, vivacious, congenial, convivial, mirthful, sportive.

jolt, n. jar, shock, jounce, jolting.

jolt, v. shake, jar, jounce.

jot, n. iota, point, tittle, bit, mite, atom, scintilla.

jotting, n. memorandum, note,

entry.

jounce, n. jolt, shake, jolting.

jounce, v. jolt, shake, jar.

journal, n. day-book, daily register, record; diary; periodical, publication, magazine, gazette.

journey, n. trip, tour, pilgrimage, excursion, travel, jaunt.

journeyman, n. craftsman, artisan. Antonyms: apprentice, amateur.

joust, v. tilt.

jovial, adj. jolly, mirthful, gay, merry, sportive, hilarious, gleeful.

joviality, n. gaiety, jollity, sportiveness, liveliness.

joy, n. gladness, exultation, jubilation, mirth, festivity, glee, elation.

joyful, adj. joyous, glad, elated, jubilant, exhilarating, happy.

joyous, adj. joyful, glad, elated.

jubilant, adj. joyful, exultant, triumphant.

jubilation, n. rejoicing, exultation, triumph.

Judas, n. betrayer, traitor.

Judas, adj. traitorous, treacherous, disloyal, perfidious.

judge, v. adjudge, adjudicate, try; discern, distinguish discriminate.

judge, n. justice, judger; arbitrator, arbiter, umpire, referee; connoisseur, critic.

judgment, n. decision, adjudication, arbitration, sentence, decree.

judicial, adj. judicative, judicatory, juridical, judiciary.

judicious, adj. prudent, discreet, well-advised.

jug, n. pitcher, ewer, demijohn, flagon.

juggler, n. prestidigitator, magician, conjurer; cheat, impostor; jongleur.

juicy, adj. succulent, sappy, lush, luscious. Antonyms: sapless, dry.

jumble, v. confuse, disarrange, entangle, mix.

jumble, n. disorder, confusion, disarray, mixture, entanglement, chaos.

jump, v. spring, bound, leap, hop, caper, vault; bounce, jolt.

junction, n. union, coalition; juncture.

juncture, n. joint, seam; crisis, conjuncture, point, exigency.

jungle, n. thicket, brake, wilderness, brush.

juryman, n. juror.

just, adj. upright, honest, conscientious, honorable, straightforward; condign, merited. Antonyms: dishonest, inequitable.

just, adv. precisely, exactly; closely, nearly, almost; barely, scarcely, only.

justice, n. justness, equity, impartiality; judge. Antonyms: inequity, injustice.

justifiable, adj. warrantable, defensible.

justification, n. vindication, exculpation, exoneration, defense.

justified, adj. reasonable, correct, right, valid, fit, proper.

justify, v. vindicate, warrant, excuse, exonerate, exculpate, absolve, defend.

justly, adv. honestly, fairly, equitably, impartially.

justness, n. justice, fairness, equity, impartiality.

jut, v. jut out, project, protrude.

juvenile, adj. youthful, young, immature.

juvenility, n. youthfulness, immaturity.

K

keen, adj. sharp, acute, trenchant; penetrating, shrewd, astute, discerning.

keep, n. custody, charge; maintenance, support; stronghold, donjon; condition, case.

keep, v. detain, restrain, hold, retain, repress, withhold; preserve.

keeper, n. warden; superintendent, curator, custodian, guardian, attendant

keeping, n. holding, restraint, custody, guard, guardianship, protection.

keepsake, n. memento, souvenir.

kernel, n. seed, grain; nucleus; gist, core, pith, substance, essence, marrow.

kerosene, n. coal oil, petroleum.

kettle, n. cauldron, pot.

key, n. pitch, tone; clue, solution, guide, explanation, elucidation.

kick, v. jolt, jerk, thrust, hit, strike; boot, punt; give up, quit, conquer, overcome.

kick, n. kicking, opposition; thrill, buzz, boost.

kicking, adj. excellent, exciting, enjoyable.

kidnap, n. abduct.

kidnapper, n. abductor, man-stealer.

kidnapping, n. abduction.

kill, v. slay, slaughter, murder, assassinate, dispatch, execute, destroy. Antonym: revive.

killer, n. slayer, murderer, assassin, assassinator, executor, destroyer.

kin, n. relationship, relatives, relations, kindred, kinfolk, kinsmen.

kind, adj. indulgent, compassionate, merciful, lenient, clement, benign, gracious.

kind, n. variety, genus, species, strain, breed, nature, genre, sort.

kind-hearted, adj. compassionate, lenient, clement, kind.

kindle, v. enkindle, fire, ignite, incite, inflame, rouse.

kindness, n. compassion, benignity, benevolence, kindliness, graciousness, clemency.

kindred, n. relationship; relatives, relations, kinfolk, kin, kinsmen.

kindred, adj. related, congenial, allied, similar.

king, n. monarch, sovereign, potentate, ruler.

kingdom, n. empire, dominion, sovereignty, monarchy, realm.

kingly, adj. royal, regal, monarchical; sovereign, august, majestic, grand. Antonyms: servile, mean, abject, slavish.

kink, v. snarl, become entangled.

kink, n. snarl, knot, entanglement, twist; crotchet, whim, caprice.

kinky, adj. snarled, tangled, knotted; crotchety, eccentric, capricious.

kinsman, n. relative.

kiss, v. osculate.

kiss, n. osculation, buss, smack, smooch, peck.

knack, n. ability, skill, talent, flair, aptitude, gift.

knave, n. villain, rascal, scamp.

knavery, n. villainy, rascality, scoundrelism, chicanery, knavishness, roguery.

knickknack, n. gimcrack, gewgaw, bauble, trinket, curio, bric-a-brac.

knife, n. dagger, stiletto, dirk, poniard, bowie-knife.

knight, n. man-at-arms: champion, gallant.

knighthood, n. chivalry.

knightly, adj. chivalrous, gallant.

knob, n. bump, lump, bulge, protuberance, protrusion.

knock, v. rap; clash, bump; strike, beat.

knock, n. blow, stroke, rap.

knoll, n. hillock, mound.

knot, n. entanglement, snarl, intricacy, complication; cluster, group.

knot, v. entangle, tie, snarl. Antonyms: disentangle, unravel, untie.

knotted, adj. knurled, gnarled, gnarly; snarled, entangled, interwoven,

knotty, adj. knotted, gnarled; intricate, difficult, complicated.

knowable, adj. ascertainable, cognizable, cognoscible, intelligible, recognizable. Antonyms: unknowable, unascertainable, unrecognizable.

knowing, adj. intelligent, sagacious, wise, clever; expressive, significant; artful, sharp, cunning.

knowingly, adv. consciously, intelligently, wittingly, designedly.

knowledge, n. learning, lore, erudition, culture, enlightenment, attainments, information. Antonym: ignorance.

L

labor, n. toil, work, drudgery, task, industry, travail.

labored, adj. studied, elaborate, overwrought, stiff, unnatural.

laborer, n. toiler, workman, stevedore, roustabout, drudge, hack.

laborious, adj. toilsome, arduous, onerous; diligent, industrious, sedulous.

labyrinth, n. maze, intricacy, complexity.

lace, n. string, cord, thong, aglet.

lacerate, v. tear, rend, mangle, harrow, wound.

laceration, n. tearing, rending, harrowing, wound.

lack, v. need, want, be in need of, require.

lack, n. want, need, deficiency, dearth, paucity, scarcity.

lackadaisical, adj. languishing, listless, lazy, apathetic, laid-back.

lacking, adj. deficient, insufficient, unsupplied, shy, wanting, devoid.

lag, v. fall behind, loiter, linger, delay, saunter.

lament, v. bemoan, weep, wail, deplore, grieve, bewail, mourn.

lamentable, adj. deplorable, grievous, pitiable, distressing, sorrowful.

lamented, adj. mourned for, deplored.

lampoon, v. libel, defame, satirize.

lance, n. spear, javelin, harpoon.

land, n. terra firma; country; freehold; ground, soil, earth; realty, real estate.

land, v. disembark, debark; capture.

landing, n. disembarkation, debarkation; wharf, dock, quay; capture.

landlord, n. host, hotel-keeper, innkeeper; owner, proprietor.

landscape, n. scene, scenery, view, prospect.

language, n. speech, tongue, vernacular; dialect; idiom, phraseology, diction.

lanky, adj. gangling, overgrown.

lapse, n. slip, misstep, indiscretion; backsliding; devolution,

large, adj. big, extensive, huge, unwieldy, vast, massive, immense.

lariat, n. lasso, riata, reata, rope.

lark, n. frolic.

lascivious, adj. lewd, libidinous, salacious.

lash, n. scourge, thong, whip.

lash, v. scourge, castigate, flagellate; satirize, scold, rate.

lashing, n. scourging, castigation, flagellation; satire, scolding, rating.

lasso, n. lariat, rope, reata.

last, adj. final, hindmost, farthest, latest, ultimate.

last, v. continue, endure, remain.

lasting, adj. enduring, durable, permanent, imperishable, abiding. Antonyms: ephemeral, transitory, fleeting, transient, fugitive, impermanent.

lastly, adv. finally.

late, adj. tardy, delayed; recent.

lately, adv. recently.

latent, adj. concealed, dormant, undeveloped, hidden.

later, adj. subsequent, posterior.

latitude, n. breadth, width; room, range, scope, extent, freedom; laxity.

laud, v. extol, praise.

laudable, adj. praiseworthy, commendable.

laugh, v. cachinnate, roar, giggle, snicker, titter, chuckle.

laughable, adj. risible, comic, ludicrous, droll, facetious, farcical, amusing.

laughing, adj. merry, gleeful, mirthful, smiling.

laughter, n. mirth, laugh, cachinnation, giggle, snicker, roar.

launch, v. set afloat; set going, start; throw, hurl.

lavish, adj. profuse, prodigal, free, unstinted; superabundant.

law, n. statute, ordinance, edict, enactment, decree, canon, usage.

law-breaker, n. criminal, malefactor, culprit, felon, delinquent, offender, sinner.

law-breaking, n. crime, misdemeanor, transgression, violation.

lawful, n. legal, legitimate, licit, legalized.

lawfulness, n. legality, legitimacy. Antonyms: unlawfulness, illegality.

lawless, adj. anarchical, riotous, licentious.

lawlessness, n. anarchy, unrestraint, abandon, license, riot.

lawmaker, n. legislator, lawgiver, Solon.

lawsuit, n. litigation, case, suit, action.

lawyer, n. attorney, counselor,

barrister, counsel, advocate, attorney-at-law.

lax, adj. loose, slack, flabby,

lay, v. deposit, place; impose, assess; impute, charge, ascribe, attribute.

layer, n. stratum, course, tier.

laziness, n. indolence, sloth.

lazy, adj. Indolent, slothful, sluggish. Antonyms: diligent, industrious, sedulous, hard-working.

lead, v. guide, conduct, escort, direct; precede; induce, entice, influence.

leader, n. guide, commander, coryphaeus, pilot, bellwether, protagonist, chief.

league, n. alliance, confederation, coalition, confederacy, union, federation, association.

lean, v. incline, slope, recline, tend; rely, depend; career.

lean, adj. thin, lank, spare, meager, poor, skinny, gaunt.

leap, v. spring, jump, vault, bound, caper, gambol, prance.

learn, v. master, acquire knowledge.

learned, adj. educated, erudite, lettered, scholarly.

learning, n. education, erudition, lore, scholarship, knowledge.

lease, v. let, demise, rent.

least, n. minimum.

leave, v. depart from, vacate, retire from; abandon, forsake, desert; abstain from.

lecture, n. discourse, address, dissertation; reproof, scolding.

leg, n. limb, shank, support.

legacy, n. bequest, devise.

legal, adj. lawful, legitimate. Antonym: illegal.

legality, n. lawfulness, legitimacy. Antonym: illegality.

legalize, v. legitimize, decriminalize, sanction, permit. Antonym: prohibit.

legend, n. fable, myth; posy, inscription, motto.

legendary, adj. mythical, traditional,

legible, adj. readable, decipherable. Antonym: illegible.

legion, n. host, army.

legitimate, adj. lawful. Antonym: illegitimate.

lend, v. loan.

lengthen, v. extend, elongate, stretch, prolong, protract; expatiate, amplify.

lengthwise, adv. longitudinally.

lengthy, adj. long, prolix, protracted, verbose.

lenient, adj. compassionate.

lenity, n. clemency, mercy, lenience.

lessen, v. reduce, diminish, minify, depreciate, minimize, decrease.

lessening, n. reduction, diminution, decrease, decrement, depreciation, mitigation, shrinkage.

lesson, n. task, exercise.

let, v. allow, permit, suffer; lease, rent.

lethargy, n. drowsiness, stupor,

let-up, n. abatement, assuagement, respite, subsidence.

level, adj. even, flat, plain, smooth, flush, plump; horizontal; steady. Antonyms: undulating, uneven, concave, convex, warped.

levity, n. lightness, buoyancy;

gaiety, frivolity.

lewd, adj. unchaste, lustful, licentious; libidinous, lecherous, incontinent. Antonyms: chaste, modest, pure,

liability, n. debt, exposure, accountability, responsibility. Antonyms: immunity, exemption.

liable, adj. exposed, subject, accountable, answerable. Antonyms: exempt, immune.

libel, n. defamation, vilification, slander. Antonym: praise.

libel, v. defame, sully, slander, malign.

libelous, adj. defamatory, slanderous, calumnious.

liberal, adj. open-handed, generous, bounteous, munificent, unstinted, princely. Antonyms: illiberal, ungenerous, stingy, limited, narrow, bigoted.

liberty, n. freedom, independence, autonomy; license, privilege, permission. Antonyms: captivity, bondage, servitude, subjection, constraint, serfdom, slavery.

license, v. legalize, permit.

licentious, adj. immoral, dissolute, profligate, lewd, libertine, rakish, lascivious

lick, v. lap; flog, thrash, chastise, castigate, trounce, drub.

licking, n. flogging, chastisement, castigation, punishment, thrashing, whipping.

lid, n. cover, top, cap.

lie, n. untruth, falsehood, fib; fiction, fabrication; subterfuge.

lien, n. encumbrance.

life, n. existence, being, animation, vitality; vivacity, spiritedness, energy.

lifeless, adj. dead, inanimate, spiritless, devitalized.

lift, v. raise, elevate, hoist.

light, adj. buoyant; easy; active nimble, deft, fleet, swift, spry.

light, v. ignite, illumine, illuminate.

light-fingered, adj. thievish, pilfering.

like, adj. similar, alike, cognate, analogous, homogeneous.

like, v. fancy, approve of; prefer, choose, wish.

likelihood, n. probability, verisimilitude. Antonyms: unlikelihood, improbability.

liken, v. compare.

likeness, n. similitude; resemblance, similarity, appearance, guise, analogy; portrait.

liking, n. fondness, partiality, affection, approval, preference, predilection. Antonyms: distaste, aversion, hatred, antipathy, disapproval.

limb, n. branch, bough.

limber, adj. flexible, pliant, limp, pliable, supple, lithe, lithesome.

limit, n. bound, boundary, confine, extent; restriction, check, restraint, limitation.

limp, adj. flaccid, flabby, limber, soft, flexible.

linen, n. napery; lingerie; damask.

linger, v. loiter, saunter, tarry, lag.

link, v. join, unite, connect, couple, concatenate

liquid, n. fluid.

list, n. catalog, inventory, roster, schedule, register.

list, v. record, catalog, register; slant, tilt, lean, incline.

listen, v. hearken; eavesdrop. Antonyms: disregard, ignore, scorn.

listless, adj. inattentive, indifferent, supine, heedless, unconcerned.

litigation, n. lawsuit, legal action.

litter, n. stretcher; disorder, untidiness, confusions, jumble, clutter, mess; trash, waste, garbage, refuse, debris, rubbish; family, brood.

little, adj. small, diminutive, minute, tiny, wee, puny, petite.

live, v. exist; dwell, reside, abide.

liveliness, n. animation, vivacity, sprightliness, briskness, activity, lilt.

lively, adj. animated, spirited, vivacious, vigorous, active, brisk. Antonyms: slow, sluggish, inactive, quiet.

livid, adj. outraged, furious, fuming; bruised, black and blue.

living, n. life, existence, being; livelihood, sustenance, subsistence.

load, v. encumber, lade, burden, freight.

loaf, v. lounge about, loiter.

loathe, v. abhor, hate, detest, abominate, despise, execrate, recoil from.

location, n. situation, locality, place.

lock-jaw, n. tetanus.

logical, adj. consistent, sound, rational, coherent. Antonym: illogical.

loiter, v. saunter, linger.

lone, adj. alone, lonely, isolated, desolate; unfrequented, solitary.

long, v. yearn for, hanker for, crave.

longshoreman, n. stevedore.

long-suffering, adj. forbearing, uncomplaining, patient.

look, v. glance, gaze, stare, see, view, observe.

look, n. glance, glimpse, inspection, scrutiny, gaze; expression.

look into, v. inspect, examine, probe, investigate.

lookout, n. observatory, watchtower, conning tower, responsibility.

look over, v. inspect, examine, scrutinize, reconnoiter.

look upon, v. regard, esteem, consider.

loophole, n. excuse, plea, pretext.

loose, v. release, disengage, free, disentangle, liberate, absolve.

looseness, n. laxity, slackness, relaxation.

loot, n. spoil, booty, plunder, prize; plundering, pillage.

lopsided, adj. unbalanced, disproportioned.

lord, n. nobleman, aristocrat, grandee; liege.

lordly, adj. overbearing, domineering, despotic, arrogant, imperious.

lose, v. miss, forfeit.

loss, n. defeat, trouncing, failure, victory, forfeiture; deficit, debit, shortfall; damage; harm, injury. Antonyms: victory, success, gain.

lost, adj. forfeited, missing; derelict, adrift; misspent, misemployed.

lot, n. destiny, doom, fortune, fate;

portion, parcel, part, allotment; much, many.

loud, adj. deafening, stentorian, resonant, clarion; clamorous, vociferous, boisterous.

lounge, v. recline, loll.

lout, n. booby, boor, bumpkin.

loutish, adj. boorish, lubberly, gawky, ungentlemanly.

lovable, adj. amiable, winsome, lovely, winning.

love, n. affection, devotion, infatuation, passion; amorousness.

lovely, adj. charming, delightful, delectable, amiable, pleasing.

lover, n. amoroso, inamorato, swain, suitor, admirer, philanderer.

loving, adj. affectionate; enamored; amative, amorous, erotic.

low, adj. blue, sad, depressed; base, mean, vulgar, raffish, ignominious, undignified.

lower, v. drop; depress, reduce; decrease, diminish, fall, humble.

lower, adj. nether, under.

lowest, adj. nethermost.

lowliness, n. humility, meekness, self-abasement.

lowly, adj. humble, meek, unassuming.

low-minded, adj. groveling, abject, sordid, base-minded.

loyal, adj. true, constant, faithful, devoted, staunch, unwavering.

loyalty, n. fidelity, constancy, faithfulness, devotion, fealty, allegiance.

lozenge, n. tablet, troche, pastille.

luck, n. fortune, chance, fortuity, haphazard, chance, hap, hazard.

lucky, adj. fortunate; favorable, auspicious, propitious.

lug, v. drag, pull, tug, haul.

luggage, n. baggage, suitcases, bags.

lukewarm, adj. tepid, indifferent, cool, unconcerned.

lull, v. hush, still, quiet, tranquillize; subside, abate.

lumbering, adj. unwieldy, ponderous, cumbersome ungraceful.

lump, n. mass, swelling, protuberance, knob, bulge.

lumpish, adj. inert, heavy; stupid, dull, stolid.

lunatic, n. madman, maniac, bedlamite.

lurch, v. sway, stagger, roll; dodge, shift, evade, bilk.

lure, n. decoy, enticement, bait.

lure, v. entice, tempt, seduce, allure, decoy.

lurk, v. prowl, loiter, lie in wait, creep around, skulk.

luscious, adj. delicious, delectable; cloying, fulsome.

lush, adj. juicy, succulent.

lust, n. yearning, desire, hunger, longing, thirst.

lust, v. yearn, desire, ache for.

luster, n. brightness, gloss, glitter, sheen, brilliancy.

lusterless, adj. dull, drab, faded.

lustful, adj. lascivious, lecherous, licentious, libidinous.

lusty, adj. robust, sturdy, stalwart, strapping, muscular.

luxuriance, n. exuberance, rampancy, richness.

luxurious, adj. voluptuous, epicurean, sybaritic.

luxury, n. lavishness, sumptuousness, opulence, magnificence, extravagance; treat, extra, bonus.

lying, adj. untruthful, false, mendacious, deceitful.

lying, n. falsehood, lie, untruth, mendacity, fabrication, fiction.

M

mad, adj. crazy, insane, demented, maniacal, raving; indignant.

madden, v. incense, anger, enrage, infuriate, provoke.

made up, adj. devised, fabricated, artificial, sham, false, counterfeit.

madhouse, n. bedlam, insane asylum.

madman, n. maniac, lunatic, bedlamite; monomaniac.

madness, n. dementia, insanity, craziness, mania, lunacy.

magazine, n. storehouse, depot, repository; periodical, publication.

magic, n. enchantment, conjuration, wizardry.

magic, adj. magical, necromantic, talismanic.

magician, n. conjurer, prestidigitator, sorcerer, wizard.

magnet, n. loadstone.

magnificence, n. grandeur, sublimity, splendor, majesty.

magnificent, adj. splendid: superb, sublime, majestic, stately, grand.

magnify, v. augment, amplify, enlarge; overstate, exaggerate.

mail, v. post.

mail carrier, n. postman, letter-carrier, courier.

main, adj. principal, leading, chief, capital, cardinal, paramount,

main, n. ocean, high sea; gross, bulk, majority; strength, power.

mainland, n. continent.

mainly, adv. principally, chiefly, largely.

maintain, v. support, sustain; affirm, assert, contend: claim; conduct.

majestic, adj. august, imperial, regal, splendid, magnificent, imposing.

majesty, n. grandeur, magnificence, augustness, splendor.

major, adj. greater, larger. Antonym: minor.

majority, n. seniority, manhood; plurality. Antonyms: minority, youth.

make, v. force, compel, coerce, constrain, require, necessitate.

make, n. construction, shape, form, structure, conformation.

make believe, adj. pretend, imaginary, feigned, mock, sham, counterfeit, spurious, simulated.

make believe, n. pretense, simulation, affectation, feint, fantasy.

make believe, v. pretend, imagine.

make good, v. fulfill, vindicate, justify, establish; indemnity, reimburse.

make headway, v. advance, progress, thrive, prosper.

make known, v. declare, announce, publish, report, proclaim.

maker, n. manufacturer, constructor, producer.

makeshift, n. expedient, substitute.

making, n. construction, fabrication, workmanship, invention.

malady, n. disorder, distemper, ailment, complaint, disease.

male, n. masculine.

malice, n. hatred, rancor, malevolence, animosity.

malicious, adj. hateful, malevolent, rancorous, malignant.

malpractice, n. misdoing, misbehavior.

man, v. mortal, person, individual, adult, someone; mankind.

manacle, n. handcuff, fetter, shackle.

manage, v. conduct, administer, supervise, manipulate, superintend.

management, n. administration, conduct, guidance, regulation, superintendence.

mandate, n. command, edict, order, injunction, precept.

mandatory, adj. obligatory, compulsory. Antonym: optional.

maneuver, n. management, ruse, stratagem, artifice, trick, finesse.

mania, n. obsession, craze, passion.

manifest, v. show, exhibit, reveal, disclose.

manipulate, v. handle, operate, manage.

manipulation, n. handling, management.

manly, adj. masculine, male. Antonym: feminine.

manner, n. mode, method, style, fashion, way; bearing, demeanor.

mannish, adj. masculine, vigorous, bold. Antonyms: effeminate, feminine.

mansion, n. palace; manor-house, hall.

mantle, n. cape, cloak; role, position; covering, layer, blanket.

manual, n. handbook.

manufacture, v. make, fabricate, construct.

manufacturing, adj. industrial.

manuscript, n. copy.

many, adj. various, numerous, sundry, divers, manifold,

map, n. chart, plat.

map, v. sketch, plan, delineate, picture.

mar, n. defacement, disfigurement, blemish, injury, defect.

margin, n. confine, border, edge, limit, skirt, brink, rim.

marine, adj. maritime, naval, nautical, oceanic.

marionette, n. puppet.

maritime, adj. marine, naval, nautical.

mark, v. note, notice, remark, observe, see; indicate, betoken.

marked, adj. designated, noticeable, conspicuous, notable, salient.

market, n. mart, emporium, exchange, market-place.

marriage, n. matrimony, wedlock; wedding, nuptials, espousals, nuptial rites.

marry, v. wed, espouse.

marsh, n. swamp, morass, fen, slough, bog, quagmire.

mart, n. market, emporium.

martial, adj. military.

marvel, n. wonder, prodigy; amazement.

marvel, v. wonder, admire.

marvelous, adj. wonderful, amazing, stupendous, astonishing.

masculine, adj. male; manly, virile, manful. Antonym: feminine.

mask, n. disguise, pretext, subterfuge, screen, cloak, veil, ruse.

mask, v. disguise, masquerade, veil.

mass, n. aggregate, aggregation, totality, lump, heap, assemblage.

massive, adj. ponderous, bulky, immense, huge, cumbersome, massy.

master, n. director, lord, commander, ruler, manager, governor.

masterful, adj. domineering, imperious, arbitrary.

masterly, adj. skillful, proficient, adroit, dexterous, finished.

mat, n. rug, carpet; matting; pad.

match, v. rival, equal, cope with; contend, pit, oppose; tally.

matchless, adj. peerless, incomparable, inimitable, unequalled,

mate, n. companion, associate, friend, chum, crony, compeer, intimate, partner.

material, n. substance, matter, fabric, stuff, cloth, staple.

matrimonial, adj. connubial, nuptial, marital; hymeneal, conjugal.

matrimony, n. marriage, wedlock.

matron, n. dame.

matronly, adj. elderly, dignified.

matted, adj. tangled, snarled, entangled.

matter, n. substance, material, body; essence, pith, embodiment.

matter, v. import, signify; be of importance, count.

matter-of-fact, adj. practical, pragmatic, unimaginative, commonplace, prosaic.

mature, adj. full-grown, ripe, developed, perfect; prepared, finished.

maturity, n. development, ripeness, perfection, completion. Antonym: immaturity.

maul, v. pound, pummel, beat, club, cudgel.

maybe, adv. perhaps, possibly, peradventure, haply.

maze, v. perplex, bewilder, confuse, puzzle.

meadow, n. pasture, field, lea.

meager, adj. poor, emaciated, gaunt; barren, sterile, unproductive, arid.

mean, adj. contemptible, despicable, low-minded, base, abject, groveling, dishonorable.

meander, v. wind, turn.

meandering, adj. winding, tortuous, crooked, serpentine, meandrous.

meaning, n. signification, significance, import, acceptation, intent.

means, n. property, possessions, wealth, resources, riches, estate.

meantime, n. interval, interim, meanwhile.

measure, n. gauge, rule; dimensions, capacity, size, extent.

measure, v. gauge, mete; appraise, estimate, compute, adjust.

measurement, n. dimensions, size, extent, area, capacity, bulk.

mechanical, adj. automatic, involuntary.

medal, n. medallion.

meddle, v. interfere, interpose, intermeddle, obtrude.

meddlesome, adj. officious, intrusive, obtrusive, nosy, prying.

mediation, n. intercession.

medical, adj. medicinal, therapeutic, curative.

mediocre, adj. middling, ordinary, medium, commonplace.

mediocrity, n. commonplaceness, indifference, middle state.

meditate, v. contemplate, muse, ponder, cogitate, reflect, think.

medium, adj. intermediate, middling, mean, average, mediocre.

medley, n. mixture, jumble, hodgepodge, potpourri, olio.

meek, adj. humble, unassuming, modest, retiring, docile, lowly.

meet, v. encounter, confront, collide, converge, engage; intercept. Antonyms: avoid, elude, escape, disperse.

meet, adj. suitable, proper, befitting, seemly, appropriate.

meeting, n. assembly, assemblage, congregation, convention, convocation, conference,

melancholy, n. despondency, hypochondria, dejection, disconsolation, melancholia.

melodious, adj. tuneful, harmonious, dulcet, musical, sweet, euphonious.

melody, n. music; descant, tune, song, air, theme. Antonyms: discord, dissonance.

melt, v. dissolve, liquefy, thaw, fuse, soften, blend, swale.

melted, adj. molten.

melting, adj. dissolving, thawing; affecting, touching.

member, n. part, organ; limb; constituent, component, part.

memento, n. souvenir, keepsake, memorial.

memoir, n. biography, autobiography.

memorandum, n. record, minute, note.

memorial, adj. commemorative.

memory, n. remembrance, recollection, reminiscence; retrospection. Antonyms: oblivion, forgetfulness, amnesia.

menace, n. threat, peril, danger.

mend, v. repair, patch; improve.

mendacious, adj. lying, untruthful, false, deceitful.

mending, n. repairing, patching, restoration; improvement.

menial, adj. serving; low, servile.

mental, adj. intellectual.

mentor, n. monitor, counselor, guide.

mercantile, adj. trading, commercial.

mercenary, adj. hired, hireling, purchased; greedy, sordid, avaricious, grasping.

merchandise, n. wares, goods, commodities.

merchant, n. trader, dealer, trafficker, shopkeeper, tradesman.

merciful, adj. pitiful, lenient, clement, compassionate, benignant, indulgent, kind.

merciless, adj. unmerciful, remorseless, cruel, pitiless, ruthless, inexorable, implacable.

mercy, n. clemency, pity, lenity, leniency, lenience, compassion.

merely, adj. purely, absolutely; simply, barely, only.

merge, v. swallow up, absorb, immerse, take in; be swallowed up, be absorbed.

merger, n. union, fusion, absorption.

merit, n. worth, value, worthiness; excellence. Antonym: demerit.

merit, v. deserve, earn, warrant.

meritorious, adj. worthy, commendable, deserving.

merriment, n. mirth, gaiety, glee, levity, laughter, sportiveness.

merry, adj. mirthful, gay, jolly, gleeful, jovial, sportive.

mesh, n. net, network.

mess, n. rations, food; mixture, medley, farrago, litter.

message, n. communication, notice, word; meaning, significance, point.

messenger, n. courier, herald, forerunner, precursor, harbinger, mercury, emissary.

meticulous, adj. timid, fearful, diffident.

mettle, n. spirit, disposition; pluck, nerve, hardihood, stamina, spirit.

midday, n. noon, meridian, noontide.

middle, adj. mean, medial: intermediate, intervening.

middle, n. center, midst.

middleman, n. factor, go-between, agent, broker, commissioner.

might, n. strength, power, force, puissance, potency.

mighty, adj. strong, powerful, potent, invincible.

mild, adj. gentle, indulgent, tender, merciful, clement, lenient. Antonyms: severe, drastic, rigorous, violent, harsh.

military, adj. martial.

military command, strategy, generalship, tactics, logistics.

mimic, n. mime, mimicker, imitator, impersonator.

mimic, v. personate, ape, imitate, mock.

mince, v. chop, hash.

mind, v. obey, regard; consider, heed, mark, note. Antonyms: disobey, disregard, ignore.

mind, n. intellect, faculties; opinion, judgment; temperament, humor, disposition.

mindful, adj. heedful, regardful, observant.

mindless, adj. irrational; unmindful, heedless, inattentive.

mingle, v. blend, mix, intermix, amalgamate, intermingle, incorporate.

minister, n. ambassador, envoy, plenipotentiary, delegate; ecclesiastic, parson.

minister, v. administer, serve; officiate.

ministry, n. ministration; cabinet, administration.

minor, adj. subordinate, secondary, less, smaller.

minority, n. nonage, pupilage.

mint, v. coin.

minute, adj. little, tiny, microscopic, diminutive; critical, precise.

minute, n. moment; memorandum, record, item, note.

miraculous, adj. supernatural, hyperphysical, incredible.

mirror, n. reflector, looking-glass; cheval glass.

mirror, v. reflect.

mirth, n. merriment, jollity, glee, gaiety, fun.

misapply, v. misemploy, pervert, misuse.

miscellaneous, adj. mixed, diversified, heterogeneous, diverse, multifarious.

misdeed, n. offense, misdemeanor.

misdemeanor, n. offense, transgression.

miserable, adj. wretched, abject; deplorable, grievous, pitiable, calamitous.

misfortune, n. disaster, calamity, frustration, mischance, reverse, affliction.

misgiving, n. doubt, suspicion, evil premonition.

misinterpret, v. misconstrue.

misleading, adj. delusive deceitful, fallacious, illusive

misrepresent, v. falsify, distort.

miss, n. failure, miscarriage; omission, oversight, default, mistake, error.

miss, v. fail, miscarry, skip, omit, overlook.

missing, adj. absent, wanting.

mission, n. commission delegation; errand, trust.

missionary, n. evangelist, missioner, revivalist, propagandist.

misstate, v. falsify, distort, misrepresent.

mist, n. vapor, fog, haze, spray, film.

mistake, n. misunderstanding, misapprehension, misconception; error, blunder, oversight.

mistreat, v. misuse, abuse, maltreat.

mistrust, v. doubt, question, suspect, distrust.

misty, adj. obscure, hazy, foggy.

misunderstand, v. confuse, misconceive, miscomprehend, misapprehend, misconstrue.

misuse, v. misapply, prostitute, pervert, profane; maltreat, abuse.

mitigate, v. meliorate, alleviate, assuage, temper.

mix, v. mingle, blend, combine, concoct, incorporate, amalgamate.

mixture, n. blending, mingling, amalgamation, incorporation, conglomeration, infusion.

mob, n. rabble, populace, riffraff; crowd, horde, mass, multitude, throng, gang.

mob, v. surround, overwhelm, set upon.

mock, adj. sham, spurious, counterfeit, imitational.

mock, v. mimic, flout, taunt, imitate, gibe, ridicule, jeer.

mocker, n. scorner, scoffer, jeerer; mimic.

mockery, n. mimicry, ridicule, derision, jeering, scorn; caricature, counterfeit, sham.

mode, n. manner, method, fashion, vogue, style.

model, n. pattern, prototype, exemplar, gauge, criterion, standard.

model, v. fashion, mold, shape.

moderate, v. temper, appease, diminish, mitigate, reduce.

moderate, adj. sparing, temperate, frugal; reasonable, calm, deliberate.

moderation, n. mitigation, diminution; temperance, restraint; calmness.

modest, adj. unassuming, shy, unpretentious, unpretending, unobtrusive, retiring.

modesty, n. unobtrusiveness, humility; delicacy, chastity, purity, decency. Antonyms: immodesty, boldness, indelicacy.

modify, v. limit, qualify, adjust.

modulate, v. inflect; harmonize, attune, adjust, adapt.

moist, adj. damp, humid, dank.

moisten, v. dampen, damp, wet.

moisture, n. dampness, humidity.

mold, v. shape, form.

moment, n. instant, minute, jiffy, trice.

momentary, adj. instantaneous, transient.

momentum, n. impetus, force, moment.

monarch, n. sovereign.

monastery, n. abbey, priory, cloister, convent.

monetary, adj. pecuniary, fiscal, budgetary.

money, n. currency, coin, capital, funds, finances, change, legal tender.

monitor, n. mentor, adviser, counselor.

monk, n. religious, monastic, cenobite, friar.

monopolize, v. engross, forestall, corner.

monotonous, adj. unvaried, uniform, uninteresting, hum-drum, tedious.

monster, adj. grotesque, hideous, monstrous, huge.

monster, n. beast, brute, monstrosity, ogre.

monstrosity, n. monster, atrocity.

monstrous, adj. enormous, colossal; atrocious.

mood, n. humor, temper, spirit, disposition; ambiance, atmosphere, aura.

moody, adj. irritable, temperamental, melancholy.

moon, n. satellite.

moot, adj. undecided, unsettled, debatable.

mope, v. brood, fret, grump, pine, pout, stew, sulk.

moral, adj. ethical; virtuous, good; accountable, responsible; probable. Antonyms: immoral, licentious.

morality, n. virtue, rectitude, probity, goodness. Antonym: immorality.

morning, n. forenoon; dawn, daybreak, aurora, sunrise. Antonym: evening.

morsel, n. bite, mouthful; fragment, crumb, scrap.

mortally, adv. fatally.

mortification, n. chagrin, humiliation, abasement, embarrassment; repression, subjection.

mother, n. mater, matron, matriarch.

mother, v. nurture, coddle, foster, parent.

motherhood, n. maternity, parenthood.

motherly, adj. maternal.

motion, n. movement, activity; gesture, signal, gesticulation. Antonyms: inertia, rest, stagnation, immobility, repose.

motionless, adj. stationary, inert, stagnant, quiescent.

motive, n. incentive, inducement,

incitement.

mount, v. ascent; bestride.

mourn, v. deplore, lament, regret, grieve, repine, sorrow, bemoan, bewail.

mournful, adj. sorrowful, lugubrious, doleful, woeful.

mourning, n. sorrow, grief, bereavement.

movable, adj. portable, mobile. Antonyms: immovable, fast, immobile.

move, v. transfer; migrate, immigrate, emigrate, remove; impel, propel.

movement, n. motion, locomotion, transference, removal.

moving, adj. stirring, poignant; motive.

mow, v. reap.

mud, n. mire, ooze, muck; silt.

muddle, v. confuse, fuddle, bewilder.

muddled, adj. confused, addled.

muddy, adj. feculent, turbid, roily; opaque, confused, involved, incoherent.

muffle, v. wrap, envelop; deaden, subdue.

muffler, n. scarf, tippet.

mull, v. ruminate, ponder, cogitate.

multitude, n. crowd, throng, host.

mum, adj. silent, speechless, dumb, mute.

mumble, v. mutter, maunder, mump.

mumbling, adj. muttering, inarticulate, indistinct, incoherent.

murky, adj. lowering, dark.

murmur, v. grumble, complain, repine.

murmur, n. plaint, complaint; babble; undertone.

murmuring, adj. complaining, querulous, repining.

muscle, n. brawn, thew; sinew, tendon.

muscular, adj. brawny, sinewy, stalwart.

muse, v. contemplate, ruminate, brood, ponder, mull, reflect.

music, n. melody, symphony, harmony; melodies, harmonics.

musical, adj. melodious, harmonious, tuneful, symphonious.

muster, v. assemble, marshal.

musty, adj. mildewed, fusty, moldy, frowzy, rank, stale.

mutinous, adj. rebellious, insubordinate, seditious, insurgent, insurrectionary.

mutiny, n. insurrection, rebellion, insubordination, revolt.

mutual, adj. reciprocal.

mutuality, n. correlation, reciprocation, interchange.

muzzle, v. restrain, repress.

mysterious, adj. inscrutable, cryptic, obscure, unexplainable, enigmatical, unfathomed.

mystery, n. secret, enigma, riddle, intricacy.

mystic, adj. occult, esoteric, cabalistic, mystical.

mystification, n. bewilderment, perplexity, obfuscation.

mystify, v. bewilder, perplex, obfuscate, befog, nonplus.

mystifying, adj. perplexing, confusing, bewildering, mysterious.

myth, n. legend, tradition, fable.

mythical, adj. fabulous, legendary,

traditional.

N

nab, v. grab, snatch, seize.

nag, v. plague, tease, twit, hector, torment, scold.

naive, adj. artless, innocent, ingenuous, frank.

naked, v. nude, undressed, bare; unexaggerated, uncolored, exact, literal.

nakedness, n. nudity, bareness; exactness, literalness, accuracy.

name, n. appellation, designation, denomination; epithet, title, cognomen.

name, v. entitle, denominate, style, call, christen, dub.

nameless, adj. unnamed; undistinguished, inglorious, unknown, obscure; anonymous.

narrate, v. recount, recite, tell about, relate.

narration, n. narrative, relation, recital, story.

narrative, n. narration, account, portrayal, story, tale.

narrow, adj. limited, circumscribed, tapered, contracted, constricted, straitened, cramped; thin, fine, slim, slender, slight. Antonym: wide.

narrow, v. contract, reduce, constrict, restrict, limit, cramp, confine; taper, tighten.

narrowing, n. contraction, reduction, constriction, limitation, circumscription.

narrow-minded, adj. illiberal, bigoted, intolerant, narrow, prejudiced, insular, intolerant.

narrow-mindedness, n. illiberality, bigotry, bias, intolerance, insularity.

nastiness, n. squalor, filthiness, pollution, filth, corruption,

nasty, adj. filthy, squalid, foul, polluted, dirty; indecent.

native, adj. natal; indigenous, natural, aboriginal, vernacular.

natural, adj. native, inborn, congenital, innate, characteristic; original.

naturalize, v. familiarize, accustom, habituate, acclimatize, adapt, acclimate.

nature, n. creation, universe, cosmos, world; kind, sort.

naughty, adj. disobedient, mischievous, perverse, froward, refractory.

nausea, n. seasickness; qualm, squeamishness, queasiness, qualmishness.

nauseate, v. sicken, disgust, revolt; recoil from; abhor, abominate.

nauseous, adj. sick, queasy, woozy; disgusting, repulsive, offensive, sickening, fulsome, distasteful.

nautical, adj. naval, marine, maritime, oceanic.

naval, adj. nautical, marine, maritime.

navigate, v. sail, cruise; guide, steer, direct; circumnavigate.

near, adj. nigh, close, adjacent, neighboring, contiguous, proximate. Antonyms: distant, remote, far.

nearness, n. closeness, proximity, propinquity, contiguity, adjacency, imminence.

near-sighted, adj. myopic, short-sighted.

neat, adj. tidy, orderly, trim, clean, cleanly; tasteful. Antonyms: dowdy, slovenly, untidy, tawdry, gaudy.

necessary, adj. requisite, essential, needed, needful, indispensable; inevitable, unavoidable. Antonyms: nonessential, unnecessary, optional, discretional, casual, needless.

necessary, n. requisite, requirement, essential.

necessity, n. requisite, necessary, requirement, essential: exigency, urgency. Antonyms: choice, option, contingency, doubtfulness, possibility.

need, n. want, necessity, extremity, strait, exigency, urgency.

need, v. require, lack, want.

needful, adj. requisite, necessary, essential, indispensable, required.

needless, adj. unnecessary, groundless, unfounded.

needy, adj. destitute, indigent, penniless, impecunious.

negation, n. denial, disavowal.

negative, n. denial, refusal. Antonym: affirmative.

neglect, n. disregard, omission, negligence, default, dereliction, remissness, oversight.

neglect, v. disregard, slight, overlook, ignore, omit.

negligence, n. neglect, remissness, oversight, heedlessness.

negligent, adj. neglectful, heedless, indifferent, slack, remiss, regardless. Antonyms: careful, attentive, heedful.

negotiable, adj. transferable.

neighborhood, n. vicinity, vicinage, locality, neighbors, venue.

neighboring, adj. adjacent, contiguous, near.

nerve, n. boldness, audacity, presumption, effrontery, courage, assurance.

nerve, v. brace, strengthen, fortify, invigorate, energize

nervous, adj. excitable, sensitive, timorous.

nestle, v. cuddle, snuggle.

network, n. system, arrangement, set of contacts, group, association; mesh, interlacement, reticulation.

neutrality, n. indifference, impartiality, objectivity. Antonym: bias.

neutralize, v. counteract, counterbalance, invalidate.

nevertheless, adv. yet, however, notwithstanding, all the same, even so.

new, adj. recent, fresh, modern, novel, newfangled, neoteric.

newly, adv. lately, recently, freshly; anew, afresh, again.

news, n. tidings, word, report.

nice, adj. fastidious, exacting, particular, punctilious, queasy, finical.

nicety, n. niceness, precision; punctilio, subtlety, fine point.

niche, n. recess, cavity, nook, tabernacle.

nick, n. notch, indentation, dent, score, dint.

nick, v. notch, mar, deface, indent.

nickname, n. sobriquet.
night, n. darkness.
nightly, adj. nocturnal.
nightmare, n. incubus, cacodemon, succubus; travail, disaster.
nimble, adj. agile, sprightly, deft, lively, swift, brisk. Antonyms: slow, sluggish, clumsy, dilatory, dull.
nip, v. pinch; clip, cut off; blast, kill; chill, deaden.
no, n. refusal, denial, negative.
nobility, n. nobleness, high-mindedness, magnanimity, excellence, superiority, dignity.
noble, adj. eminent, exalted, magnanimous, superior; stately, magnificent.
noble, n. nobleman, peer, grandee. Antonyms: commoner, proletarian, plebeian.
nobody, n. nonentity, jackstraw.
nod, n. bow.
noise, n. sound; racket, clamor, din, outcry, clatter, uproar. Antonym: silence.
noiseless, adj. still, silent, quiet, inaudible.
noisy, adj. clamorous, boisterous, vociferous, turbulent, riotous.
nonchalant, adj. indifferent, cool, unconcerned, insouciant.
nonconformist, n. dissenter, rebel, maverick, free spirit, individualist, oddball.
nonconformity, n. eccentricity, originality, oddness, quirkiness.
nondescript, adj. ordinary, unexceptional, dull, uninteresting, commonplace, plain. Antonym: special.
nonessential, adj. unimportant, incidental, adventitious.
nonsense, n. absurdity, twaddle, bosh, fudge, silliness.
nook, n. retreat, corner, recess.
noon, n. meridian, noonday, noontide, midday.
normal, adj. natural, regular, ordinary, common. Antonyms: abnormal, unnatural.
nose, n. snout, nozzle, spout, proboscis, muzzle.
nostalgia, n. homesickness, reminiscence, wistfulness, longing.
notable, adj. noticeable, conspicuous, plain, evident; signal, remarkable, famous.
notch, v. nick, score, indent, crenellate.
notched, adj. serrated, crenate, incised, emarginated.
note, n. billet; memorandum, minute, record; remark, comment.
noted, adj. celebrated, renowned, eminent; distinguished, famous.
noteworthy, adj. memorable, remarkable.
nothing, n: nonexistence, nonentity; bagatelle; naught, cipher, zero, null.
nothingness, n. nihility, nonexistence, nullity.
notice, n. observation, cognizance, note, heed, attention, regard.
notice, v. see, observe, note, heed, recognize, perceive. Antonyms: ignore, connive, skip, neglect, slight, overlook, disregard.
noticeable, adj. observable, appreciable, conspicuous, salient, prominent. Antonyms: unobservable, inappreciable, in-

conspicuous.

notify, v. inform, acquaint, tell, apprise, give notice to.

notion, n. conception, idea, concept; opinion, judgment, belief.

notoriety, n. disrepute, infamy, dishonor, bad name, ill repute.

notorious, adj. infamous, disreputable, talked of, evident, obvious, noted.

notwithstanding, conj. despite, nevertheless, however.

nourish, v. feed, nurture; support; encourage, foster, cherish.

nourishing, adj. nutritious.

nourishment, n. nutrition; food, nutriment.

novel, adj. new, recent, fresh, unusual, rare, unique, innovative.

novel, n. fiction, romance, story, tale.

novelty, n. newness; change, curiosity, innovation.

novice, n. tyro; probationer, proselyte, convert, novitiate.

now, adv. instantly, immediately, at once.

now and then, adv. occasionally, at intervals, infrequently, intermittently, sometimes, periodically, once in a while.

noxious, adj. injurious, baneful, unwholesome, noisome.

nucleus, n. kernel, core, heart, center.

nudge, v. poke, elbow, shove, prod.

nuisance, n. plague, pest, bane, infliction, bore, offense.

null, adj. invalid, nugatory.

nullify, v. invalidate, abrogate, cancel, repeal, countermand.

numb, adj. deadened, unfeeling, insensible, benumbed.

numb, v. benumb, deaden.

number, v. enumerate, figure up, count, numerate.

number, n. numeral, figure, digit, integer; collection, multitude.

numerous, adj. many, plentiful, multitudinous.

numskull, n. dolt, dullard, dunce, simpleton.

nuptials, n. wedding, marriage, espousal.

nurse, v. suckle; nourish, cherish, foster, succor, foment, encourage.

nurture, n. care, training; food, nourishment.

nurture, v. feed, nourish, nurse; educate, train, school.

nutriment, n. nourishment, food, aliment.

nutrition, n. nourishment, feeding; nutriment, food.

nutritious, adj. nourishing, nutritive, healthy, wholesome.

O

oar, n. paddle, scull.

oath, n. adjuration, pledge, sworn promise; curse, profanity, swearing.

obedience, n. compliance, submission, subservience; dutifulness. Antonyms: disobedience, incompliance, defiance, revolt, insubordination.

obedient, adj. submissive, tractable, deferential, subservient, compliant. Antonyms: intractable, disobedient.

obey, v. comply, submit to, heed, regard, be ruled by.

object, v. disapprove, oppose, demur, contravene, gainsay, except, cavil.

object, n. thing, article; goal, purpose, aim, motive, intent.

objection, n exception, scruple, demurrer, cavil. Antonyms: approval, acquiescence.

objectionable, adj. exceptionable, offensive, obnoxious, undesirable, displeasing.

obligation, n. accountableness, responsibility, incumbency, duty, indebtedness; agreement.

obligatory, adj. binding, incumbent, imperative, coercive. Antonyms: optional, discretional.

oblige, v. constrain, obligate; please, gratify, accommodate; coerce, compel.

obliging, adj. gracious, accommodating, affable, debonair, deferential, yielding.

obliterate, v. efface, erase, blot out, remove, destroy, expunge.

oblivious, adj. unmindful, unconscious, forgetful, heedless, unaware.

obnoxious, adj. subject, liable; offensive, odious, hateful, displeasing.

obscene, adj. smutty, lewd, gross, indecent, immodest, indelicate.

obscenity, n. lewdness, smut, ribaldry, indecency, bawdiness, immodesty.

obscure, adj. abstruse, vague, recondite, indefinite, ambiguous; humble.

obscure, v. darken, obfuscate, bedim, eclipse; involve, dissemble.

obscurity, n. ambiguity, vagueness; privacy, seclusion, retirement; darkness.

obsolete, adj. disused, archaic, antiquated, unfashionable, old-fashioned.

obstacle, n. obstruction, barrier, impediment, hindrance, stumbling block.

obstinate, adj. incompliant, intractable, mulish, perverse, dogged, contumacious, stubborn. Antonyms: amenable, yielding, tractable, submissive, compliant, obedient.

obstruct, v. impede, oppose, retard, barricade, blockade, clog.

obtain, v. gain, get, procure, acquire, win, attain, secure.

obtainable, adj. procurable, attainable, accessible. Antonyms: unobtainable, unprocurable, unattainable, inaccessible.

obtrusive, adj. officious, meddlesome, intrusive, forward. Antonyms: unobtrusive, retiring.

obvious, adj. plain, evident, palpable, manifest, patent, self-evident.

occult, adj. mystic, mystical, abstruse, recondite, secret, unrevealed.

occupant, n. occupier, tenant, holder, incumbent, possessor, lessee.

occupation, n. occupancy, tenure, incumbency; vocation, employment.

occupational, adj. vocational.

occupy, v. hold, keep, possess,

fill; engage, absorb.

odd, adj. unmatched, single, uneven; singular, peculiar, unusual, unique,

oddity, n. oddness, singularity; curiosity, marvel, wonder.

odds and ends, n. remnants, fragments, orts, scraps.

odious, adj. detestable, abominable, execrable, offensive, repulsive, hateful, loathsome.

odor, n. smell, aroma, fragrance, scent, redolence, perfume, savor; stink.

odorless, adj. inodorous, savorless, scentless.

odorous, adj. odoriferous, fragrant, savory, aromatic, balmy, scented.

offend, v. displease, affront, provoke, mortify, exasperate.

offender, n. delinquent, wrongdoer, trespasser, malefactor, culprit, criminal.

offense, n. crime, wrong, sin, outrage, indignity; displeasure.

offensive, adj. obnoxious, displeasing: noisome, distasteful, insolent, abusive.

offer, v. tender, proffer, propose, propound, volunteer, bid.

offer, n. tender, proposition, bid, overture, proffer.

offering, n. overture, proposition, bid; sacrifice, oblation; offertory.

offhand, adj. extemporaneous, impromptu, improvised, unstudied.

office, n. duty, function, service, work, charge, trust, business.

officer, n. office-holder, magistrate, dignitary; incumbent.

offset, n. set-off, counterbalance, equivalent.

offset, v. counterbalance, counterpoise.

offshoot, n. scion, branch.

offspring, n. children, issue, progeny, posterity, descendants.

often, adv. frequently, repeatedly, oftentimes. Antonyms: seldom, infrequently.

oil, v. lubricate, grease.

oily, adj. unctuous, oleaginous, lubricous; glib, fluent, plausible.

old, adj. aged, elderly, senescent, decrepit, venerable, patriarchal.

old-fashioned, adj. antiquated, archaic, passé, antique, obsolete.

old-time, adj. late, former, quondam.

omen, n. foretoken, sign, augury, portent, presage, prognostic, auspice.

ominous, adj. portentous, monitory, premonitory, threatening.

omission, n. default, oversight, neglect, pretermission.

omit, v. leave out, skip, disregard, neglect, overlook, ignore, delete.

one, n. unit.

oneness, n. unity, singleness, individuality, unanimity.

onerous, adj. laborious, difficult, arduous.

one-sided, adj. unilateral; partial, unfair, inequitable, ex parte.

onlooker, n. bystander, spectator, beholder, witness, eye-witness.

ooze, v. filter, exude, percolate, transude, seep.

opaque, adj. obscure, unintelligible.

open, adj. accessible, clear, unobstructed, unrestricted; ajar, unlocked.

open, v. spread, expand, unfold, evolve; reveal, disclose.

opening, adj. beginning, introductory, initiatory, preliminary,

openly, adv. publicly, unreservedly, candidly.

open-mouthed, adj. gaping, yawning; greedy, clamorous, ravenous, rapacious, eager.

opinion, n. belief, judgment, impression; decision, ruling, verdict, sentence.

opponent, n. adversary, antagonist, rival, competitor.

opportune, adj. timely, seasonable, apropos, felicitous, appropriate.

oppose, v. combat, resist, confront, withstand, oppugn, impugn. Antonyms: yield, acquiesce, concur, agree.

opposing, adj. conflicting, antagonistic, contending, opposite, adverse.

opposite, adj. contrary, adverse, diametrical, antagonistic, inverse, reverse.

opposition, n. resistance, counteraction, hostility, repulse, rebuff, antagonism, disagreement; opponent, challenger, enemy, rival, foe. Antonyms: friendliness, ally.

oppress, v. burden, overwhelm, aggrieve, tyrannize, persecute, overpower.

oppression, n. tyranny, persecution, extortion, hardship, severity.

oppressive, adj. rigorous, tyrannical, extortionate, burdensome.

oppressor, n. tyrant, persecutor, bully.

option, n. choice, preference, election, discretion, alternative. Antonyms: constraint, coercion, compulsion.

optional, adj. discretional, elective. Antonyms: compulsory, coercive, obligatory.

oral, adj. spoken, verbal, vocal, nuncupative.

oration, n. declamation, rhetoric.

ordeal, n. trial, torment, tribulation.

order, n. mandate, command, precept, direction, decree.

order, v. methodize, systematize, regulate; bid, command, dictate, enjoin.

ordering, n. distribution, disposition, regulation.

orderly, adj. systematic, methodical, well-regulated, regular; peaceable.

ordinary, adj. common, regular, conventional, commonplace, mediocre, average, usual.

organic, adj. constitutional, vital, fundamental, essential, inherent, instrumental.

organization, n. organism; formation, construction, making, structure; association, corporation.

organize, v. arrange, systematize, form.

origin, n. source, beginning, derivation, rise, origination.

original, adj. first, primeval, aboriginal, primitive, archetypal, primordial. Antonyms: derivative, copied.

ornament, n. decoration, embellishment, adornment, garniture, ornamentation.

ornamentation, n. adornment, garniture, embellishment.

ornate, adj. ornamented, decorated, embellished, florid, adorned.

oscillate, v. fluctuate, vacillate.

ostentatious, adj. showy, pompous, spectacular, gaudy, pretentious.

oust, v. eject, evict, dispossess, dislodge, remove, displace, expel, depose.

out, adv. away, absent, abroad; outright, aloud, audibly.

out and out, adj. wholly, completely, openly, absolute, unqualified, undisguised.

outbreak, n. eruption, outburst, uprising.

outburst, n. eruption, outbreak, paroxysm, access, ebullition.

outcast, n. pariah, castaway, reprobate.

outcome, n. consequence, outgrowth, result, issue, upshot, eventuation.

outdo, v. excel, surpass, best, outstrip, exceed.

outer, adj. external, exterior.

outermost, adj. extreme, uttermost, utmost.

outfit, n. equipment; group, company, team, unit.

outfit, v. equip, furnish.

outflow, n. effusion, outpouring.

outlandish, adj. grotesque, bizarre, barbarous, unconventional, freakish.

outlast, v. outwear, survive.

outlaw, n. bandit, desperado, criminal, brigand.

outlaw, v. proscribe, forbid, ban, prohibit, bar.

outlay, n. expenditure, disbursement.

outlet, n. egress, vent, exit.

outline, n. contour, circumference, periphery, profile, sketch, draught, scenario.

outlive, n. survive.

outlook, n. prospect, view, vista; watch-tower; foresight.

outlying, adj. remote, detached, distant, frontier.

out of order, adj. disordered, disarranged, jumbled, chaotic, disorganized.

out of place, adj. inappropriate, inapt, unbefitting, incongruous, incompatible, misplaced; improper, unbecoming.

out of reach, adj. impracticable, unlikely, not viable, inaccessible, unattainable.

outrage, n. indignity, affront, insult, assault.

outrageous, adj. atrocious, nefarious, wanton, flagrant, unwarrantable, furious, monstrous, villainous.

outright, adv. unconditionally, utterly.

outside, n. exterior, fascade.

outside, adj. external.

outskirt, n. edge, border, purlieu, suburb, frontier.

outspoken, adj. unreserved, frank, explicit, blunt, ingenuous.

outward, adj. external, exterior, outer, superficial, surface, extrinsic.

outweigh, v. overweigh, overbalance, preponderate.

outwit, v. circumvent, outgeneral, defeat.

oval, adj. elliptical.

over, adv. across, crosswise, athwart, transversely.

overbearing, adj. haughty, arrogant, dictatorial, magisterial, lordly, dogmatic.

overcharge, n. extortion.

overcoat, n. great coat, topcoat, Ulster, raglan, Inverness.

overcome, v. surmount, conquer, subdue, master, vanquish, overpower, subjugate.

overcoming, adj. conquering, overmastering, overwhelming, irresistible.

overconfident, adj. rash, presumptuous, incautious.

overdo, v. overwork, overtax, exhaust; exaggerate.

overeat, v. gorge, glut, satiate.

overfeed, v. surfeit, stuff, satiate, gorge, pamper.

overfill, v. surcharge.

overflow, n. deluge, flood, inundation: exuberance, superabundance, profusion.

overflow, v. inundate, deluge, engulf.

overflowing, n. overflow, inundation; exuberance, copiousness, superabundance.

overhang, n. projection.

overhead, adv. aloft, above.

overlook, v. supervise, oversee; inspect, overhaul, examine, neglect, ignore, miss, disregard; excuse, condone, pardon, wink at, forgive.

overpower, v. vanquish, subdue, conquer, overcome, defeat, crush, overwhelm.

overpowering, adj. overwhelming, conquering, irresistible, overmastering, intense, consuming.

override, v. trample upon, supersede, annul, abrogate.

overrule, v. annul, rescind, abrogate, revoke, supersede, set aside.

overruling, adj. predominant, prevailing, controlling.

overruling, n. abrogation, cancellation, rescission.

overrun, v. infringe, invade.

oversee, v. superintend, supervise.

overseer, n. superintendent, supervisor, inspector, taskmaster, foreman, monitor.

oversight, n. supervision, care, inspection, surveillance, control; mistake, omission, lapse.

overstate, v. exaggerate.

overstep, v. exceed, trespass, infringe, encroach.

oversupply, n. excess, superabundance, surfeit, glut, repletion.

overt, adj. public, apparent, unconcealed, patent.

overthrow, v. upset, overturn; demolish, prostrate, subvert, defeat.

overthrow, n. overthrowing, demolition, subversion, undoing, reversal, prostration.

overvalue, v. overrate, overestimate, overprize.

overweight, adj. heavy, cumbersome; corpulent, obese.

overwhelm, v. overflow, submerge, engulf, drown, overpower, crush.

overwhelming, adj. irresistible, overpowering.

owing, n. indebtedness.

owing, adj. due, payable, unpaid; ascribable, traceable, imputable.

own, v. admit, acknowledge, confess, allow, concede, grant; possess. Antonyms: disown, deny.

owner, n. proprietor.

ownership, n. proprietorship, claim, title.

P

pacify, v. appease, quiet, calm, mollify, propitiate, tranquilize.

pack, n. bundle, bale, parcel, package; multitude, number.

pack, v. compress, stow, truss; load, encumber.

package, n. bundle, packet, bale, parcel, pack, budget.

pact, n. compact, covenant, concordat.

pad, n. cushion, bolster; saddle-cloth, housing.

page, n. footboy; folio.

pail, n. bucket, canister, vessel.

pain, v. hurt, torture, rack; distress, grieve, afflict,

pain, n. punishment, penalty; suffering: ache, smart. Antonyms: ease, comfort, relief, solace.

painful, adj. distressing, agonizing, excruciating, dolorous, racking.

painstaking, adj. diligent, particular, precise, scrupulous. Antonyms: slovenly, negligent.

paint, n. pigment; cosmetic, rouge.

paint, v. delineate, portray, limn, depict, picture, sketch.

pair, n. two, brace, couple, span, team, yoke.

pai, n. partner, mate, confederate, associate, accomplice.

palace, n. mansion, castle.

pale, adj. pallid, wan, colorless, ghastly, blanched, cadaverous. Antonyms: ruddy, flushed.

paleness, n. whiteness, pallor, pastiness, colorlessness. Antonyms: rosiness, darkness.

palliate, v. excuse, apologize for, gloss over, extenuate; moderate.

palliation, n. extenuation, glossing over, excuse, apology; moderation.

pamper, v. overfeed, feed luxuriously; indulge, gratify, spoil.

pamphlet, n. brochure, booklet, tract.

pan, n. basin, chafer.

pancake, n. griddlecake, flapjack, fritter.

panic, n. consternation, terror, alarm.

panic-stricken, adj. panic-struck, alarmed, dismayed, terrified, appalled.

pant, v. gasp; long, hunger, yearn, thirst.

panther, n. puma, cougar, jaguar.

panting, v. gasping; longing, hungering, desiring.

paper, n. document; essay, dissertation, article; journal, newspaper.

par, n. equality, equivalence.

parade, n. pomp, display, ostentation, show; procession, pageant.

parade, v. display, flaunt, show off.

paradise, n. garden of Eden; Elysium; Heaven; nirvana, utopia.

parallel, adj. like, similar, equal, analogous.

paralyze, v. benumb, deaden, stun, unnerve.

paraphernalia, n. equipment, accouterments, ornaments.

parasite, n. hanger-on, toady, sycophant, fawner.

parcel, n. bundle, package; collection, lot; tract, plot, piece.

pardon, n. absolution, remission, amnesty, forgiveness. Antonyms: retribution, vengeance; retaliation, implacability, penalty.

pardon, v. absolve, remit, forgive, condone.

pardonable, adj. venial, excusable. Antonyms: unpardonable, inexcusable.

pare, v. peel, skin, strip, trim; cut back, scale down, reduce.

parentage, n. extraction, descent, pedigree, ancestry, family, birth, lineage.

parsonage, n. rectory; manse; living, benefice.

part, n. portion, fraction, division, piece, constituent, installment.

part, v. divide, sever, disunite, dissever, sunder, dissociate.

partake, v. share, participate in.

partaking, n: participation.

parted, adj. separated, divided, severed, disunited, isolated, detached.

partial, adj. warped, biased, prejudiced; imperfect, incomplete.

partiality, n. bias, favoritism; pre-

dilection, inclination, fondness.

particular, adj. special, especial, specific; minute, precise, detailed. Antonyms: indiscriminate, general.

particular, n. detail, instance, item.

parting, adj. farewell, valedictory.

parting, n. division, disunion, severance, separation; leave-taking, farewell.

partition, n. division, distribution, apportionment, allotment.

partner, n. colleague, associate, confederate.

party, n. clique, faction, set, circle, ring, cabal.

pass, v. elapse, lapse; transmit, deliver, hand; go, move.

pass, n. passageway, defile, passage; thrust, lunge.

passable, adj. navigable, traversable, penetrable; tolerable, mediocre. Antonyms: impassable, impervious, impenetrable.

passage, n. transit; fare; clause, sentence, paragraph; enactment.

passing, adj. exceeding, surpassing; transient, momentary, transitory.

passion, n. suffering, pain, agony; emotion, ardor, feeling.

passionate, adj. irascible, quick-tempered, choleric, excitable.

passionless, adj. impassive, phlegmatic, stoical, unemotional, dispassionate, apathetic.

passive, adj. inactive, quiet, inert, receptive, quiescent; patient.

passport, n. pass, permit, safe-conduct; visa, credentials.

password, n. countersign; watchword, sesame.

past, adj. bygone, elapsed; historical, previous, earlier, former, ancient, bygone.

pastime, n. amusement, sport, diversion, recreation, divertissement, entertainment.

patch, n. tract, plot, parcel.

patch, v. mend, repair, vamp, revamp.

patent, adj. evident, obvious, manifest, apparent.

path, n. footway, runway, course, passage, route, avenue.

pathetic, adj. plaintive, pitiable, piteous, mournful, sad.

patience, n. long-suffering, fortitude, resignation, submission, sufferance; indulgence. Antonyms: impatience, restiveness, resistance.

patient, adj. uncomplaining, submissive, resigned, passive, long-suffering, indulgent; diligent.

patron, n. supporter, promoter, defender, guardian, benefactor; customer.

pattern, n. model, exemplar, original, prototype, archetype; specimen.

pause, n. intermission, suspension, break; hesitation.

pause, v. stop, hesitate, desist, waver, intermit.

pawn, v. pledge, impawn.

pay, v. compensate, remunerate, recompense, requite, indemnify, reward. Antonyms: repudiate, protest, bilk, defraud.

payable, adj. due, unpaid, outstanding; remunerable.

pay back, v. reimburse, refund, restore, repay, requite.

paying, adj. profitable, lucrative, gainful, remunerative.

payment, n. paying, compensation, remuneration, liquidation, discharge, reparation. Antonyms: nonpayment, protest, repudiation, default.

peace, n. concord, amity, harmony; tranquility, quietness.

peaceable, adj. amicable, inoffensive; tranquil, serene, undisturbed. Antonyms: bellicose, belligerent, contentious, rebellious, pugnacious.

peaceably, adv. amicably.

peaceful, adj. amicable, tranquil, peaceable, halcyon.

peacemaker, n. mediator, intercessor, pacificator, makepeace, arbitrator, intermediary.

peace-offering, n. atonement, reparation, amends.

peak, n. apex, pinnacle, summit, crest, spire, point.

peaked, adj. pointed; sickly, thin, pale, emaciated.

peculation, n. embezzlement.

peculiar, adj. individual, personal, particular; singular, eccentric, erratic.

peculiarity, n. characteristic, trait, attribute, idiosyncrasy, eccentricity, oddness.

peddle, v. hawk, vend.

pedigree, n. lineage, ancestry, descent, extraction, genealogy.

peek, v. peep.

peel, n. rind, skin.

peel, v. pare, decorticate. Antonym: pulp.

peep, v. chirp, cheep; peer, peek,

pry.

peevish, adj. petulant, querulous, captious, spleeny, fretful, impatient, cross.

penalty, n. punishment, retribution; forfeiture, fine.

pending, adj. undecided, unsettled.

pending, prep. during.

penetrable, adj. permeable, pervious. Antonym: impenetrable.

penetrate, v. pierce, perforate; comprehend, understand; explore; interpenetrate.

penetration, n. piercing, perforation; acuteness, discernment, sharpness; interpenetration.

penitence, n. contrition, repentance, remorse, compunction. Antonym: impenitence.

penitentiary, n. prison.

penniless, adj. impecunious, indigent, destitute.

pensive, adj. meditative, dreamy, lackadaisical, introspective, thoughtful; sad, grave.

people, n. folks; inhabitants, population; citizens; populace, commonalty.

people, v. populate, colonize.

peppery, adj. pungent; irascible, hot-tempered, choleric.

perceive, v. see, discern, observe; apprehend, comprehend, understand.

perception, n. cognizance, discernment; sensation, feeling.

perchance, adv. perhaps, peradventure, possibly, maybe.

percolate, v. ooze, strain, filter, transude.

perfect, adj. consummate, fault-less, flawless, exquisite, inviolate. impeccable.

perfect, v. consummate, elaborate, retouch, develop.

perforate, v. bore through, pierce, penetrate, drill.

perform, v. accomplish, execute, do.

performance, n. execution, achievement, accomplishment; trick, feat, exploit.

perfume, n. fragrance, aroma, redolence, sachet, incense.

perhaps, adv. perchance, possibly, haply.

perilous, adj. dangerous, hazardous, imperiled, unsafe.

period, n. interval.

perishable, adj. destructible, impermanent, mortal. Antonyms: imperishable, permanent.

permanent, adj. stable, immutable, durable, imperishable, unchangeable. Antonyms: impermanent, evanescent, ephemeral, transient.

permeable, adj. penetrable, holey, leaky, porous. Antonym: impermeable.

permission, n. consent, allowance, license, leave, permit, authorization. Antonyms: refusal, denial, embargo, injunction, veto.

permit, v. allow, consent to, suffer, tolerate, let, authorize. Antonyms: refuse, disallow, prohibit, resist.

permit, n. warrant, license, leave, permission.

perpendicular, adj. upright, vertical. Antonyms: horizontal, oblique.

perplex, v. bewilder, puzzle, pose, confuse, mystify, distract.

perplexity, n. bewilderment, distraction, confusion, disconcertion, doubt, uncertainty.

persecute, v. harass, oppress, tyrannize, torment.

perseverance, n. persistence, diligence, constancy.

persevere, v. persist, continue.

persevering, adj. persistent, steadfast, untiring, indefatigable, pertinacious, unremitting; indomitable. Antonyms: inconstant, fickle.

persist, v. persevere, hang on; continue, endure.

persistency, n. perseverance, doggedness, pertinacity, obstinacy, contumacy, insistence.

persistent, adj. persevering, insistent, pertinacious, tenacious, relentless, determined.

personality, n. individuality, character, qualities.

personally, adv. individually.

personate, v. impersonate.

perspire, v. sweat.

persuade, v. induce.

persuasion, n. inducement, suasion, incitement; creed, belief. Antonyms: dissuasion, coercion, constraint.

pertain, v. apply, concern, relate, refer to.

pertinence, n. relevancy, applicability, propriety. Antonyms: impertinence, irrelevance.

pertinent, adj. relevant, apposite, applicable, proper. Antonyms: impertinent, irrelevant.

perturb, v. disquiet, excite, disturb, agitate, discompose, distress.

perturbed, adj. excited, distressed, worried, discomposed, agitated.

perusal, n. reading, scrutiny, inspection.

perverse, adj. perverted, misdirected, erring, depraved, vitiated; intractable.

pessimistic, adj. gloomy, foreboding, hopeless.

pest, n. plague, scourge; curse, nuisance, annoyance.

pester, v. plague, badger, harass, harry, tease, torment.

pestilence, n. plague, scourge, epidemic.

pet, n. fondling, darling, favorite.

pet, v. humor, coddle, fondle, cosset, caress, indulge.

petition, n. entreaty, supplication, prayer.

petitioner, n. suppliant, applicant, solicitor.

petrify, v. harden, fossilize, solidify; frighten, terrify, scare, alarm, horrify.

petty, adj. small, insignificant, trivial, trifling.

phantom, n. specter, apparition, ghost.

phase, n. aspect, appearance.

phase, v. disconcert, disturb, discompose, affect.

phlegmatic, adj. unemotional, cold, dull, sluggish.

phrase, n. idiom, diction, phraseology.

physical, adj. material, bodily.

pick, v. pluck; pick out, select, choose, cull, glean.

picket, n. stake, pale, paling; sentry, guard, watchman, sentinel.

pickle, n. brine; dilemma, predicament, plight; marinade.

picture, v. delineate, sketch, draw, represent, depict.

picture, n. drawing, painting, engraving, photograph, print.

piddling, adj. trifling, inconsiderable, insignificant, inconsequential.

piece, n. scrap, swatch, clout, chunk, slice, clipping.

pier, n. wharf, dock, jetty, buttress.

pierce, v. transfix, stab, impale, gore; penetrate.

piercing, adj. penetrating, keen, sharp, thrilling, poignant.

piety, n. sanctity, godliness, holiness.

pigheaded, adj. stubborn, perverse.

pig pen, n. sty, pigsty, piggery.

pile, n. heap, stack, accumulation.

pilfer, v. filch, purloin.

pilgrim, n. wayfarer, traveler, sojourner, crusader.

pilgrimage, n. journey, expedition, sojourn, crusade.

pillage, n. devastation, plundering, spoliation; spoil.

pillar, n. column, pier, shaft, post.

pillow, n. cushion, bolster.

pilot, n. steersman, helmsman; director, guide, conductor.

pinch, v. squeeze, compress, twinge, tweak, gripe, nip; arrest.

pine, v. droop, languish, waste; yearn, long.

pious, adj. religious, devout, saintly, righteous, reverent. Antonym: impious.

pipe, n. tube, conduit, aqueduct.

piquancy, n. pungency, sharpness, spiciness; raciness, liveliness.

pit, n. hollow, role, excavation, cavity; abyss.

pitch, n. slope, declivity, slant.

pitch, v. cast, hurl, toss, throw, fling, heave, chuck.

pitfall, n. snare, trap, pit.

pitiful, adj. tender-hearted, compassionate, merciful, lenient, ruthful, clement.

pittance, n. dole, trifle.

pity, n. compassion, mercy, commiseration, condolence, sympathy.

pity, v. have pity for, condole with, commiserate.

place, n. position, site, situation, locality; rendezvous.

place, v. deposit, locate, dispose, put, set, station.

plague, n. pestilence.

plague, v. hector, tantalize, tease, badger, pester.

plain, adj. evident, manifest, explicit, obvious, unmistakable, apparent. Antonyms: ambiguous, equivocal, indistinct, indecipherable, elaborate, luxurious.

plain-spoken, adj. frank, candid, unreserved, outspoken.

plaintiff, n. complainant.

plan, v. scheme, project, intend, devise, contrive, design, purpose.

plant, v. sow; settle; establish.

plastic, adj. formative, creative; impressible, fictile.

platform, n. rostrum, stage, dais.

plausible, adj. reasonable, believable, credible, probable, likely. Antonym: implausible.

play, v. frolic, sport, gambol, disport, frisk, skip.

play, n. game, pastime, amusement, recreation, diversion, sport.

playful, adj. sportive, frolicsome, prankish, jocular, sprightly.

plaything, n. bauble, gimcrack, toy.

plead, v. reason, argue; apologize, defend, advocate, intercede.

pleader, n. intercessor, defender, advocate.

pleasant, adj. agreeable, genial, congenial, affable, amiable, enjoyable. Antonyms: unpleasant, disagreeable, uncongenial, repellent.

pleasantry, n. badinage, banter, raillery, witticism, joke, jest.

please, v. rejoice, gladden, delight, gratify, cheer; elate.

pleasing, adj. pleasant, delightful, gratifying, delectable, gracious, winning.

pleasure, n. gratification, enjoyment, happiness, delectation, delight: amusement. Antonym: displeasure.

pledge, n. gage, security, hostage, guarantee.

pledge, v. swear, vow, vouchsafe, promise, oath, assurance, plight.

plentiful, adj. abundant, bounteous, ample, galore, copious, full. Antonyms: scarce, deficient, inadequate, insufficient, scant.

plenty, n. abundance, sufficiency, plenitude.

pliability, n. flexibility, suppleness,

pliancy, limberness, ductility, malleability. Antonyms: inflexibility, rigidity.

pliable, adj. flexible, pliant, supple, limber, lithesome, lithe. Antonym: inflexible.

plight, n. condition, state, dilemma, predicament, situation, scrape.

plight, v. pawn, pledge; promise, betroth.

plot, v. conspire, intrigue, cabal, complot, machinate, scheme.

pluck, v. pull, draw; pick, gather.

plump, adj. fleshy, bouncing, chubby, fat, portly, stout.

plunder, n: booty, spoil, loot, pillage, robbery.

plunge, v. souse, immerse, submerge, dip, douse; dive, pitch.

pocketbook, n. purse, wallet.

poem, n. sonnet, ballad, verse, distich, lyric.

poetry, n. verse, rhyme, poems, poesy. Antonym: prose.

poignant, adj. heartrending, moving, touching; piercing.

point, v. aim, level, direct; show, indicate, designate.

pointed, adj. sharp, picked, peaked, tapering, conical. Antonyms: pointless, dull.

pointer, n. indicator, index.

poise, n. equipoise, balance, equilibrium, dignity, composure, aplomb.

poise, v. balance, hover, float, perch.

poison, n. venom, virus, toxin, toxicant.

poisonous, adj. toxic, venomous,

noxious, baneful.

poke, v. stir up, excite; punch, thrust.

poke fun at, v. ridicule, deride.

poky, adj. slow, dull, tiresome, tedious, prosaic.

polish, n. gloss, luster, sheen, glaze, glazing.

polite, adj. courtly, civil, courteous, suave, urbane, deferential.

politeness, n. courtliness, courtesy, civility, suavity, urbanity.

politic, adj. political; judicious, discreet, shrewd, astute; diplomatic.

politician, n. statesman; demagogue.

pollute, v. defile, contaminate, corrupt, infect, debase, vitiate.

pompous, adj. stately; imposing, august; pretentious, grandiose.

pond, n. lake small; lagoon.

ponder, v. meditate, reflect, ruminate, think, muse.

ponderous, adj. massive, heavy, cumbersome; dull, spiritless; momentous, important.

poor, adj. indigent, impecunious, needy, poverty-stricken, straitened, necessitous.

poorhouse, n. almshouse, infirmary.

populace, n. commonalty, proletariat, rabble.

popular, adj. approved.

popularity, n. favor, esteem, approbation, celebrity.

population, n. inhabitants.

porch, n. piazza, stoop, veranda.

porous, adj. permeable, penetrable, pervious.

port, n. harbor, haven; embrasure; larboard.

portion, n. part, section, piece; allotment, quota, share.

portly, adj. dignified, imposing, stately, commanding; fleshy, obese.

portray, v. delineate, depict, picture, draw, sketch, paint, describe.

position, n. situation, post; attitude, posture; situation, place.

positive, adj. definite, precise, unequivocal, explicit, categorical, unmistakable.

posse, n. crowd, throng, multitude.

possess, v. own; have, hold, occupy, seize, take, appropriate.

possession, n. ownership, occupancy, tenure, fruition, retention, occupation.

possessor, n. owner, proprietor; occupant, tenant, holder.

possibility, n. potentiality, contingency. Antonym: impossibility.

possible, adj. potential, contingent, practicable. Antonym: impossible.

possibly, adv. maybe, perhaps, perchance, peradventure, haply.

post, n. column, pillar, pilaster; position, seat, station.

post, v. placard, announce; mail.

posted, adj. informed.

poster, n. placard, bulletin, bill.

posterior, adj. later, subsequent, ensuing, succeeding; hinder, rear.

postpone, v. defer, delay, put off, procrastinate, adjourn, prorogue.

postponement, n. deferring, delay, procrastination.

posture, n. attitude.

potent, adj. powerful, forcible, cogent, effective, strong.

pound, v. beat; comminute, pulverize, bray, triturate.

pour, v. decant; flow, gush, stream.

poverty, n. penury, indigence, need, destitution, privation, neediness.

powder, n. dust, residue.

powder, v. crush, grind, pulverize.

power, n. potency, might, cogency, efficacy, force.

powerful, adj. mighty, potent, drastic, efficacious, intense, strong.

powerless, adj. impotent.

practicability, n. feasibility.

practical, adj. pragmatic, tenable, sensible, convenient. Antonyms: impractical, Utopian, chimerical.

practice, n. custom, usage, habit; exercise, application, drill, rehearsal.

practice, v. exercise, apply, do, train, drill, rehearse.

praise, n. commendation, laudation, approbation, encomium. Antonyms: condemnation, dispraise, disapprobation, disparagement.

praise, v. laud, extol, commend, eulogize, panegyrize, applaud. Antonyms: condemn, denounce, disparage, deprecate, criticize.

praiseworthy, adj. laudable, admirable, worthy, commendable. Antonym: blameworthy.

prance, v. cavort, caper, frolic, gambol.

prank, n. trick, antic, frolic, caper.

prankish, adj. playful, frolicsome, sportive, mischievous, gamesome.

pray, v. invoke, supplicate, entreat, implore, beg, petition, intercede.

prayer, n. invocation, orison, collect, suffrage, supplication.

preach, v. exhort, expound, lecture; indoctrinate, proselytize.

preacher, n. cleric, vicar, rector, parson, reverend, evangelist, revivalist.

preaching, n. sermon, homily, exhortation.

precarious, adj. shaky, unstable, uncertain, insecure, doubtful; risky, dangerous, hazardous, perilous. Antonyms: stable, safe.

preceding, adj. foregoing, previous, earlier, prior, former, past.

precept, n. commandment, maxim, rule, adage, behest, injunction.

precious, adj. costly, expensive; valuable; dear, beloved, adored, idolized.

precise, adj. exact; formal, punctilious, particular, prim, prudish.

precision, n. exactness, accuracy; formalness, prudery.

predatory, adj. greedy, rapacious, grasping, voracious, predacious, plundering.

predestination, n. foreordination, foreordainment.

predict, v. prophesy, foretell, prognosticate, forebode, portend.

prediction, n. prophecy, soothsaying, divination, augury, prognostication.

predominant, adj. dominant, overruling, ascendant, supreme.

preface, n. prologue, prelude.

prejudice, n. prejudgment, bias;

harm, mischief, detriment.

preposterous, adj. absurd, ridiculous, irrational, inconsistent, foolish.

present, n. gift, donation, largess, gratuity, douceur.

preserve, n. conserve, jam, jelly; realm, domain, territory.

preserve, v. protect, conserve, safeguard, save; maintain, uphold, carry on.

press, n. pressure, urgency.

press, v. squeeze, crowd, compress: urge.

pressing, adj. urgent, importunate, exigent.

pretend, v. claim; simulate, feign, affect.

pretense, n. assumption, claim, pretension; simulation, affectation; pretext.

pretty, adj. comely, fair; personable, considerable. Antonyms: plain, homely, uncomely, ugly.

prevent, v. thwart, hinder, obstruct preclude, obviate,

prevention, n. obstruction, thwarting, interruption, hindrance, preclusion.

preventive, adj. deterrent, obviating, defensive, precautionary.

previous, adj. former, foregoing, antecedent, prior, anterior.

prey, n. spoil, loot, plunder, booty; victim, quarry.

prick, v. puncture, pierce, perforate; goad, spur, incite; sting.

pride, n. self-esteem, self-respect; haughtiness, arrogance, hauteur, superciliousness. Antonyms: humility, shame, self-abasement, modesty, lowliness.

priestly, adj. sacerdotal, clerical.

prim, adj. formal, precise, demure, prudish.

primitive, adj. pristine, primordial, primeval, primal; antique.

principal, adj. leading, chief, cardinal, paramount, main, foremost.

prior, adj. previous, former, antecedent, anterior.

priority, n. antecedence, anteriority, precedence.

prison, n. penitentiary, jail, poky, house of corrections, clink, brig.

privacy, n. retirement, seclusion; retreat, solitude, concealment.

private, adj. personal, individual; secret, secluded, covert, sequestered.

privation, n. deprivation, degradation; destitution, poverty, need; absence.

privilege, n. liberty, right, franchise, prerogative, immunity, advantage.

prize, v. value, esteem.

prize-fighter, n. pugilist, boxer.

probability, n. likelihood, verisimilitude, credibleness.

probable, adj. likely, credible, reasonable.

probe, v. investigate, examine.

procession, n. parade, cavalcade, cortege, train, retinue, file.

procure, v. get, obtain, acquire.

prodigal, adj. wasteful, extravagant, lavish, profuse.

profane, v. violate, desecrate; debase, prostitute, defile.

profane, adj. unconsecrated, secular; unsanctified, unholy; blasphemous.

profess, v. acknowledge, avow,

admit; claim, pretend.

profession, n. vocation, calling, line of work, occupation, job, career, business.

proficient, adj. expert, adept, skilled.

profit, n. gain, emolument, dividend.

profitable, adj. remunerative, lucrative, gainful, beneficial.

profound, adj. abysmal, deep; abstruse, recondite. Antonym: shallow.

progress, n. progression, advancement, improvement.

prominent, adj. protuberant; conspicuous, salient; eminent, distinguished.

promise, n. pledge, word, parole, plight, betrothal, troth.

promise, v. pledge, covenant, assure, plight.

promote, v. advance, forward; exalt, elevate, raise.

promotion, n. preferment, exaltation, advancement, furtherance.

prompt, adj. quick, expeditious, ready; punctual, timely.

pronunciation, n. utterance; articulation, enunciation, elocution.

proof, n. verification, corroboration, attestation, certification, confirmation. Antonyms: disproof, refutation.

proper, adj. appropriate, meet, suitable, seemly, condign, pertinent. Antonyms: improper, inappropriate, unsuitable.

property, n. attribute, trait; estate, wealth, chattels, goods.

prophecy, n. prediction, foretelling, divination, soothsaying, prognostication.

prophet, n. prognosticator, vaticinator, soothsayer, diviner, oracle, seer.

prosperity, n. weal, success, wellbeing. Antonyms: adversity, reverses, disaster.

protect, v. shield, defend, guard, fortify, screen, shelter, befriend.

protection, n. defense, shield, shelter, tutelage, refuge.

protector, n. defender, guardian, patron.

proud, adj. arrogant, vain, haughty, overbearing, supercilious.

provable, adj. demonstrable, verifiable.

prove, n. verify, corroborate, substantiate, demonstrate. Antonyms: disprove, refute.

provide, v. supply, furnish; stipulate, covenant, agree.

provider, n. furnisher, caterer, purveyor, supplier, contributor, donor, giver.

provoke, n. incite, stimulate, instigate, rouse; exasperate, displease.

prudence, n. discretion, caution.

prudent, adj. discreet, cautious, circumspect, provident. Antonyms: imprudent, incautious.

publish, v. promulgate, proclaim, circulate, blazon, announce. Antonyms: suppress, withhold.

pull, v. draw, tug, haul, tow, drag.

pulverize, v. grind, crush, macerate, pulp, mash, pound, squash, smash, puree.

pump, v. interrogate, question, quiz.

punch, v. push, poke; pierce, bore, perforate, puncture.

puncture, v. prick, perforate, pierce.

pungent, adj. pricking, stinging; poignant, sharp, excruciating, severe.

punish, v. chastise, castigate, chasten, discipline.

punishment, n. chastisement, castigation, scourging, discipline, penalty. Antonyms: immunity, impunity, acquittal, exoneration.

puny, adj. undeveloped, small, undersized, diminutive, stunted.

pup, n. puppy, whelp.

pupil, n. scholar: learner, disciple, catechumen.

purchase, v. buy, procure, acquire.

pure, adj. chaste, virtuous, innocent, undefiled, unpolluted,

purification, n. depuration, expurgation, refinement, cleansing.

purify, v. cleanse, refine, expurgate, sublime, clarify.

purity, n. chastity, virtue; clarity; homogeneity.

purport, n. meaning, signification, import.

purport, v. mean, intend, signify, import.

purpose, n. aim, object, design, intent, goal, view, drift.

push, v. shove, impel.

push, n. energy, spiritedness, enterprise, aggressiveness.

pushy, adj. enterprising, energetic, intrusive, forward, officious, obtrusive, aggressive.

put back, v. replace, restore, reinstate; retard, impede, delay, hinder.

put down, v. deposit; crush, quell, suppress, repress, vanquish.

put in, v. insert, inject, interpolate, interpose, thrust in.

put out, v. eject, oust, remove, evict, dispossess, dislodge.

puzzle, v. mystify, pose, nonplus, perplex, bewilder, confuse.

puzzle, n. enigma, conundrum, intricacy, maze, crux, riddle.

puzzling, adj. enigmatical, perplexing, inexplicable, inscrutable, intricate, bewildering.

Q

quack, n. charlatan, empiric, pretender, mountebank, impostor, fake, fraud, swindler, con artist, sham.

quaint, adj. fanciful, whimsical, odd, curious, grotesque, old-fashioned.

quake, v. quiver, tremble, shake, shudder, vibrate.

quake, n. agitation, trembling, shaking, vibration, quivering.

qualification, n. condition, restriction, modification, limitation; endowment.

qualified, adj. modified, limited; competent: eligible, fitted, capable.

qualify, v. modify, limit, restrict, condition; fit, prepare.

qualify, n. nature, character, sort, strain, condition; characteristic.

qualm, n. misgiving, doubt, apprehensiveness, uneasiness, foreboding, trepidation, disquiet; compunction, regret, uneasiness, scruple.

quandary, n. perplexity, predicament, dilemma, puzzle, difficulty, strait.

quantity, n. amount, magnitude, size, number.

quarrel, n. altercation, disagreement, dispute, brawl, affray, fray.

quarrel, v. wrangle, altercate, dispute, contend, squabble, bicker.

quarrelsome, adj. disputatious, contentious, irascible, choleric, litigious.

quarry, n. stone pit; game, prey.

quarters, n. rooms, lodging; posts, stations, cantonment, barracks.

quash, v. crush, subdue, extinguish; quell, suppress; annul, overrule.

quaver, v. shake, tremble, quiver.

queen, n. monarch, sovereign, ruler, consort.

queer, adj. odd, erratic, eccentric, peculiar, singular, unusual.

quench, v. slake; extinguish, stifle, suppress.

query, n. question, interrogatory; request.

quest, n. search, seeking, pursuit; request, desire, solicitation, inquiry.

question, n. interrogation, inquiry, query, quizzing, quiz, examination.

questionable, adj. suspicious, disputable, doubtful, debatable, problematical.

questioner, n. inquirer, interrogator, inquisitor, quizzer.

questioning, adj. interrogatory, inquisitive, quizzical, inquisitorial, catechistic.

quibble, n. shift, evasion, cavil, sophism, subterfuge, subtlety.

quibbling, adj. trifling, evasive, caviling, elusive, sophistical, hairsplitting, pedantry.

quick, adj. hasty, swift, fast, speedy, fleet, hurried, rapid. Antonyms: slow, dilatory, sluggish.

quicken, v. revive, vivify, vitalize, resuscitate, animate, excite. Antonyms: impede, retard, hinder, obstruct, check.

quickness, n. fleetness, expedition, rapidity, celerity, alacrity, agility.

quiet, adj. calm, still, pacific, motionless, unmoved, stagnant, placid. Antonyms: noisy, tumultuous, boisterous, rude, stormy.

quiet, v. still, hush, lull, appease, allay, compose. Antonyms: arouse, aggravate, exasperate, intensify, increase.

quietness, n. stillness, quiescence, quiet, repose, calmness, tranquillity.

quilt, n. coverlet, throw, comforter, counterpane.

quirk, n. evasion, subterfuge, shift, quibble, prevarication, equivocation.

quit, v. cease, stop, desist, discontinue, forbear, break off. Antonyms: continue, persist, stay.

quiver, v. tremble, shake, shudder, quake.

quivering, adj. trembling, tremulous, shuddering, shaking.

quiz, v. puzzle; question, ask, interrogate, cross-examine, grill, interview.

quiz, n. puzzle, conundrum, poser; examination.

quota, n. portion, share, allotment, apportionment.

quotation, n. citation, excerpt.

quote, v. cite, repeat, paraphrase, excerpt.

R

rabbit, n. hare, coney, bunny,

rabid, adj. violent, raging, furious; intolerant, fanatical, uncompromising.

rack, n. pain, torture, agony.

rack, v. stretch, strain, torture, agonize; harass.

racy, adj. fine-flavored, pungent, rich; spirited, piquant, fresh and lively. Antonyms: insipid, vapid, tasteless, flavorless, dull.

radiance, n. effulgence, refulgence, brilliancy, brightness.

radiate, v. shine, beam, gleam; diverge.

radiated, adj. divergent.

radiation, n. irradiance, irradiation; divergence. Antonym: convergence.

radical, adj. original, fundamental; extreme, thorough-going; primitive. Antonyms: conservative, moderate, slight, trifling, derivative.

radically, adv. extrenmely, severely, drastically, fundamentally.

raffle, n. lottery, drawing, sweepstakes.

raft, n. float, catamaran.

rag, n. tatter, flitter, shred, patch, frazzle, fragment.

ragamuffin, n. tatterdemalion, scarecrow.

rage, n. fury, wrath, passion, frenzy; vogue, mode, fashion, craze, fad, fashion.

rage, v. storm, fume, rave, seethe, thunder.

raging, adj. furious, raving, infuriated, frenzied.

raid, n. foray, incursion.

railroad, n. railway.

railroad, v. force, coerce, bulldoze, intimidate, browbeat; frame.

rain, n. drizzle, mist, shower, precipitation, downpour, mizzle; volley. Antonym: drought.

rain, v. pour, drizzle, shower, sprinkle.

rainbow, n. iris.

rainy, adj. wet, showery, pluvial. Antonym: dry.

raise, v. uplift, lift; hoist, heave; erect, build.

raising, n. uplifting, lifting, elevation, hoisting; erection, rearing.

rally, v. collect, reunite; recover, recuperate; assemble.

ram, v. cram, stuff, compress.

ramble, v. rove, range, stroll, stray, straggle, roam, wander.

rambling, adj. roving, wandering; discursive, digressive, incoherent.

rampage, n. debauchery, passion, excess, unrestraint.

rampant, adj. exuberant, luxuriant, rank, wanton, excessive.

rampart, n. fortification, bulwark, bastion, wall.

rancid, adj. musty, tainted, rank, frowzy.

rancorous, adj. malevolent, vindictive, malignant, hateful, virulent, bitter.

random, adj. haphazard, chance, stray, aimless.

range, v. arrange, rank, class, classify; rove, roam.

range, n. extent, reach, sweep, compass, scope, latitude.

rank, adj. exuberant, luxuriant, rampant, vigorous; violent, extreme.

rank, n. row, line, range, order, tier, series.

ransack, v. rummage, plunder, loot, pillage.

ransom, n. release, liberation, redemption, deliverance.

ransom, v. redeem, rescue, liberate, deliver.

rant, v. declaim, spout, rave,

ranting, adj. bombastic, shouting, raging; incoherent.

rap, v. knock, tap.

rap, n. knock, thump, thwack, blow, tap.

rapacious, adj. predatory, predaceous, ravenous.

rapid, adj. swift, fast, fleet, expeditious, cursory, quick.

rapidity, n. swiftness, celerity, velocity, haste, speed, fleetness.

rapidly, adv. swiftly, fast, post, haste.

rapture, n. ecstasy, transport, delight, bliss, beatitude.

rapturous, adj. ecstatic, beatific, delightful; ravishing, transporting.

rare, adj. uncommon, unusual, strange, infrequent, singular, curious.

rarely, adv. infrequently, seldom.

rascal, n. rogue, scoundrel, scamp, knave, villain.

rash, adj. incautious, precipitate, overhasty, indiscreet, inconsiderate.

rash, n. exanthema, eruption, efflorescence, outbreak, inflammation.

rashness, n. temerity, precipitancy, indiscretion, incaution, recklessness.

rate, v. estimate, value, appraise; access; scold, censure.

ratification, n. confirmation, sanction, substantiation, corroboration.

ratify, v. confirm, sanction, substantiate, corroborate.

ration, n. allowance, portion, allotment.

rational, adj. reasoning; intelligent, sane, sound, judicious, wise. Antonyms: irrational, insane, injudicious, unwise, unreasonable.

rationale, n. explanation, exposition, reason.

rattle, v. clatter; chatter, prate, babble.

ravage, n. plunder, pillage, devastation, spoliation, sack.

rave, v. rage, rant, storm.

ravenous, adj. voracious, rapacious, ravening, insatiable.

ravine, n. gorge, defile, clough, gully, gulch.

raving, adj. irrational, delirious, maniacal, wild, frenetic.

ravish, v. transport, enrapture, enchant.

ravishing, adj. rapturous, ecstatic,

transporting, beatific, delightful.

ravishment, n. ecstasy, transport, rapture.

raw, adj. uncooked; unprepared, crude; immature, unripe.

ray, n. beam, gleam.

reach, v. attain, achieve; contact; convey.

reachable, adj. attainable, accessible.

react, v. repeat; resist, oppose; rebound, recoil.

read, v. peruse, study, scan.

readable, adj. legible. Antonyms: unreadable, illegible.

readiness, n. promptness, speediness, facility, alacrity; willingness, eagerness, inclination. Antonyms: unwillingness, delay.

reading, n. perusal; recitation, recital; interpretation, analysis, evaluation.

real, adj. genuine, veritable, actual, true. Antonyms: fictitious, unreal, spurious, ostensible, artificial.

reality, n. actuality, verity. Antonyms: unreality, phantasm, simulation, phantom.

realization, n. fulfillment, effectuation.

realize, v. effectuate, accomplish; comprehend, grasp, understand.

really, adv. actually, truly, indeed, veritably, verily.

realm, n. kingdom, dominion; domain, region, sphere,

rear, n. back, stern. Antonym: front.

rear, v. raise, lift, elevate; erect, build; bring up.

reason, n. motive, consideration, design, purpose, rationality, logic.

reason, v. ratiocinate, argue, remonstrate, expostulate.

reasonable, adj. rational; logical, just; conscionable, fair, moderate, equitable.

reasoning, n. ratiocination, argumentation, syllogism, reckoning.

rebate, n. deduction, discount, allowance.

rebel, n. insurgent, mutineer, revolutionary, radical, dissenter, turncoat.

rebel, v. revolt, mutiny, rise up, defy, dissent

rebellion, n. insurrection, insurgency, mutiny, sedition, revolt, insubordination.

rebellious, adj. insurgent, seditious, mutinous, insubordinate, refractory. Antonyms: dutiful, submissive, docile, compliant.

rebound, v. recoil, ricochet; reverberate.

rebound, n. rebounding, resilience, repercussion, recoil, ricochet.

rebuff, n. repulse, resistance, opposition, repellence.

rebuke, v. reprove, upbraid, censure, reprehend, chide, admonish.

rebuke, n. reproof, censure; chastisement, punishment.

recall, v. revoke, annul, retract, recant, rescind, repeal.

recant, v. retract, abjure.

recapitulate, v. summarize.

receipt, n. receiving, reception; formula, recipe, formulary; voucher.

receive, v. take, accept; admit, allow; welcome; hold, contain.

receiver, n. recipient, beneficiary; handset. Antonym: sender.
recent, adj. new, late.
receptacle, n. container, repository.
reception, n. receipt, receiving; levee, soiree, function.
recess, n. retreat, withdrawal, alcove, niche.
recipe, n. formula, receipt.
recipient, n. receiver, beneficiary.
reciprocity, n. reciprocation, interchange.
recital, n. recitation, narration, narrative.
recite, v. relate, recount, repeat, deliver.
reckless, adj. heedless, inconsiderate, unmindful, thoughtless, temerarious, rash.
reckon, v. compute, calculate, count, enumerate; esteem, regard.
reckoning, n. computation, calculation, enumeration; settlement, adjustment.
reclaim, v. tame, domesticate; reform.
reclining, adj. recumbent, leaning, lying.
recluse, adj. solitary, eremitic.
recluse, n. solitary, eremite, anchorite, hermit.
reclusion, n. seclusion, eremitism.
recoil, v. rebound, react; flinch, shrink, quail.
recollect, v. remember, recall, reminisce. Antonym: forget.
recollection, n. remembrance, memory, reminiscence.
recommend, v. commend, praise.
recommendation, n. commenda-

tion.
reconcile, v. propitiate, pacify; harmonize, adjust, settle. Antonyms: estrange, disaffect, alienate.
reconciliation, n. conciliation, pacification, appeasement, reunion.
record, n. register, memoir, diary, chronicle, minute, memorandum; evidence, proof, documentation, testimony; disc, vinyl, LP, single, release, recording, soundtrack; top score.
record, v. tape, video, film; log, chronicle, note.
record, adj. best, greatest, top.
records, n. minutes, proceedings, account, report, archives.
recover, v. regain, reclaim, retrieve, repair, recoup.
recoverable, adj. retrievable.
recovery, n. retrieval, recuperation, regaining, restoration, convalescence.
recreation, n. pastime, amusement, relaxation, diversion, sport, fun.
rectify, v. correct, amend.
rectitude, n. probity, integrity, uprightness, honesty, virtue.
rector, n. pastor, clergyman, priest.
rectory, n. parsonage.
red, n. carmine, crimson, scarlet, cerise, garnet, vermilion.
red, adj. florid; blushing, flushed, ruby, ruddy.
redeem, v. repurchase; regain, recover; ransom, rescue, deliver.
redeemer, n. rescuer, deliverer,

savior, liberator.

redemption, n. ransom, salvation, deliverance, rescue.

redoubtable, adj. formidable, terrible; valiant, courageous, brave.

redress, n. reparation, amends, indemnification, relief.

reduce, v. diminish, lower, degrade, minimize, depress, debase.

reduction, n. diminution, abatement, minimization, decrement, debasement; subjugation.

redundant, adj. superabundant, superfluous, excessive, plethoric; repetitive.

reek, v. stink, smell.

reek, n. stench, stink, smell, odor.

reel, v. stagger.

refer, v. allude.

referable, adj. attributable, ascribable, traceable, assignable.

referee, n. umpire, judge, arbitrator, arbiter.

refine, v. purify, clarify, sublimate, sublime.

refined, adj. exquisite, polished, fine, well-bred, courtly, cultured.

refinement, n. culture, elegance, polish, fastidiousness; purification. Antonyms: vulgarity, coarseness, crudity, barbarity.

reflect, v. mirror; rebound, revert; meditate, ruminate, consider, contemplate.

reflection, n. meditation, contemplation, rumination; stricture.

reform, v. reclaim, regenerate, convert, amend.

reformation, n. reform, reclamation, betterment, improvement.

refraction, n. deflection.

refrain, v. restrain, curb, check;

forbear, abstain, desist.

refresh, v. revive, enliven, reanimate; renovate, renew, restore.

refreshing, n. reviving, reanimating, cooling, reinvigorating.

refreshment, n. collation, lunch, refection, regalement.

refuge, n. stronghold, asylum, retreat, covert; shelter.

refugee, n. fugitive, runaway.

refund, v. repay, return, restore.

refusal, n. dissent, denial, snub, negation, rebuttal, repudiation, rebuff.

refuse, v. deny, decline; reject, rebuff, repulse.

refutation, n. confutation, disproof.

refute, v. rebut, disprove, contradict, dispute.

regain, v. recover, retrieve.

regal, adj. kingly, royal.

regard, v. heed, observe, consider.

regard, n. respect, esteem, estimation, opinion; respect. Antonyms: disregard, heedlessness.

regardful, adj. mindful, heedful, attentive, observant.

regardless, adj. heedless, careless, unmindful, inattentive, indifferent.

regards, n. compliments, respects.

region, n. district, quarter, locality, neighborhood, vicinity.

register, n. list, roll, schedule, roster; registrar, recorder.

register, v. record, enroll, matriculate.

registration, n. registry, enrollment, matriculation.

regret, n. sorrow, compunction, deprecation, rue.

regret, v. deplore, be sorry for, rue, deprecate.

regular, adj. formal, normal, steady.

regularity, n. uniformity, symmetry, shapeliness, constancy, order. Antonyms: irregularity, inconstancy, disorder.

reign, n. sovereignty, rule, dominion, supremacy, control.

reject, v. cast away, discard; refuse, decline, rebuff, repulse.

rejection, n. refusal, declination, rebuff, repulse, discarding.

rejoice, v. glory, exult; gladden, cheer, delight, please, exhilarate.

rejoicing, n. joy, gladness, exultation, delight, pleasure.

relate, v. recount, narrate, tell.

related, adj. allied, cognate, germane, agnate, akin, kindred.

relation, n. connection, bearing, relationship, reference, correlation, alliance.

relationship, n. kindred, affinity, alliance, kinship, cognation.

relative, adj. relating, referring, respecting, pertaining; comparative; context-sensitive.

relative, n. relation, kinsman, kinswoman, family member.

relax, v. loosen, slacken; abate, diminish, mitigate.

relaxation, n. loosening, slackening; diversion, recreation, rest.

relay, v. pass on, communicate, transmit.

release, v. liberate, loose, discharge, free, acquit; announce, issue, emit. Antonyms: withhold, hold.

release, n. liberation, discharge, deliverance, relief, freedom, emancipation; announcement, statement.

relentless, adj. ruthless, implacable, unrelenting, inexorable, unmerciful.

relevance, n. significance, bearing, application.

relevant, adj. pertinent, germane, apposite.

reliability, n. dependability, trustworthiness.

reliable, adj. trustworthy, trusty, dependable.

reliance, n. dependence, confidence, trust.

reliant, adj. confident, trusting.

relics, n. leavings, remains, remnants.

relief, n. alleviation, mitigation, comfort, ease, succor.

relieve, v. assuage, alleviate, allay, lesson.

relieve, v. assuage, alleviate, allay, lesson, remedy.

religious, adj. pious, godly, devout, righteous, devotional; strict.

relinquish, v. surrender, waive, forego, renounce, cede, abandon, desert.

relinquishment, n. surrender, abandonment, renunciation.

reluctance, n. unwillingness, disinclination, aversion.

reluctant, adj. disinclined, unwilling, averse, loath, indisposed.

rely, v. depend, remainder, residue, remnant, balance, rest, surplus.

remaining, adj. residual, outstand-

ing, left over, enduring, lasting.
remains, n. relics, debris, remnants, leftovers, vestiges, residue.
remand, v. recommit, send back.
remark, v. notice, observe, heed, see, note.
remark, n. comment, observation.
remarkable, adj. noteworthy, striking, extraordinary, wonderful, notable.
remedy, v. heal, cure, repair, relieve, redress, alleviate.
remedy, n. medicine, cure, antidote, corrective, specific.
remember, v. recollect, recall.
remembrance, n. recollection, memory, reminiscence; souvenir, keepsake. Antonyms: forgetfulness, amnesia, amnesty, oblivion.
reminder, n. prompt, cue; souvenir, memento, keepsake.
remiss, adj. negligent, derelict, careless, slack, heedless, neglectful.
remission, n. surrender, relinquishment; discharge; abatement.
remnant, n. remainder, residue, rest; fragment, piece.
remorse, n. self-reproach, sorrow, regret; penitence; pity, compassion, sympathy.
remorseless, adj. implacable, ruthless, merciless, unmerciful.
remote, adj. distant, isolated; aloof, detached.
removal, n. displacement, dislodgement, transference, expulsion, elimination, dismissal.
remove, v. move, displace, transfer, dislodge; dismiss, discharge.

remunerative, adj. profitable, lucrative.
rend, v. tear, rive, lacerate, cleave, sunder.
render, v. repay, restore; translate, interpret, construe.
rendering, n. repayment, restoration; contribution, surrender.
renegade, n. deserter, recreant, backslider, turncoat; rebel.
renew, v. renovate, rejuvenate, restore, rebuild, remodel, reconstruct.
renewal, n. renovation, repair, restoration, regeneration, reconstruction.
renounce, v. disclaim, disown, repudiate; reject.
renovation, n. restoration, renewal, rehabilitation, reconstruction.
renown, n. celebrity, repute, fame, notoriety, note.
renowned, adj. famous, celebrated, eminent, far-famed, illustrious. Antonyms: unrenowned, obscure, inglorious, unknown.
rent, v. lease, let, hire.
renter, n. lessee, tenant.
renunciation, n. abjuration, denial, disownment, disclaimer.
repair, v. mend, restore, patch, tinker, revamp, darn.
repair, n. renovation, restoration, reconstruction, reparation, rehabilitation.
reparation, n. restoration, rehabilitation, instauration, renovation; atonement, restitution, compensation, reimbursement.
repay, v. refund, restore, reimburse; recompense.

repeal, v. revoke, rescind, abrogate.

repeat, v. iterate, reiterate, echo, recur.

repel, v. repulse, rebuff, resist, oppose.

repentance, n. penitence, contrition, compunction, remorse. Antonym: impenitence.

repetition, n. iteration, reiteration, recurrence.

replace, v. restore, refund, repay.

replacement, n. restoration, reinstatement.

reply, v. answer, respond, rejoin, retort.

report, n. rumor, hearsay, bruit; account, statement.

report, v. announce, communicate, describe. Antonyms: suppress, withhold, reserve.

repose, n. rest, inactivity, motionlessness; composure, tranquillity.

repository, n. depository, storehouse, depot, magazine.

represent, v. show, typify, symbolize; personate.

representative, n. deputy, delegate, vicar, proxy, agent, substitute.

repress, v. quell, subdue, suppress, overpower, restrain.

repression, n. suppression, restraint, quelling, check.

reproach, v. censure, upbraid, rebuke, reprimand, revile.

reproachful, adj. upbraiding, opprobrious, abusive; shameful, disgraceful, scandalous.

reprobate, adj. abandoned, depraved, profligate, incorrigible.

reprobate, n. castaway, outcast, wretch, degenerate, good-for-nothing, troublemaker.

reproduce, v. portray, duplicate, imitate; generate, beget, propagate.

reproduction, n. duplication, copy, imitation; generation, procreation, propagation.

repudiate, v. reject, renounce, disavow, abjure, disclaim.

repugnance, n. aversion, reluctance, unwillingness, hostility, antipathy.

repugnant, adj. hostile, contrary, refractory, adverse, offensive.

repulse, v. repel, reject.

repulsive, adj. repellent, offensive, forbidding, revolting.

reputation, n. repute, name, credit, esteem, honor.

repute, n. reputation, esteem, credit.

request, n. asking, solicitation, demand, instance, prayer.

request, v. ask, supplicate, petition, beg, entreat.

require, v. demand, claim, exact, need, want, necessitate, enjoin.

requirement, n. demand, requisition, requisite; command, essential, need.

requisite, adj. necessary, required, essential, indispensable.

requital, n. remuneration, retribution, retaliation, reprisal.

rescue, n. deliverance, liberation, salvation, ransom.

rescue, v. release, deliver, liberate, recapture, redeem, save.

resemblance, n. likeness, similitude, similarity, analogy.

resentment, n. dudgeon, umbrage, displeasure, grudge.

reserve, n. reticence, constraint, uncommunicativeness.

reserved, adj. retained, withheld, excepted; uncommunicative.

residence, n. dwelling, domiciliation, abode, house, home, habitation.

resident, n. denizen, inhabitant, dweller, occupant, tenant.

residue, n. remainder, remnant, residuum, rest, balance.

resign, v. demit, abdicate, withdraw, surrender, relinquish, submit.

resignation, n. surrender, abdication, forbearance, acceptance, acquiescence. Antonym: defiance.

resigned, adj. surrendered; uncomplaining, submissive, reconciled, acquiescent, patient. Antonym: resistant.

resist, v. oppose, withstand, impugn, oppugn, defy.

resistance, n. confrontation, fight, struggle, opposition, renitence, defiance, challenge Antonyms: surrender, acceptance.

resistant, adj. resisting, opposing, renitent.

resolute, adj. determined, unwavering, unflinching, steadfast, firm, pertinacious.

resolution, n. firmness, determination, pertinacity, persistence, steadfastness.

resolve, v. determine; dissolve, liquefy.

resolve, n. resolution, determi-

nation, intention, purpose, design.

resound, n. echo, reverberation.

resounding, adj. resonant, echoing; emphatic, definite.

resource, n. resort, expedient, device, shift.

resources, n. assets, means.

respect, n. care, caution, regard; esteem, veneration.

respect, v. esteem, venerate, revere, honor, reverence.

respectable, adj. reputable, honorable, estimable; moderate, fair, average.

respectful, adj. deferential, courteous, polite, obeisant, reverent. Antonyms: disrespectful, discourteous, defiant.

respective, adj. relative; particular, own.

respects, n. compliments, regards, devoirs.

response, n. reply, answer, rejoinder, retort.

responsibility, n. accountability, liability, duty, trust.

responsible, adj. accountable, answerable, amenable. Antonyms: irresponsible, unaccountable, independent.

responsive, adj. responding, antiphonal.

rest, n. quiet, quietness, inactivity, repose, east, tranquillity. Antonyms: activity, agitation, unrest, commotion.

rest, v. stop, halt, pause, desist; repose, recline.

restaurant, n. café, chophouse, refectory, buffet, bistro, eatery.

resting, adj. reclining, lying, incumbent.

restitution, n. repayment, restoration, return, indemnification; reparation.

restive, adj. restless, impatient, fidgety, intractable, uneasy.

restless, adj. restive, fidgety, agitated, unquiet, uneasy.

restlessness, n. restiveness, uneasiness, agitation, turbulence.

restoration, n. return, restitution; replacement, reinstatement, reparation.

restore, v. repair, renew, reconstruct, rehabilitate.

restrain, v. repress, suppress, check, bridle, curb, constrain.

restraint, n. repression, constraint, check, suppression, limitation prevention.

restrict, v. restrain, limit, confine, repress, curb, circumscribe.

restriction, n. restraint, constraint, confinement, repression, circumscription, limitation.

result, v. terminate, end, eventuate, issue, accrue, ensue.

result, n. consequence, effect, issue, event, outcome.

resume, n. recapitulation, summary, abstract.

resurrection, n. resurgence, revivification, renaissance, renewal, revitalization.

retain, v. keep, hold, reserve.

retaliate, v. avenge, requite, repay.

retaliation, n. revenge, requital, retribution.

retard, v. impede, hold back, check, delay.

retentive, adj. tenacious. Antonyms: irretentive.

reticence, n. reserve, uncommunicativeness, taciturnity.

reticent, adj. taciturn, reserved, uncommunicative.

retire, v. withdraw, retreat, recede, retrocede, leave, secede.

retired, adj. secluded, sequestered, unfrequented, withdrawn.

retiring, adj. diffident, shy, coy, shrinking, reserved, modest.

retract, v. recant, rescind, recall, disavow.

retreat, n. retirement, withdrawal; refuge, asylum, seclusion.

retreat, v. retire, withdraw, recede.

retribution, n. retaliation, repayment, requital.

retrograde, v. retrocede, recede, decline, deteriorate.

return, v. restore, repay, refund, replace; recur, regress.

return, n. restoration, restitution, repayment, requital, retribution, redress.

returning, adj. recurrent, recurring, intermittent.

reveal, v. disclose, unveil, expose, divulge, impart.

revel, n. carousal, festivity, saturnalia.

revel, v. carouse; luxuriate, wanton.

revelation, n. disclosure, divulgement, exposition, apocalypse.

revenge, v. avenge, retaliate.

revenge, n. vengeance, retaliation, payback, retribution, reprisal.

revengeful, adj. vindictive, implacable, resentful, rancorous.

revenue, n. income, proceeds, assets, earnings, receipts.

revere, v. venerate, reverence, honor, respect.

reverence, n. veneration, devotion, awe, homage.

reverence, v. revere, venerate.

reverent, adj. reverential, humble.

reverse, v. invert; overthrow, subvert, overturn; revoke, annul.

reverse, n. opposite, contrary, counterpart, reversal; misfortune, failure.

review, v. reconsider, revise, reexamine, retrace.

review, n. reexamination, reconsideration, retrospect, revision.

revision, n. revisal, amendment, emendation, modification, alteration, improvement.

revival, n. revitalization, reanimation, resuscitation, restoration, renewal, restoration, stimulation, recovery.

revive, v. resuscitate, reanimate, quicken, revivify, revitalize.

revocation, n. recall, repeal, reversal, abjuration, recantation.

revoke, v. repeal, reverse, recant, rescind, abrogate.

revolt, n. rebellion, sedition, uprising, mutiny, insurrection.

revolt, v. rebel, mutiny; disgust, nauseate, shock, offend.

revolting, adj. nauseating, repulsive, fulsome, abhorrent, disgusting.

revolution, n. rotation, gyration; rebellion, revolt.

revolve, v. rotate, spin, gyrate, turn; devolve; brood over.

revolver, n. pistol, repeater.

revolving, adj. rotary, gyrating, gyratory.

reward, n. recompense, requital, remuneration, prize, compensation, bonus. Antonym: penalty.

reward, v. requite, recompense, compensate. Antonym: penalize.

rhyme, n. jingle, poetry.

ribald, adj. indelicate, gross, indecent, obscene, lewd.

rich, adj. wealthy, opulent, affluent, well-to-do, moneyed; abundant. Antonyms: poor, infertile, indigent, plain.

richness, n. opulence, wealth, affluence; abundance, profusion. Antonyms: poverty, infertility.

rid, adj. free, clear, disencumbered.

rid, v. free, disburden, relieve, disencumber, dispose of, dispatch.

riddle, n. enigma, puzzle, problem.

ridicule, n. mockery, gibe, jeer, burlesque.

ridicule, v. deride, satirize, scoff, rally, banter.

ridiculous, adj. preposterous, absurd, farcical, burlesque, ludicrous.

rifle, v. strip, fleece, despoil, pillage, devastate.

right, adj. just, true, equitable, honest, rightful, lawful.

right, v. correct, rectify, emend; make restitution, redress.

right, n. prerogative, privilege, immunity, exemption; uprightness, rectitude, probity, integrity.

right away, adv. immediately, straightway, right off, instantly, at once, instantaneously.

righteous, adj. pious, religious, devout, godly; saintly.

righteousness, n. godliness, holiness, sanctity. Antonym: unrighteousness.

rigid, adj. inflexible, stiff, unyielding; rigorous, severe.

rigidity, n. stiffness, inflexibility, severity, rigor.

rigmarole, n. nonsense, flummery, balderdash, twaddle.

rigor, n. rigidity, inflexibility, austerity, severity.

rigorous, adj. severe, stringent, strict, unyielding; inclement, severe.

rile, v. roil; anger, vex, offend.

rim, n. brim, margin, edge, brink, verge, border.

rind, n. skin, peel. Antonym: pulp.

ring, v. sound, resound, reverberate; toll, knell, chime.

ring, n. circle, hoop; grommet.

ringing, n. sounding, resounding, reverberation, tolling, clang.

ringlet, n. tress, curl, lock.

riot, n. tumult uproar; revelry.

rioter, n. reveler, carouser, roisterer.

riotous, adj. wanton, luxuriant, unrestrained; seditious.

rip, n. rent, tear.

ripe, adj. mature, ripened; consummate, complete, perfect.

ripen, v. mature, maturate, develop, mellow.

ripeness, n. maturity, completeness, development.

rise, v. ascend, mount, arise, levitate; tower; swell, increase.

rise, n. ascent, spring, source, origin, beginning.

rising, adj. ascending, ascendant.

rising, n. ascent, ascension, rise, levitation, emergence.

risk, n. danger, peril, jeopardy, hazard, imperilment, menace. Antonym: safety.

risk, v. hazard, endanger, peril, imperil, jeopardize.

rite, n. ceremony, ordinance.

ritual, n. rite, service, ceremony, sacrament; custom, habit, practice, convention, tradition.

ritual, adj. ceremonial, procedural; customary, habitual, usual, normal, routine, traditional, conventional.

rival, n. competitor, emulator, antagonist.

rival, adj. competing, competitive, emulative.

rival, n. competition, emulation, contention.

road, n. thoroughfare, avenue, highroad, highway, street, lane.

roam, v. ramble, stray, rove, range, wander.

roar, n. bellow, shout, rumble.

roar, v. bellow; boom, peal, resound, thunder.

roast, v. bake: torrefy, parch; criticize, mock.

rob, v. plunder, pillage, fleece, despoil, rifle.

robber, n. bandit, brigand, buccaneer, burglar.

robbery, n. larceny, burglary, theft, plundering, piracy.

robe, n. gown, housecoat.

robust, adj. strong, sinewy, muscular, brawny, stalwart, vigorous, sound.

rogue, n. knave, miscreant, scamp, rascal.

roll, n. scroll; roster, record; convolution.

roll, v. wheel, whirl, revolve, rotate, turn, gyrate, spin.

rolling, adj. rotating; undulating.

romantic, adj. imaginary, impractical, chimerical, picturesque, fanciful, fantastic.

room, n. space, compass, range, scope, latitude; apartment.

roomer, n. lodger, boarder, tenant.

roomy, adj. spacious, capacious, commodious.

roost, n. perch.

root, n. etymon, stem, radix, radical.

rope, n. cordage, cable, hawser, lasso, lariat.

rosy, adj. rose-colored, roseate, ruddy, alluring.

rot, n. decomposition, decay, putrescence, corruption, putridity. Antonyms: preservation, incorruption, soundness.

rotary, adj. turning, rotating.

rotate, v. revolve, turn, gyrate, whirl.

rotation, n. turning, revolution; succession.

rotten, adj. decayed, putrid, putrescent, carious, corrupt, decomposed.

rough, adj. uneven, jagged, craggy, rugged, cragged, scraggy.

rough, n. bully, ruffian, rowdy.

round, adj. circular, spherical, orbicular, orbed, globular.

round, n. revolution, cycle, rotation, series, succession.

roundabout, adj. circuitous, indirect, tortuous; encircling, ambient.

roundness, n. circularity, globularity, rotundity; plumpness, chubbiness.

rousing, adj. exciting, stirring; astounding: startling.

route, n. course, road, passage.

routine, n. custom, round, course.

rove, v. range, ramble, straggle.

rowdy, n. ruffian, rough, bully, hoodlum.

royal, adj. kingly, regal, imperial, monarchic.

royalty, n. kingship, sovereignty, regality, regency; sovereign, majesty.

rub, n. friction; hindrance, impediment, obstruction.

rub, v. abrade, chafe, scrape, grate, fret; embrocate.

rubbing, n. friction, abrasion, attrition, chiding, fraying.

rubbish, n. trash, litter, lumber, refuse, debris, garbage.

rude, adj. crude, unpolished, raw, rough, indelicate, unrefined, coarse.

rudiment, n. origin, seed, embryo, kernel.

rudimentary, adj. rudimental, elementary, basic, primary, fundamental.

rue, v. regret, deplore.

rueful, adj. woeful, sad, lugubrious, mournful.

ruffian, n. monster, villain, rowdy, desperado.

ruffle, n. ruff, frill, flounce.

rugged, adj. irregular, rough, uneven, scraggy.

ruin, n. wreck, destruction, undoing, dilapidation, disorganization.

ruin, v. overthrow, subvert, destroy, wreck, impoverish.

ruination, n. ruin, undoing, downfall.

rule, n. regulation, prescript, prescription, order, ruling; standard.

rule, v. govern, dominate; restrain, influence, sway, prevail.

ruler, n. governor, sovereign, monarch, president, king.

ruling, n. government; decision, verdict, edict, judgment, decree.

ruminate, v. meditate, muse, ponder, reflect.

rummage, v. ransack, search, delve.

rumor, n. hearsay, gossip.

rumple, v. crumple, wrinkle, pucker, crease.

rumpus, n. disturbance, quarrel, affray, brawl, row, fracas.

run, v. sprint, lope, scamper, scud, speed.

run, n. running, spring, sprinting; course, series.

run after, v. pursue, follow, tag.

runaway, n. fugitive, absconder, deserter, truant, renegade.

runaway, adj. fugitive, absconding, truant.

run away, v. flee, escape, desert, elope, abscond.

run down, v. decline, deteriorate; decry, belittle, disparage, derogate.

runner, n. racer, sprinter, messenger, courier.

running, adj. successive, consecutive; flowing, easy, cursive; continuous.

run out, v. expire, finish, end; extend, spread; expatiate, descant; become extinct.

run through, v. squander, dissipate; transfix, impale, pierce.

rural, adj. rustic, country, countrified, pastoral,

ruse, n. artifice, wile, trick, stratagem, maneuver.

rush, v. press, hurry, run, dash, sprint, flash, charge; precipitate, hasten. Antonym: dawdle.

rush, n. haste, hurry; blast, current, gale, gust, draft.

rust, v. corrode; degenerate.

rustic, adj. rural, country, pastoral, bucolic; unpolished, countrified. Antonym: urban.

rustling, adj. whispering, susurrus.

rusty, adj. corroded, oxidized, tarnished; out of practice.

rut, n. groove; roaring of waves, rote.

ruthless, adj. pitiless, cruel, truculent, relentless, implacable, fell, hard-hearted.

ruthlessness, n. truculence, implacability, cruelty, mercilessness.

S

sack, n. bag, pouch.

sacred, adj. consecrated, hallowed; venerable, sainted, religious.

sacrifice, n. oblation, immolation; surrender, giving up.

sacrifice, v. offer, immolate; surrender, give up, forego.

sacrilege, n. desecration, profanation, violation.

sacrilegious, adj. impious, profane, irreverent.

sad, adj. sorrowful, pathetic, plaintive, doleful, piteous.

sadden, v. depress, dishearten; tone down, subdue.

sadness, n. melancholy, pathos, sorrow, gravity, soberness, seriousness.

safe, adj. unharmed, intact, unscathed, immune; trustworthy, reliable. Antonyms: unsafe, endangered, insecure.

safe-conduct, n. convoy, guard, escort; pass, passport.

safeguard, n. defense, security, palladium, protection.

safeguard, v. guard, defend, protect, shield.

safekeeping, n. guardianship, care, custody, charge, preservation.

safety, n. security, custody; immunity, exemption.

sagacious, adj. intelligent, knowing, shrewd, discerning.

sagacity, n. intelligence, shrewdness, cleverness, ingenuity, wisdom.

sail, v. navigate, cruise, embark.

sailcloth, n. canvas, duck, tarpaulin.

sailor, n. mariner, navigator, seaman, seafarer.

sainted, adj. holy, pious, saintly, consecrated; canonized.

salable, adj. vendible, marketable. Antonyms: unsalable, unmarketable.

sale, n. auction; transaction, deal, vending, selling. Antonym: pur-

chase.

salient, adj. prominent, conspicuous, noticeable, striking.

salt, n. seasoning, flavor, savor, taste.

salty, adj. saline, brackish, briny; amusing, indecent.

salute, v. address, greet, hail, welcome, accost,

salute, n. salutation, greeting, address, signal.

salvation, n. redemption, deliverance.

salve, n. ointment, emollient, balm.

same, adj. identical, invariable, uniform, analogous, similar.

sameness, n. identity, identicalness, similarity, correspondence, uniformity.

sample, n. specimen, example, illustration, exemplification, instance, pattern.

sanction, n. confirmation, ratification, authorization; penalty, punishment.

sanction, v. confirm, ratify, approve, countenance.

sanctity, n. godliness, saintliness, inviolability, sacredness.

sanctuary, n. shrine, sanctum, adytum; Holy of Holies, church, temple.

sand, v. rub down, smooth, polish.

sandy, adj. grimy, gritty, grainy; brownish yellow.

sane, adj. rational, sound, lucid.

sanity, n. saneness, rationality.

sappy, adj. juicy, lush, succulent.

sarcastic, adj. satirical, taunting, ironical, derisive. sneering.

satchel, n. handbag, valise.

satire, n. irony, sarcasm, ridicule.

satirical, adj. bitter, sarcastic, ironical, caustic, mordacious.

satisfaction, n. gratification; contentment, complacency, content, comfort; reparation.

satisfactory, adj. sufficient, satisfying, conclusive, gratifying, atoning.

satisfy, v. gratify, content, appease, satiate, suffice.

saucy, adj. impertinent, insolent, pert, impudent, malapert, flippant.

savage, adj. uncivilized, barbarous; ferocious, ravenous, fierce, untamed.

savage, n. barbarian, beast, ruffian.

save, v. rescue, deliver, redeem, salvage; preserve, conserve, keep, hoard, bank.

save, prep. or conj. but, except, excepting, reserving, apart from.

saving, adj. preserving, redemptory, redeeming; preservative, conservative; frugal. Antonyms: lavish, extravagant, prodigal, unthrifty, profuse, wasteful.

savory, adj. flavorful, palatable, toothsome, fragrant. Antonym: unsavory.

savvy, v. understand, comprehend.

savvy, n. understanding, comprehension, know-how, savoir-faire.

say, v. utter, express, mention, pronounce, speak, declare, tell, articulate.

saying, n. utterance, declaration, statement, pronunciation, mention.

scramble, v. sprawl, shamble; jostle; jumble, shuffle, confuse.

scamp, n. rascal, knave, miscreant.

scamper, v. hasten away, scud, hie, run, scuttle, scatter.

scandal, n. reproach, opprobrium, disgrace, odium, shame; slander.

scandalize, v. shock, offend, displease; disgrace; slander, defame, vilify.

scandalous, adj. defamatory, libelous, slanderous; infamous, disgraceful.

scant, adj. scanty, meager, insufficient, inadequate; sparing.

scantiness, n. smallness, narrowness, inadequacy; insufficiency, meagerness.

scarce, adj. rare, limited, meager, sparse, insufficient, deficient. Antonyms: plentiful, abundant.

scarcity, n. dearth, deficiency, insufficiency, lack, drought, rarity.

scare, v. frighten, intimidate, terrify, daunt, cow, appall. Antonym: reassure.

scare, n. fright, alarm, terror, panic.

scary, adj. timid, apprehensive, alarming, frightful.

scatter, v. dissipate, disperse, dispel, separate.

scatter-brained, adj. giddy, thoughtless, flighty, careless.

scattering, n. dispersion, spreading, diffusion, distribution.

scene, n. spectacle, show, exhibition, display, view, scenery.

scenery, n. view, landscape, prospect.

scent, n. odor, smell, perfume.

scepter, n. royal mace, sovereignty.

schedule, n. list, catalogue, timetable, itinerary.

scheme, n. design, plan, project, machination, intrigue.

scheme, v. devise, excogitate, plan, machinate, plot, design.

schismatic, n. nonconformist, dissenter, separatist, heretic, sectary.

scholar, n. pupil, student, learner, disciple.

scholarly, adj. erudite, scholastic.

scholarship, n. erudition, learning, knowledge, attainments.

school, n. institute, academy, seminary, college; faction, group.

school, v. train, educate, drill, teach.

schooling, v. education, training, nurture, discipline; tuition.

scoff, v. deride, ridicule, mock, sneer, gibe, jeer, contemn.

scold, n. shrew, vixen, virago, termagant.

scolding, n. chiding, censure, rating, reprimand, reprehension, rebuke, berating.

scoop, n. ladle; cavity, hollow.

scope, n. design, purpose; opportunity, space, room, liberty.

scorch, v. singe, char, torrefy, burn, parch.

score, n. tally, account; notch, incision; motive, account.

score, v. notch, scratch, cut; record, enter.

scorn, n. contempt, disdain, derision, contumely, mockery, slight.

scorn, v. despise, reject, contemn, disregard, scout, spurn.

scornful, adj. disdainful, con-

temptuous, contumelious, defiant.

scoundrel, n. villain, knave, rascal, scamp, rogue.

scout, v. explore, reconnoiter, investigate, survey.

scout, n. spy, pathfinder, guide.

scowl, v. glower, frown, lower, glare, grimace.

scowl, n. frown, glare, glower, grimace. Antonyms: smile, beam.

scraggy, adj. craggy; scrawny, lank, gaunt, skinny.

scramble, v. scrabble, clamber; struggle, contend, strive.

scrap, n. bit, fragment, morsel, crumb; excerpt, extract.

scrapbook, n. commonplace book, album.

scrape, n. difficulty, predicament, dilemma.

scrape, v. abrade, rasp, grate; gather, collect; erase, remove.

scrawl, n. scribble, doodle, jot, scratch.

scrawny, adj. angular, lank, meager, scraggy, bony.

scream, n. shriek, screech, yell, outcry.

screech, n. shriek, scream.

screechy, adj. discordant, unmelodious, unmusical, strident.

screen, n. shield, protection, guard, defense, traverse, fender.

screw, v. twist, wrench, force, squeeze.

scribe, n. writer, scrivener, amanuensis, copyist.

scrimmage, n. skirmish, scuffle, scrabble, fight.

scrimp, v. economize, limit.

scrub, n. clean, scour, wash; jungle, thicket, brushwood.

scrubby, adj. stunted, dwarfed, undeveloped, scrub, insignificant.

scrumptious, adj. fine, elegant, excellent, fastidious, particular.

scrupulous, n. conscientious, exact, strict, punctilious, particular.

scuffle, n. tussle, struggle, encounter, contest, fight, fray.

sculpture, n. statuary, figurine, carving.

scurry, v. hurry, scamper, dash, dart, rush, bustle, scuttle.

scuttle, v. hurry, scamper, dash, dart, rush, bustle, scurry; spoil, ruin, foil, wreck, sink.

seacoast, n. seaboard, seashore, seaside, beach.

seal, n. signet; assurance, ratification, attestation, authentication.

seal, v. ratify, authenticate, confirm, attest.

sealing, n. confirmation, ratification, authentication, attestation.

seaman, n. sailor, seafarer, mariner.

sear, v. cauterize, scorch.

search, v. examine, explore, hunt, seek, overhaul; rummage.

search, n. quest, research, pursuit.

searcher, n. seeker, explorer, pursuer.

seashore, n. seacoast, seaside, seaboard.

season, v. habituate, inure, harden, accustom, acclimatize.

seasonable, adj. opportune, timely, suitable, apropos, convenient.

seasoning, n. condiment, spice, relish, sauce, flavor, salt.

seat, n. site, abode, situation, station; fundament; chair, bench, stool.

seat, v. usher, place, settle.

secluded, adj. sequestered, isolated, retired, withdrawn, covert, lonely.

seclusion, n. sequestration, isolation, solitude, loneliness, retirement.

second, n. backer, supporter, assistant.

second, v. back, support, abet.

secondary, adj. subordinate, second, inferior, minor, collateral.

secondary, n. subordinate, deputy, delegate, proxy, underling, auxiliary.

second-class, adj. inferior, second-rate.

secrecy, n. seclusion, privacy, retirement concealment, confidence.

secret, adj. hidden, concealed, unrevealed, esoteric, mysterious. Antonyms: overt, revealed, open, exoteric, manifest.

secretary, n. amanuensis, clerk, writer, scribe; writing-desk.

secrete, v. bury, hide, conceal, shroud, disguise, cloak.

secretive, adj. uncommunicative, taciturn, reserved, silent, wary.

secrets, n. confidences, mysteries.

sect, n. school, party, denomination.

section, n. portion, part, division, segment, piece; paragraph.

secular, adj. temporal, worldly, laic, civil.

secure, adj. safe, protected, confident, assured, fast, immovable, stable, indemnified. Antonyms: insecure, risky, hazardous.

secure, v. procure, obtain, get, acquire.

security, n. safety, confidence, assurance certainty, warranty.

sedate, adj. staid, demure, imperturbable, composed, calm.

sedative, n. anesthetic, narcotic, opiate, hypnotic.

sediment, n. residue, deposit, dregs, remains.

seduce, v. entice, tempt, betray, allure.

seducement, n. seduction, enticement.

seductive, n. alluring, attractive, siren, enticing.

see, v. perceive, descry, view, behold, witness. Antonyms: overlook, ignore, miss, skip.

seed, n. origin, source, inception, root, first principle; kernel, grain, pip, ovule.

seed, v. sow, plant seeds.

seedy, adj. shabby, tacky, threadbare; spiritless.

seeing, n. perception, viewing, espial, descrying, beholding; discernment. Antonym: blindness.

seek, v. search for, hunt; aim at, strive after, attempt.

seeming, n. appearance, show, semblance, speciousness, guise, look.

seemingly, adv. apparently, ostensibly.

seemly, adj. becoming, suitable, proper, appropriate, meet, befitting.

seep, v. percolate, drip, ooze, trickle.

seer, n. prophet, vaticinator, predictor, diviner.

segment, n. section, part, portion, piece.

seize, v. apprehend, snatch, clutch, catch, grasp.

seizure, n. apprehension, grasping; capture; confiscation, usurpation.

seldom, adv. infrequently, rarely.

select, v. pick out, choose, prefer, cull, single out, elect.

select, adj. choice, top quality, first-class, excellent, exclusive. Antonym: inferior.

selection, n. choice, election, preference, pick; collection, assortment.

self, n. ego, person, individual.

self-conceit, n. egotism, overweening, priggishness, vanity.

self-denial, n. self-abnegation, asceticism, self-sacrifice, abstemiousness. Antonyms: self-indulgence, sensuality, voluptuousness.

self-denying, adj. self-sacrificing, unselfish, ascetic, abstemious.

self-evident, adj. apparent, axiomatic, obvious, clear, plain. Antonyms: mysterious, hidden.

self-examination, n. introspection, reflection.

self-explanatory, adj. obvious, plain, clear.

self-importance, n. pompousness, pomposity, vanity, conceit.

self-righteous, adj. pharisaic, sanctimonious.

self-sufficiency, n. self-complacency.

sell, v. vend, barter, exchange, betray; deceive, impose upon, cheat.

seller, n. vendor, retailer, supplier, broker, peddler, hawker. Antonym: buyer.

send, v. dispatch, commission, delegate; transmit, forward.

send back, v. return, remand, recommit.

seniority, n. eldership, superiority.

sensation, n. consciousness, feeling, perception; excitement.

sensational, adj. amazing, astounding, breathtaking, thrilling, magnificent, incredible; shocking, scandalous, melodramatic, lurid. Antonyms: boring, ordinary.

sense, n. perception, sensation, sensibility, feeling.

sense, v. perceive, recognize.

senseless, adj. insensible, unconscious; absurd, silly, nonsensical.

senselessness, adj. insensibility, unconsciousness; fatuity, absurdity.

sensible, adj. apprehensible, perceptible; susceptible, impressible; conscious. Antonyms: insensible, unconscious.

sensitive, adj. susceptible, impressible; sentient; irritable.

sensual, adj. unspiritual, carnal, fleshy, sensuous; voluptuous.

sentence, n. opinion, decision, determination, judgment.

sentiment, n. thought, feeling; judgment, notion, opinion.

sentimental, adj. romantic, sappy, schmaltzy, gushy, maudlin, impressible, emotional. Antonyms: unsentimental, matter-of-fact, pragmatic.

sentinel, n. guard, sentry, watchman, picket.

separable, adj. divisible, independent, detachable, severable. Antonym: inseparable.

separate, v. divide, dissolve, detach, sunder, sever, disconnect.

separate, adj. detached, disconnected, disjoined, separated, apart.

separation, n. division, segregation, disunion, disconnection, sequestration.

sequel, n. continuation, conclusion, consequence, result, outcome.

sequence, n. succession, series, following; result, sequel, consequence.

sequestered, adj. secluded, isolated, quarantined.

serene, adj. calm, placid, composed, tranquil, unruffled, unclouded.

serenity, n. calmness, composure, tranquility; cloudlessness, clearness.

serious, adj. grave, earnest, thoughtful, solemn, staid, sober.

seriousness, n. gravity, significance, importance, weightiness. Antonyms: levity, frivolity, triviality.

sermon, n. homily, exhortation religious, discourse.

servant, n. domestic, subaltern, subordinate, helper.

serve, v. attend, wait upon; promote, advance, contribute.

service, n. labor, employment, office, duty, business, function.

servile, adj. slavish, abject, cringing, groveling.

servitude, n. bondage, enslavement.

set, v. place, put, fix, establish, locate, station.

set, adj. fixed; immovable, rigid, firm, obstinate, inflexible.

set, n. clique, group, class, party.

set aside, v. displace, supersede.

setback, n. hindrance, holdup, impediment, stumbling block, obstruction, obstacle.

settle, v. fix, establish; ordain, install; adjust, determine.

settlement, n. establishment; ordination, installation; colonization.

settler, n. pioneer, colonist.

sever, v. part, divide, disunite, separate, disjoint, detach, disconnect.

several, adj. various, diverse, manifold, divers, sundry.

severe, adj. drastic, harsh, stern, rigorous, exact, cruel.

severity, n. rigor, rigorousness, harshness, exactness, cruelty, austerity.

sew, v. stitch; baste.

shabby, adj. seedy, threadbare, tacky.

shackle, n. handcuff, manacle, fetter.

shade, n. umbrage, shadow; darkness, obscurity, gloom.

shade, v. screen; obscure, dim, obfuscate, cloud, darken, eclipse.

shadowy, adj. unsubstantial, visionary, illusory, chimerical.

shake, v. agitate, jar, jolt, convulse, concuss, jounce.

shake, n. jar, shivering, jolt, shaking, shudder.

shallow, adj. shoal; superficial, frivolous, senseless.

sham, n. pretense, feint, delusion, imposition, mockery, fraud.

sham, adj. counterfeit, spurious, pretended, dummy, unreal, false, mock, simulated.

shame, n. ignominy, dishonor, reproach, derision, contempt.

shame, v. humiliate, mortify, disconcert; disgrace, degrade.

shameful, adj. indecent, immodest, obscene; scandalous, disgraceful.

shameless, adj. immodest, unabashed, indelicate, indecent, unblushing, audacious.

shanty, n. hut, hovel, shack.

shape, v. form, mould, fashion, frame; adjust, regulate.

shape, n. form, figure, guise, appearance.

shapeless, adj. misshapen, unsymmetrical, unshapely, formless, amorphous.

shapely, adj. symmetrical, well-formed, comely, well-proportioned.

share, v. apportion, divide; partake, participate in.

share, n. portion, allotment, quota, dole, proportion.

shark, v. sharper, trickster, cheat, swindler; fraud, trickery.

sharp, adj. pointed, trenchant, incisive, keen; poignant, piercing.

sharpen, v. intensify, aggravate, quicken; hone, grind.

sharpness, n. keenness, poignancy, acuteness, edge; asperity.

shatter, v. smash, break, splinter, ruin, destroy, wreck, crush, demolish.

shave, v. shear, cut, trim, cut off.

sheath, n. case, scabbard; covering.

shed, v. discard, cast off.

shed, n. lean-to, shack, shanty, hut.

sheen, n. shine, luster, gloss, brightness, splendor.

sheepish, adj. bashful, shy, overmodest.

sheer, adj. thin; unadulterated, pure, unmixed; precipitous.

shelf, n. mantel, mantelpiece; bracket, console; ledge.

shell, n. armature, case, exoskeleton, shale

shell, n. framework; bomb, torpedo, shrapnel, grenade.

shelter, n. protection, screen, cover, shield, defense.

shelter, v. shield, protect, defend, screen, ensconce, cover. Antonym: expose.

shield, v. defend, protect, safeguard; ward off, repel.

shift, v. veer, change, turn; quirk, quibble.

shift, n. subterfuge, device, contrivance, evasion, stratagem.

shifting, adj. unstable, variable, changeable.

shiftless, adj. improvident, unthrifty, wasteful. Antonym: industrious.

shine, v. beam, radiate, gleam, irradiate, glisten.

shine, n. luster, polish, gloss, sheen, radiance.

shining, adj. radiant, beaming, lustrous, luminous, glowing.

ship, n. vessel, craft, liner, boat.

ship, v. transport, dispatch; deport; dismiss, send away.

shipment, n. shipping, transportation; consignment.

shipping, n. shipment, transportation, navigation.

shipwreck, n. wreckage; disaster, destruction, ruin, subversion.

shirk, v. avoid, evade, neglect.

shiver, n. splinter, sliver; tremor, quiver, shudder, quake.

shock, v. dismay, horrify, appall, terrify, frighten.

shock, n. impact, blow, collision, concussion, onset.

shocking, adj. scandalous, appalling, offensive, outrageous, heinous, dire.

shoddy, adj. sham, spurious, mock.

shoestring, n. shoelace.

shoot, v. discharge, fire; eject, hurl, emit; dart, dash, zip, zoom; film, photograph; aim, direct, point at.

shooting, adj. darting, piercing.

shop, n. workshop, factory; store; warehouse; atelier, studio.

shore, n. beach, coast, strand.

short, adj. brief, contracted, terse, concise, condensed. Antonyms: diffuse, prolix, long.

shortage, n. deficiency, insufficiency, inadequacy, deficit.

shortcoming, n. defect, imperfection, fault, foible, failure.

shorten, v. abridge, abbreviate,

curtail, reduce, epitomize.

shortening, n. abbreviation, abridgement, contraction, curtailment, reduction.

short-lived, adj. ephemeral, fleeting, transitory.

shortness, n. brevity, briefness, conciseness, laconism; inadequacy.

short-sighted, adj. myopic, near-sighted; unwise, imprudent, indiscreet.

shot, n. discharge; projectile, bullet, ball: marksman.

shout, n. vociferation, halloo, outcry, call, hoot, clamor, acclamation.

show, n. exposure, exhibition, exposition, demonstration, representation.

show, v. exhibit, present, display, uncover, reveal, disclose.

showing, n. demonstration, exhibition, presentation, revelation, disclosure.

showy, adj. spectacular, pageant, ostentatious, pompous, garish, gaudy. Antonyms: inconspicuous, plain, modest, unostentatious, quiet, subdued.

shred, n. fragment, tatter, rag, strip, frazzle.

shrewd, adj. astute, sharp; cunning, crafty.

shrewdness, n. acumen, astuteness, sharpness.

shriek, n. screech, yell, scream.

shrill, adj. piercing, acute, strident.

shrink, v. contract, shrivel, decrease, dwindle; flinch.

shrinkage, n. contraction, reduction, decrease. Antonym: growth.

shrinking, adj. coy, shy, diffident, bashful, modest, retiring.

shroud, v. hide, veil, swathe, mask, screen, cloak, conceal.

shrub, n. bush; shrubbery, thicket, boscage, bosket.

shudder, n. tremor, jolt, agitation, shake, trembling.

shudder, v. tremble, shake, shiver, quake.

shuffle, v. jumble, intermix; equivocate, prevaricate.

shuffle, n. artifice, evasion, prevarication, trick.

shun, v. avoid, elude, evade, spurn, reject, eschew, shirk, reject. Antonym: court.

shut, v. close; debar, exclude, preclude.

shy, adj. timid, coy, backward, retiring, diffident, wary.

shyness, n. diffidence, coyness, timidity, bashfulness.

shyster, n. knave, impostor, rogue, cheat.

sick, adj. ill, unwell, ailing, indisposed, diseased, out of sorts.

sicken, v. nauseate, disgust, pall, surfeit, decay, languish.

sickening, adj. nauseating, disgusting, fulsome, nauseous, revolting.

sickly, adj. invalid, unwell, unhealthy, ailing; unwholesome.

sickness, n. illness, malady, ailment, complaint, disorder, distemper.

side, adj. lateral, collateral, incidental.

sidetrack, v. shunt; switch off, divert.

sideways, adv. sidewise, askance, obliquely, laterally.

siege, n. investment, blockage, besiegement.

sieve, n. strainer, sifter.

sift, v. filter, separate, strain; investigate, examine, select.

sight, n. vision; seeing, view, perception; visibility; spectacle.

sign, n. omen, auspice, portent, prodigy.

sign, v. signify, mark, indicate, betoken; subscribe.

signal, n. sign, ensign, beacon.

signal, adj. memorable, remarkable, noticeable, notable.

signer, n. subscriber, signatory.

significance, n. meaning, import; consequence, importance, force.

significant, adj. momentous, important, major, momentous, noteworthy; considerable, large, major, hefty, substantial. Antonyms: insignificant, unimportant, paltry, trivial.

signify, v. indicate, betoken, denote; mean; matter.

silence, n. stillness, quietness; taciturnity, muteness, reserve, secrecy.

silence, v. still, hush, quiet, suppress, lull.

silent, adj. still, quiet, noiseless, inaudible.

sill, n. ledge, shelf, ridge, projection; threshold.

silliness, n. folly, foolishness, puerility, stupidity.

silly, adj. witless, foolish, simple, fatuous, inane.

similar, adj. like, corresponding, resembling, homogeneous, analogous.

similarity, n. analogy, homogeneity, likeness, similitude, correspondence.

simple, adj. easy, straightforward, uncomplicated, effortless; plain, unadorned, down-to-earth, unpretentious. Antonyms: complex, difficult, complicated, intricate, artful, crafty, elaborate.

simpleton, n. dolt, dunce, numskull, oaf.

simulate, v. pretend, feign.

simultaneous, adj. contemporaneous, synchronal, synchronous.

sin, n. iniquity, transgression, wickedness, delinquency.

sin, v. do wrong, trespass, transgress.

sincere, adj. heartfelt, genuine, unfeigned, earnest, frank. Antonym: insincere.

sincerity, n. honesty, genuineness, earnestness, unaffectedness, authenticity.

sinful, adj. wrong, immoral, wicked, evil, corrupt, aberrant, depraved. Antonym: pure.

sinfulness, n. iniquity, immorality, depravity, wickedness.

sing, v. carol, warble, chant, hymn, hum.

singe, v. scorch, burn, char, sear.

singer, n. vocalist, songster, songstress, minstrel, chanter.

single, adj. individual, alone, particular, isolated, sporadic, solitary.

single, v. single out, choose, select, separate, isolate, segregate.

single-minded, adj. artless, undesigning, guileless.

singular, adj. unusual, unconventional, uncommon, strange, peculiar.

singularity, n. peculiarity, idiosyncrasy, individuality; curiosity, freak.

sinister, adj. left; unlucky, inauspicious, evil, wrong, forbidding.

sink, v. subside, descend, decline, fall; immerse.

sinking, n. subsidence, fall, decrease, decline.

sinless, adj. innocent, guiltless, undefiled, perfect, blameless, faultless.

sinner, n. wrongdoer, delinquent, miscreant, trespasser.

site, n. location, place, spot, position.

situation, n. position, place, post, employment, job, location.

size, n. magnitude, volume, dimensions, amplitude, bulk.

skedaddle, v. run away, flee, decamp, scuttle.

skeptic, n. unbeliever, infidel.

skeptical, adj. doubtful, disbelieving, incredulous. Antonym: credulous.

skepticism, n. doubt, incredulity, infidelity. Antonym: credulity.

sketch, n. draft, outline, plan, drawing, design, scenario.

skill, n. adroitness, ingenuity, cleverness, technique, dexterity. Antonyms: quackery, inexpertness, clumsiness.

skillful, adj. skilled, expert, adroit, dexterous, adept, masterly. Antonyms: unskillful, empirical, maladroit.

skimpy, adj. scant, skimp, meager, sparse.

skin, n. hide, pelt, coat; casing, covering, membrane, crust, film.

skin, v. graze, scrape; peel, pare.

skin-deep, adj. superficial.

skinflint, n. miser, penny pincher, tightwad.

skinny, adj. emaciated, gaunt, rawboned, thin.

skip, v. omit, pass, disregard; caper, gambol.

skit, n. reflection, jeer, gibe, satire, squib.

skittish, adj. wary, jumpy, edgy, restless.

sky, n. firmament, empyrean, azure, the heavens.

slack, adj. lax, loose, relaxed; remiss, negligent, careless.

slacken, v. moderate, retard, slack, reduce; loosen, relax.

slackness, n. looseness, laxity, negligence, remissness, carelessness.

slander, v. malign, defame, traduce, asperse, vilify.

slanderous, adj. defamatory, malicious, vituperative, calumnious, libelous.

slant, n. slope, incline, inclination, obliquity.

slant, v. slope, incline.

slap, v. hit, smack, cuff, whack, strike.

slap, n. smack, whack, cuff, wallop.

slash, n. incision, gash, cut, slit.

slave, n. vassal, bond servant, bondsman.

slave, v. drudge, toil, moil.

slavery, n. bondage, enslavement, servitude, captivity.

sled, n. sleigh, sledge, toboggan, luge.
sleek, adj. smooth, glossy.
sleep, v. slumber, repose; doze, drowse; lie dormant; hibernate.
sleep, n. slumber, repose; nap, doze, drowse, snooze, dozing.
sleepiness, n. drowsiness, somnolence.
sleeping, adj. asleep, slumbering, dormant.
sleepless, adj. wakeful, insomnious, restless.
sleepy, adj. drowsy, somnolent, dozy; soporiferous, somniferous.
sleigh, n. cutter, sled, sledge, bobsled, toboggan.
slender, adj. slim, slight, thin, spare, lank.
slice, n. piece, sliver, wedge, portion, segment; share, cut, percentage.
slice, v. cut, carve.
slick, adj. sleek, smooth.
slide, n. slip; flume, shoot, chute.
slide, v. slip, glide, lapse, elapse, skid.
slight, adj. inconsiderable, trivial, insignificant, trifling, petty.
slight, n. neglect, inattention, disregard, snub.
slight, v. overlook, neglect, disregard, ignore.
slightly, adv. somewhat; superficially, cursorily, hastily.
slim, adj. thin, gaunt, poor, lank, spare, spindling, meager.
slip, n. lapse, error, indiscretion, transgression.
slippery, adj. smooth, glib; inconstant, unstable; loose.

slipshod, adj. slovenly, careless, negligent.
slit, n. gash, incision.
sliver, n. splinter, slice.
slobber, v. drivel, drool, slaver; smear.
slogan, n. motto, saying, jingle, watchword, catchphrase.
slope, v. slant, incline, tilt, lean.
slope, n. inclination, slant, obliquity; acclivity; declivity.
sloping, adj. oblique, slanting; declivous.
slosh, n. slush, sludge.
sloth, n. sluggishness, indolence, laziness.
slothful, adj. dronish, lazy, indolent, supine, sluggish, idle, inactive.
slouchy, adj. slouching, ungainly, awkward.
slow, adj. deliberate, moderate, gradual; dilatory, languid.
slow, v. slacken, relax, moderate, delay, retard
sluggish, adj. idle, lazy, slothful; inactive, slow, inert.
slump, v. slouch, droop, hunch, sag; plummet, plunge, decline.
slump, n. decline, depression.
slur, n. stain, mark; innuendo, reproach, brand.
sly, adj. cautious, nimble, skillful, arch, wary, knowing, shrewd.
smack, n. slap, punch, cuff; kiss, buss; crack, snap.
smack, v. slap, hit, strike, punch, cuff.
small, adj. little, minute, diminutive, petty, slight, inconsiderable.

smart, v. hurt, sting.

smart, adj. acute, bright, clever, apt, brilliant, gifted; elegant, stylish, well-dressed, chic. Antonyms: dull, inapt, dowdy, tawdry.

smash, v. crush, shatter, break, demolish, destroy.

smash, n. accident, collision, fender-bender; great success.

smell, n. aroma, fragrance, odor, savor, scent; stink, stench, reek.

smell, v. reek, stink; sniff, sense.

smile, v. grin, beam.

smirk, n. simper, sneer.

smite, v. strike, buffet; blast, destroy, afflict, chasten, visit.

smoke, n. fume, reek, effluvium; smudge.

smoke, v. reek; fume; fumigate; smolder.

smoky, adj. sooty, hazy, cloudy, murky. Antonym: clear.

smooth, v. even, plane, sleek, flatten.

smooth, adj. even, plaint, flat, level, abraded.

smoothness, n. evenness, levelness, sleekness; volubility.

smother, v. suffocate, stifle; extinguish, repress, suppress; smolder.

smut, n. soot, dirt; mildew, blight.

smutty, adj. obscene, lewd, ribald, indecent, gross.

snake, n. serpent, reptile.

snake, v. wind, bend, turn, twist, meander.

snaky, adj. serpentine, winding; insinuating, subtle, deceitful.

snap, n. spell, period, season, interval.

snappish, adj. captious, irascible, testy, petulant.

snare, n. catch, wile, trap, gin, lure, decoy.

snarl, v. entangle, complicate, involve, knot; confuse. Antonyms: disentangle, unravel, extricate.

snarl, n. complication, entanglement, intricacy, knot; confusion; growl.

snatch, v. seize, grasp, gripe, wrest, pluck, grab, twitch.

sneak, v. skulk, slink, lurk, snoop.

sneaky, adj. devious, sly, shifty, lurking, skulking, underhanded, covert, stealthy.

sneer, v. mock, gibe, scoff, flout, jeer.

snicker, n. giggle, titter, snigger.

snide, adj. tricky, deceptive, dishonest, fraudulent.

sniff, v. inhale, breathe in, snuffle; snivel, sob, blubber. Antonym: exhale.

sniff, n. smell, breath, inhalation.

snob, n. upstart, pretender, parvenu.

snobbish, adj. snooty, high and mighty, superior, pretentious, assuming, overbearing, stuck-up; arrogant, conceited, patronizing. Antonyms: humble, modest.

snub, v. slight, ignore, disregard.

snub, n. slight, check, rebuke.

snug, adj. cozy; concealed, close; comfortable, compact.

snuggle, v. nestle, cuddle.

soak, v. drench, saturate; absorb, imbibe.

soaked, adj. drenched, saturated, sodden.

soaking, adj. drenching, saturating.

sob, v. weep, cry, snivel, blubber, bawl.

sober, adj. temperate, abstinent, abstemious. Antonym: intoxicated.

sobriety, n. abstemiousness, temperance; gravity, seriousness, solemnity.

sociable, adj. affable, friendly, companionable, genial, social, unreserved. Antonym: unsociable, hostile.

social, adj. civil, civic; sociable; festive, convivial.

society, n. association, fraternity, club.

sod, n. sward, turf; peat.

soft, adj. quiet, gentle, low, mellifluous, muted, mellow; yielding, squashy, spongy, elastic, malleable, bendable; smooth, silky, supple, velvety. Antonyms: hard, rough, loud.

soften, v. intenerate, mollify, palliate, extenuate, qualify.

softness, n. mellowness, gentleness, smoothness, quietness; elasticity.

soil, n. ground, earth, dirt, humus, land.

soil, v. dirty, defile, pollute, besmear, contaminate, taint.

soldier, n. warrior; private; cadet; recruit; veteran.

solemn, n. serious, sober, grave; Impressive.

solemnity, n. gravity, earnestness, seriousness.

solicit, v. ask, seek, petition, request, invite.

solicitation, n. request, instance, entreaty, invitation.

solid, adj. dense, compact, hard, impenetrable, firm.

solidness, n. solidity, firmness, compactness, stability.

solitary, adj. unfrequented, secluded, lonely; single, individual.

solitude, n. loneliness, isolation, seclusion, eremitism.

solution, n. melting, liquefaction; explanation, resolution, answer, key.

solvent, adj. in the black, in the money. Antonym: bankrupt.

sometimes, adv. at intervals, now and then, occasionally.

song, n. hymn, chant, lay, ditty, ballad.

soothe, v. compose, tranquilize, pacify, assuage, mollify, calm.

soothing, adj. bland, emollient, demulcent, gratifying.

soothsayer, n. seer, prophet, diviner, oracle, clairvoyant, foreteller.

sophisticated, adj. complicated, difficult, stylish; urbane, classy, refined; mature, experienced; complex, advanced; high-level, erudite.

sorcerer, n. conjurer, necromancer, magician, enchanter, wizard.

sorcery, n. necromancy, magic, enchantment, witchcraft, black art.

sore, adj. painful, tender, stinging, raw, inflamed; irritated, angry, cross, resentful, bitter.

sore, n. wound, abscess, lesion, eruption, blister, boil.

sorrow, n. grief, regret, remorse, misery, heaviness.

sorrow, v. grieve, mourn, regret, deplore, bewail, lament.

sorry, adj. melancholy, mournful, dismal, depressing, sad.
sort, n. kind, species, character, description.
sort, v. assort, classify; conjoin; choose, select.
so-so, adj. middling, passable, tolerable, mediocre, ordinary, average.
soul, n. spirit, psyche.
sound, adj. whole, intact, perfect, flawless, unimpaired.
sound, n. tone, noise, ring, echo; strait, narrows, channel.
sound, v. fathom, gauge; examine, try, test, probe.
soup, n. broth, bouillon, consommé,
sour, adj. acid, tart, bitter, acerbic, acrid, vinegary; disagreeable, unpleasant, bitter, resentful. Antonym: sweet.
sour, v. curdle, turn; taint, ruin, spoil, embitter.
source, n. origin, spring, fountain, rise.
sourness, n. acidity, tartness, acerbity, sharpness.
souvenir, n. keepsake, reminder, memento; trophy.
sovereign, adj. supreme, chief, paramount, predominant.
sovereign, n. ruler, monarch.
sovereignty, n. dominion, supremacy, sway, empire.
sow, v. propagate, disseminate, scatter, plant.
space, n. room, freedom, liberty, legroom, vacancy; gap, break, hole, opening, interval, pause; outer space, cosmos; area, plot, place, seat.

spacious, adj. capacious, roomy, vast.
spare, v. forbear, refrain, be merciful.
spare, adj. thin, lean, poor, gaunt, meager.
sparing, adj. economical, frugal, saving, parsimonious, chary.
spark, v. flash, ignite, incite, activate; court, woo.
sparkle, v. glimmer, coruscate, glisten, scintillate, twinkle.
sparkle, n. scintillation, glitter, gleaming, brilliancy.
sparkling, adj. glittering, flashing, brilliant, twinkling.
sparse, adj. scattered, thin, innumerous, meager.
spasm, n. convulsion, paroxysm, fit, throe.
spasmodic, adj. intermittent, fitful, convulsive.
spat, n. tiff, quarrel, dispute, dissension.
speak, v. utter, pronounce, say, articulate, enunciate, express. Antonyms: repress, suppress.
speaker, n. orator, discourser, spokesman, prolocutor.
spear, n. lance, javelin, harpoon.
special, adj. particular, especial, specific, exceptional.
specialty, n. particularity; expertise, field, discipline.
species, n. group, class, kind, brood, sort, variety.
specific, adj. definite, precise, specified; characteristic, particular, special.
specify, v. designate, particularize, individualize, name.
specimen, n. example, sample,

model, copy, pattern.

speck, n. spot, stain; atom, mite, particle.

spectacle, n. scene, sight, show, exhibition, pageant.

spectator, n. beholder, witness, bystander, onlooker, observer.

speculate, v. theorize, meditate, conjecture, guess, think.

speculation, n. theory, supposition, conjecture; contemplation, thought.

speculative, adj. contemplative, meditative; theoretical, supposititious.

speech, n. utterance, speaking; language, talk, conversation.

speechless, adj. dumb, mute, aphasic, inarticulate.

speed, n. velocity, swiftness, rapidity, celerity, haste.

speed, v. hurry, hasten; accelerate, expedite, quicken.

speedy, adj. swift, quick, fast, rapid, fleet, hasty.

spell, n. charm, incantation, enchantment, hex; period, season, interval.

spell, v. mean, denote, imply.

spellbound, n. fascinated, charmed, enchanted, bewitched.

spend, v. expend, disburse.

spender, n. payer, financier.

spending, n. expenditure, disbursement.

spendthrift, n. wastrel, spender, squanderer.

spent, adj. exhausted, tired, consumed, worn out.

sphere, n. globe, ore, ball; province.

spice, n. condiment; piquancy, pungency.

spicy, adj. aromatic, fragrant; piquant, pungent, sharp.

spin, v. whirl, twirl, revolve, gyrate.

spine, n. backbone, vertebrae; bristle, needle, spike, thorn.

spineless, adj. invertebrate; cowardly, gutless, timid.

spinning, n. whirling, twirling.

spiral, adj. winding, twisting, curved, coiled, corkscrew.

spiral, n. coil, twist, whirl, helix.

spiral, v. escalate, increase, rise, mushroom, rocket; corkscrew, curl, twine. Antonym: plummet.

spire, n. steeple; shoot, stalk, blade, spear.

spirit, n. soul; shade, apparition, specter, ghost.

spirited, adj. animated, lively, ardent, mettlesome, fervent, passionate.

spite, n. malignity, malice, rancor, hate, resentment.

spiteful, adj. malicious, malign, malignant, rancorous, hateful.

spleen, n. anger, spite, malice, choler; melancholy, depression.

splendid, adj. bright, brilliant; magnificent, grand, superb.

splendor, n. brilliancy, brightness; magnificence, pageantry, pomp.

splice, v. interweave, unite, braid together.

splinter, n. sliver, fragment, chip, particle, piece.

splinter, v. crack, shatter, disintegrate.

split, v. crack, rent, fissure, rift, rip, tear; divide; break up, part, divorce; go, exit, leave.

split, adj. cleft, divided, sundered.

split, n. tear, crack, rip, gash; division, rift.

splitting, n. fission, cleavage, riving, sundering, rupture.

spoil, v. ruin, destroy; indulge, pamper, cosset; decay, rot.

spoils, n. plunder, pillage, booty, prize, gain, loot.

spoke, n. radius, ray; rung, round.

spoken, adj. oral, nuncupative, stated, verbal.

spokesman, n. speaker, mouthpiece, prolocutor.

sponsor, v. back, support, pay for, subsidize, fund.

sponsor, n. godparent; backer, supporter, guarantor, patron, benefactor.

spontaneous, adj. instinctive, voluntary, impulsive, unforced.

spook, n. ghost, spirit, specter, apparition.

sporadic, adj. intermittant, irregular, erratic; separate, single, isolated.

sport, n. amusement, game, recreation, fun, play, diversion.

sport, v. frolic, play, caper, disport; exhibit.

sportive, adj. frolicsome, merry, boon, frisky, sprightly, prankish, gamesome.

spot, n. speck, speckle, mark, blot, discoloration.

spotless, adj. immaculate, stainless, unsullied.

spout, n. nozzle; conduit, trough.

spread, v. extend, stretch, expand, dilate; unfurl, unroll.

spreading, n. extension, expansion, dilation; dissemination.

spree, n. carousal, debauch, revelry, orgies.

sprig, n. shoot, slip, twig, spray.

sprightly, adj. energetic, spry, full of beans, active, nimble.

sprightliness, n. animation, liveliness, vivacity, activity, briskness.

sprightly, adj. lively, brisk, animated, debonair, vivacious.

spring, v. shoot; bound, leap, jump, hop, vault.

spring, n. coil, spiral; bounce, elasticity; leap, bound, jump.

springy, adj. elastic, resilient, rebounding recoiling.

sprinkle, v. scatter: strew; besprinkle, bedew, asperse.

sprinter, n. runner, dasher, athlete.

sprout, v. germinate, pullulate, bourgeon, grow, vegetate.

spry, adj. agile nimble, quick, brisk, sprightly, alert.

spunky, adj. mettlesome, plucky, spirited.

spur, v. goad, incite, urge, stimulate, instigate, impel.

spurious, adj. counterfeit, sham, false, mock.

spurn, v. reject, snub, slight, rebuff, disdain.

spurt, n. gushing, spouting, jet, ejection.

spurt, v. gush, spout, jet.

spy, n. secret agent, mole, scout.

spy, v. discover, detect; spot, espy, glimpse, see.

spying, n. espionage, espial.

squabble, n. wrangle, dispute, altercation.

squad, n. band, gang, knot, bevy, company.

square, adj. equitable, true, just, honest, impartial.

square, v. adjust, fit, suit; balance, conform.

squat, v. crouch, cower.

squeak, v. creak; betray, tell, confess.

squeal, v. cry, yell; tell, betray, confess.

squeeze, v. compress, grope, pinch; oppress, extort.

squeeze, n. compression, pressure; exaction, extortion.

squelch, v. crush, silence, quell, stifle, abash.

squirm, v. wriggle, writhe, twist.

stab, v. pierce, thrust, gore, transfix; backbite, malign.

stability, n. fixedness, firmness, permanence, constancy, steadiness. Antonyms: instability, unsteadiness.

stable, adj. steady, firm, immovable, unwavering, constant, permanent.

stack, n. pile, rick, heap.

staff, n. rod, stick, cane.

stage, n. platform, rostrum; scaffold, staging; theater.

stagger, v. reel, totter, sway; shock; astound, dumfound.

stagnant, adj. motionless, standing; quiet; inactive, dull, sluggish.

stain, n. mark, blemish, spot, blot.

stain, v. soil, sully, defile, taint.

stairway, n. stairs, staircase, flight of stairs; escalator.

stake, n. picket, pale, post; pledge, wager.

stake, v. venture, risk, hazard, wager, bet, pledge.

stale, adj. vapid, musty, fusty, flat, insipid.

staleness, n. vapidity, mustiness, insipidity; triteness.

stall, n. stable; booth, stand; seat.

stamp, v. impress, imprint; stomp.

stamp, n. impression, imprint, die; hallmark; pestle.

stamp out, v. extinguish, crush, quell.

stand, v. endure, bear, weather, brook, suffer, tolerate; situate, set, locate, park; remain, continue, prevail; halt, stop, pause; rise, get up, arise.

stand, n. attitude, opinion, stance, standpoint, outlook; stop, stay, rest, halt; stall, booth; frame, easel, shelf.

standard, n. criterion, model, type, pattern, norm, benchmark; flag, banner, ensign, pennant, streamer.

standard, adj. normal, average, regular, traditional.

standing, adj. erect: stagnant; lasting, permanent, persistent.

standing, n. status, rank, position, station, footing.

standing out, adj. prominent, projecting, protuberant, jutting out; conspicuous, salient.

standoff, n. argument, confrontation, quarrel, disagreement, altercation.

stand out, v. be obvious, stick out; project, overhang, jut, protrude.

standpoint, n. stance, position, viewpoint.

star, n. luminary, planet; asterisk; celebrity, leading light, personality. Antonym: nobody.

star, adj. brilliant, celebrated, major, well-known, leading.

starched, adj. stiff, ceremonious, prim, formal.

start, v. set out, go, initiate, launch, institute, embark; jump, recoil, jerk.

start, n. beginning, birth, commencement, outset, inception; shock, fright.

startle, v. scare, surprise, shock, amaze.

starve, n. famish, go hungry, waste away.

state, n. condition, plight, category, situation, pass, predicament.

state, v. assert, affirm, aver, allege, say, specify, declare.

statehouse, n. capitol.

stately, adj. imposing, dignified, august, pompous, majestic, formal.

statement, n. assertion, affirmation, specification, avowal.

station, n. standing, rank, status; depot; situation, place.

staunch, adj. loyal, steadfast, constant, true, unwavering, sound.

statue, n. image; figurine, effigy, sculpture, bust.

status, n. standing, rank, station, condition.

statute, n. law, decree, ruling.

staunch, adj. loyal, steadfast, constant, true, unwavering, sound.

stay, v. sojourn, tarry, lodge, remain, continue, abide.

stay, n. sojourn, abidance, stop; dependence, support, upholder.

steadfast, adj. firm, fixed; constant, unswerving, unwavering.

steady, adj. steadfast, constant; stable, firm, fixed, unremitted.

steal, v. pilfer, filch, peculate, purloin, poach, abstract.

stealing, n. theft, larceny, robbery, pilfering, peculation, thievery.

stealthy, adj. clandestine, sly, secret, furtive, skulking, underhand.

steam, v. vapor, reek, fume, emanation, effluvium.

steel, v. fortify, brace, nerve.

steep, adj. precipitous, abrupt, sheer, perpendicular; excessive, immoderate.

steep, n. precipice, cliff, abrupt declivity; escarpment, scarp.

steep, v. soak, macerate, imbrue, infuse.

steeple, n. spire, tower, turret; minaret.

steer, v. guide, pilot, control, govern.

steering, n. guiding.

steersman, n. helmsman, pilot.

stem, n. trunk, body.

stem, v. oppose, withstand, resist, check, staunch.

stench, n. reek, stink.

step, n. pace; stair, round; footstep, footprint, footmark.

step, v. pace, stride.

sterile, adj. barren, unproductive, unfruitful, unprolific.

sterility, v. barrenness, infecundity, unproductiveness.

stern, adj. austere, rigorous, exacting, strict, hard-hearted.

sternness, n. austerity, severity, rigor, strictness.

stew, v. simmer, bubble, poach, cook; fret, brood.

stick, n. switch, rod, birch.

stick, v. pierce, stab, penetrate, impale, transfix, gore.

sticker, n. label; decal.

stickiness, n. tackiness, gumminess, adhesiveness, viscosity.

sticking, n. adhesion, adherence, coherence, cleaving.

stickler, n. haggler, nit-picker, pedant, perfectionist, martinet.

sticky, adj. adhesive, viscous, viscid, mucilaginous, glutinous.

stiff, adj. inflexible, rigid, firm, unbending, inelastic, stark. Antonyms: limber, flaccid, limp, flexible, lithe.

stiffness, n. inflexibility, rigidity, firmness; constraint. Antonyms: pliability, limpness, flexibility, flaccidity, ease, relaxation, informality.

still, n. motionless, unruffled, stagnant, quiescent, inert, stationary.

still, v. calm, compose, quiet, silence, hush.

stimulant, n. provocation, stimulus, spur, goad, pick-me-up.

stimulate, v. excite, incite, instigate, arouse, provoke, goad, spur.

stimulus, n. incentive; stimuli.

sting, v. smart, tingle, prick, hurt.

stinginess, n. parsimony, illiberality, penuriousness, closeness, avarice. Antonyms: liberality, generosity.

stingy, adj. parsimonious, illiberal, close, penurious, miserly. Antonyms: liberal, generous.

stink, n. stench, fetor, odor, reek.

stinking, adj. fetid, malodorous, offensive, noisome, ill-smelling.

stint, n. limit, restraint, restriction; assignment, allotment.

stir, v. move, budge.

stir, adj. agitation, tumult, bustle, commotion, flutter, ado.

stirring, adj. animated, lively, strenuous, active, enterprising.

stock, n. goods, merchandise, wares, reserve.

stock, v. replenish, supply, furnish.

stockings, n. hosiery, hose, nylons, tights.

stocky, adj. stout, plump.

stolen goods, n. booty, loot, spoil, plunder, pillage.

stomach, v. brook, tolerate, suffer, put up with, abide, stand, endure, take.

stomach, n. abdomen, belly, tummy.

stone, n. rock, pebble; calculus, concretion; flint, granite.

stone, n. gem, jewel, diamond, brilliant, beryl, emerald. Antonyms: paste, gewgaw, gimcrack, tinsel.

stony, adj. rocky, flinty, pebbly, gritty, gravelly; unrelenting, pitiless, unyielding, flinty, compassionless, hard.

stool, n. footstool, cricket, hassock, ottoman.

stoop, v. bend; condescend, deign, descend.

stoop, n. condescension, descent; porch, veranda, piazza.

stop, v. obstruct, close up; stanch; arrest, hinder, impede. Antonyms: continue, persist.

stop, n. cessation, discontinuation, surcease, pause, suspension, intermission.

store, n. shop; accumulation,

stock, abundance, plenty, hoard, supply.

storehouse, n. warehouse, repository, depot, store,

storm, n. tempest, squall, hurricane, blizzard, typhoon; outburst, eruption, flare-up.

storm, v. assault, attack, besiege; rage, fume, rant.

storminess, n. inclemency, tempestuousness, boisterousness, violence.

stormy, adj. tempestuous, boisterous, inclement, rugged, impetuous; violent, furious. Antonyms: calm, pacific, serene.

story, n. fiction, tale, anecdote, romance; novel, fable, legend.

stout, adj. strong, powerful, vigorous, enduring, durable, tough.

straight, adj. perpendicular, vertical, plumb, erect, upright. Antonyms: indirect, oblique, crooked, devious, circuitous.

straightaway, n. immediately; at once, directly, forthwith.

strain, v. stretch, tighten; sprain, wrench; percolate, filter.

strain, n. pedigree, race, lineage, extraction sort, kind.

strained, adj. tense, unnatural, forced, artificial, agonistic,

strait, n. narrows, channel; dilemma, difficulty, pinch, exigency, restriction.

strait-laced, adj. uncompromising, rigorous, strict. prudish, prim, precise.

stranded, adj. wrecked, aground, beached.

strange, adj. foreign, unfamiliar, exotic, outlandish; novel, odd. Antonyms: familiar, accustomed, wonted, commonplace, conventional,

stranger, n. foreigner, alien, outsider, visitor.

strap, n. thong, strop, leash.

strapping, adj. stalwart, able-bodied, large, muscular, brawny.

stray, v. wander, rove, roam, swerve, deviate; err, sin.

stray, adj. lost, wandering, abandoned, homeless.

streak, n. stripe, wale, welt, ridge, vein.

stream, n. current, river, creek, brook.

streamer, n. ensign, pennon, banner, banderole, flag.

street, n. highway, avenue, thoroughfare, boulevard.

strength, n. force, vigor, power, might, hardihood, potency. Antonyms: debility, delicacy, fragility, weakness, impotency, frailty, infirmity.

strengthen, v. invigorate, brace, nerve, steel, fortify, harden.

strengthening, adj. invigorating, tonic, fortifying.

strenuous, adj. zealous, ardent, valiant, intrepid, vigorous, active, energetic.

stress, n. urgency, pressure; emphasis, accent; severity, inclemency.

stretch, v. extend, elongate, lengthen, spread; overstate, exaggerate.

strict, adj. rigorous, stringent, exacting, rigid. Antonyms: lax, remiss, indulgent.

strife, n. conflict, struggle, contention, emulation, competition, battle.

strike, v. hit, smite, buffet, knock, beat, thump, whack.

striking, adj. impressive, noticeable, astonishing, surprising, forcible.

string, n. cord, line, twine, warp.

stringent, adj. binding, restrictive, rigid, severe, rigorous, exact.

strip, v. deprive, divest, dispossess, dismantle; plunder, desolate.

stripping, n. deprivation, divestiture, dismantling.

strive, v. struggle, try, endeavor, contend, vie, cope.

stroll, v. ramble, rove, range, stray, straggle, wander.

strolling, adj. wandering, nomadic, itinerant, roving, vagrant.

strong, adj. tough, enduring, hale, sound, robust. Antonyms: weak, vulnerable, frail, fragile.

struggle, n. conflict, contest, strife.

struggle, v. strive, cope, grapple, labor.

stubborn, adj. unyielding, obstinate, obdurate, mulish, refractory.

stuck-up, adj. proud, arrogant, haughty, vain, overbearing, cavalier.

study, n. research, excogitation, lucubration, cogitation.

stuff, n. material, fabric, cloth; trash, refuse, rubbish, goods.

stuffing, n. filling, forcemeat, dressing, wadding, padding, innards.

stumbling-block, n. difficulty, obstruction, hindrance, barrier.

stun, v. overcome, stupefy, dumfound, bewilder.

stunning, adj. overpowering, stupefying; astonishing, striking, fine.

stunted, adj. atrophied, undeveloped, scrubby, undersized.

stupefy, v. dull, benumb, hebetate, blunt, besot.

stupid, adj. dull, stolid, obtuse, sluggish, inept. Antonyms: shrewd, sharp, apt, spirited, lively, exciting, interesting.

stupor, n. lethargy, insensibility, unconsciousness, trance, daze.

sturdy, adj. obstinate, stubborn, pertinacious; strong, hardy, robust.

style, n. mode, vogue; fashion: manner, way, method.

stylish, adj. modish, fashionable, in vogue.

suave, adj. urbane, courteous, debonair, bland, affable.

subdue, v. conquer, vanquish, subject, overpower, subjugate.

subdued, adj. vanquished, conquered, submissive, tame.

subject, adj. exposed, liable, prone; answerable, amenable. Antonyms: exempt, immune, independent, free.

subject, v. subordinate, expose.

subject, n. dependant, subordinate: topic, matter, theme, issue, point, question.

subjection, n. subjugation, conquest, subordination, helplessness, weakness.

sublime, adj. exalted, grand, magnificent, glorious, majestic.

submerge, v. plunge, immerse, sink, submerse; overflow, flood.

submerging, n. submergence, submersion, immersion, inundation.

submission, n. compliance, acquiescence, surrender, resignation, obedience.

submissive, adj. yielding, obedient, tractable, meek, resigned, passive. Antonyms: defiant, intractable, rebellious, refractory.

submit, v. yield, surrender, succumb, acquiesce, comply, tolerate, stand. Antonyms: resist, rebel, disobey, revolt.

subservient, adj. subordinate, subject, inferior.

subside, v. collapse, fall down, dip; lessen, abate, decrease, diminish, dwindle.

substantiate, v. verify, corroborate, confirm, prove.

substantiation, n. corroboration, confirmation, verification.

substitute, v. exchange, commute.

substitute, n. deputy, proxy, representative, agent.

subterfuge, n. artifice, evasion, shift, sophistry, excuse.

subtle, adj. artful: cunning, sly, designing, crafty, refined, discriminating.

succeeding, adj. subsequent, following.

success, n. prosperity, triumph, victory, good fortune.

successful, n. prosperous, victorious, triumphant, fortunate.

succession, n. sequence, consecution; chain, line, series.

successive, adj. consecutive, succeeding, following.

successor, n. follower; heir, descendant. Antonym: predecessor.

sudden, adj. unexpected, abrupt, unlooked for.

sue, v. prosecute, litigate, charge, seek damages.

suffering, n. distress, agony, discomfort.

sufficiency, n. enough, adequacy, competence.

sufficient, adj. adequate. Antonyms: insufficient, inadequate.

suggest, v. allude to, hint, intimate, insinuate, propose, recommend.

suggestion, n. intimation, hint, allusion, proposal, instance, insinuation.

suit, n. wooing, courtship, addresses; prosecution, action, lawsuit.

suit, v. fit, adapt, adjust; please, gratify, satisfy.

suitable, adj. fitting, accordant, proper, becoming.

sulky, adj. sullen, morose, surly, moody.

sullen, adj. morose, sulky, intractable.

sum, n. amount, total, aggregate, sum total, totality, whole, balance, result.

sum, v. cast up, add, compute; summarize.

summary, n. recapitulation, epitome, resume, synopsis.

sunrise, n. daybreak, dawn, aurora.

super, adj. wonderful, great, fantastic, marvelous, fabulous, tremendous, excellent, splendid, terrific, superb, brilliant; superior, better, enhanced, improved, outstanding. Antonym: awful.

superabundance, n. redundancy, excess, surfeit, superfluity.

superb, n. magnificent, grand, august, elegant.

superintendent, n. overseer, guardian, supervisor, custodian, director, manager.

superior, adj. more excellent, surpassing, paramount, predominant.

superiority, n. preeminence, ascendency, supremacy, advantage, dominance, lead, control, authority; arrogance, haughtiness, condescension, disdain, snootiness.

supernatural, adj. miraculous, preternatural, hyperphysical, paranormal.

supersede, v. replace, displace, supplant.

supple, adj. flexible, plaint, lithe.

supplement, n. continuation, appendix, postscript, addition, addendum.

supply, v. furnish, afford, yield, replenish, recruit, stock.

support, v. prop, brace, bolster, uphold, sustain. Antonyms: desert, undermine, weaken, repudiate.

supporter, n. advocate, adherent, defender, pillar.

suppose, v. assume, conjecture, presume, imagine, believe, imply, surmise.

supposed, adj. assumed, presumed, putative.

supposition, n. hypothesis, conjecture, surmise, assumption.

suppress, v. quell, overpower, put down; check, repress, restrain.

suppression, n. quelling, overthrow; repression, restraint; concealment, secretion.

supreme, adj. transcendent, preeminent, superlative, paramount, predominant.

sure, adj. certain, inevitable; positive, confident, assured. Antonyms: uncertain, doubtful, dubious.

sureness, n. certainty, inevitability, assurance, certitude, safety.

surety, n. sureness, certainty; security, pledge, guarantee.

surface, n. exterior, outside, superficies.

surmise, v. suppose, conjecture, suspect, guess, opine.

surmount, v. conquer, overcome, prevail, conquer, triumph, defeat. Antonym: fail.

surpass, v. exceed, beat, better, outdo, top.

surplus, n. extra, excess, residue, remainder, leftovers, superfluity, overage, oversupply

surplus, adj. extra, excess, spare, leftover, remaining, additional, over, superfluous, excessive.

surprise, v. amaze, astonish, astound.

surprise, n. amazement, astonishment.

surprising, adj. astonishing, amazing, astounding, marvelous.

surrender, v. relinquish, yield,

abandon, capitulate, waive, remit.

surrender, n. relinquishment, capitulation, yielding.

surround, v. enclose, encircle, encompass, environ.

surrounding, adj. circumambient, encompassing, encircling, ambient, enveloping.

susceptible, adj. sensitive, impressionable, impressible, tender.

suspect, v. mistrust, distrust, doubt; conjecture, surmise.

suspense, n. uncertainty, wavering, hesitation, irresolution.

suspension, n. pendency; delay, respite, postponement, abeyance.

suspicion, n. mistrust, misgiving, distrust; surmise, conjecture, supposition.

swallow, v. ingurgitate, gulp, bolt, engorge.

swap, v. exchange, trade.

swarming, adj. teeming.

sway, n. dominion, domination, rule.

swear, v. blaspheme, curse, imprecate, use profane language; declare, affirm, promise.

swearing, n. profanity, oath, blasphemy.

sweat, v. perspire; exude.

sweet, adj. saccharine, honeyed, sugary. Antonyms: bitter, acrid, tart, sour.

sweetheart, n. lover, inamorato, beau, darling, beloved.

sweets, n. confectionery, sweetmeats.

sweet-smelling, adj. fragrant, redolent, balmy, aromatic, savory, sweet-scented,

swell, v. distend, dilate, expand, bloat, puff up.

swell, n. swelling, augmentation, increase: protuberance, bulge; fop, dandy.

swell, adj. fashionable, elegant, distinguished, exquisite.

swelling, n. bulge, bump, blister, abscess, inflammation.

swerve, v. deviate, deflect, diverge, turn aside.

swift, adj. fleet, rapid, fast, speedy, quick.

swiftness, n. celerity, velocity, speed, rapidity, fleetness, quickness.

swine, n. hog, pig; brute, beast.

swing, v. oscillate, vibrate; sway; brandish, flourish, wave.

swipe, v. strike; steal, pluck, snatch.

switch, v. whip, flog; shunt, shift.

swollen, adj. tumid, bloated, puffed up.

sword, n. rapier, saber.

swordfight, n. fencing, swordplay.

symbolic, adj. typical, emblematical.

symmetry, n. proportion, regularity, balance, equilibrium, evenness.

sympathetic, adj. compassionate, commiserating, pitiful, kind, tender.

sympathize, v. have sympathy, commiserate, condole with; agree, be in accord.

sympathy, n. fellow-feeling, tenderness; pity, commiseration, compassion. Antonyms: antipathy, disagreement, incompatibility.

symptom, n. indication, mark,

sign, evidence, diagnostic.

synopsis, n. syllabus, compendium, abstract, summary, epitome, digest.

system, n. method, order. Antonyms: chaos, confusion, disorder.

systematic, adj. methodical, orderly. Antonyms: unsystematic, chaotic.

systematize, v. methodize, classify.

T

tab, n. account, reckoning, check, tally, score.

table, n. tablet; schedule, synopsis, index, list.

taboo, adj. prohibited, forbidden, interdicted, proscribed.

tackle, n. gear, implements, equipment, rigging, apparatus.

tacky, adj. sticky, adhesive; dowdy, shabby, unkempt, seedy.

tadpole, n. polliwog.

taint, v. imbue, impregnate, corrupt, infect, vitiate, sully.

taint, n. infection, contamination, vitiation, defilement, pollution.

take, v. seize, grasp, clutch, procure, clasp; catch; confiscate.

take back, v. recant, retract, recall, revoke, rescind, disavow, resume.

take the place of, v. supplant, displace, substitute.

taking, adj. captivating, attractive, enchanting, intriguing, winning, charming, delightful.

talent, n. endowment, faculty, gift, forte, knack, genius, aptitude.

talented, adj. gifted, endowed, clever, precocious, skillful.

talk, v. speak, converse, confer, confabulate, consult; babble.

talk, n. conversation, converse, colloquy, conference, confabulation, chat, parley.

talkative, adj. garrulous, loquacious, chatty, verbose, longwinded. Antonyms: reserved, reticent, uncommunicative, silent, still.

talkativeness, n. garrulity, loquacity, communicativeness. Antonyms: reserve, reticence, taciturnity.

talker, n. conversationalist: interlocutor; chatterer, babbler, magpie, chatterbox.

tall, adj. lofty, high, towering.

tally, n. mate, match, counterpart; score, account, record.

tally, v. match, conform, agree, correspond, coincide.

tame, v. domesticate, reclaim, break; discipline, subjugate, conquer.

tamed, adj. domesticated, controlled, restrained, disciplined.

tamper, v. meddle, tinker.

tangible, adj. palpable, tactile, material; substantial, evident, perceptible, obvious.

tangle, v. snarl, entangle, interweave. Antonyms: disentangle, unravel, extricate.

tangle, n. snarl, complication, intricacy. Antonyms: disentanglement, extrication.

tangled, adj. entangled, complicated, snarled, intricate, involved.

tantalize, v. torment, plague, vex, disappoint.

tardy, adj. slow, sluggish; dilatory, reluctant, behindhand, late. Antonyms: punctual, prompt.

tarnish, v. dim, sully, besmirch, blacken, deface.

task, n. work, labor, assignment, stint; study, lesson, exercise.

taste, n. flavor, tang; try, sample, bite, test; discrimination, discernment, refinement; preference, predilection, leaning.

taste, v. sample, try, test, eat, bit, nibble; savor, experience, feel, undergo.

tasteful, adj. attractive, refined, discerning, sophisticated, elegant, stylish, classy.

tasteless, adj. insipid, flat, unpalatable, vapid; cheap, garish, flashy, loud.

tasty, adj. delicious, flavorsome, yummy, succulent; neat.

tattle, v. tell, divulge, blab.

tattler, n. tale-bearer, gossip, quidnunc, busybody, snitch, informant.

taunt, v. ridicule, deride, mock, reproach, revile, jeer, twit, gibe.

taunting, adj. reviling, derisive, jeering, sarcastic.

tax, n. assessment, toll, excise, levy, tribute, custom, duty.

taxable, adj. assessable.

teach, v. instruct, inform, educate, discipline, train, indoctrinate, school.

teachable, adj. docile, tractable, apt, bright.

teacher, n. instructor, tutor, master, pedagogue, preceptor.

teaching, n. instruction, education, breeding, enlightenment.

tear, n. rent, fissure, rip.

tearful, adj. lachrymose, weeping, maudlin.

tearing, n. rending, laceration, ripping.

tease, v. torment, plague, tantalize, hector, taunt, harass, badger.

tedious, adj. tiresome, wearisome, irksome, humdrum, monotonous.

teeth, n. incisors, molars, bicuspids, grinders.

tell, n. mention, recount, relate, narrate, numerate, advise. Antonyms: suppress, reserve, withhold, forbear.

telling, n. notification, apprising, communication, relation, narration, recital, divulgement.

temper, v. qualify, modify, moderate appease; anneal.

temper, n. mood, disposition, humor; passion.

temperament, n. constitution, nature, temper, disposition.

temperate, adj. moderate; dispassionate, calm; abstemious, sober, self-denying.

temple, n. church, sanctuary, tabernacle.

temporal, adj. secular, worldly; temporary; political, civil.

temporary, adj. transitory, transient, temporal, impermanent, ephemeral, fleeting.

tempt, v. seduce, entice, decoy, allure; provoke, incite, instigate.

temptation, n. seduction, allurement, enticement, attraction.

tempting, adj. enticing, alluring,

seductive.

tenacious, adj. retentive; cohesive, tough; pertinacious, persistent.

tend, v. conduce, contribute; attend, accompany, guard; incline, lean.

tendency, n. drift, inclination, proclivity, proneness, propensity, bent, predisposition.

tender, adj. delicate, fragile, sensitive, susceptible; touching, sympathetic. Antonyms: tough, strong.

tender, n. attendant; offer, proposal, overture, proposition.

terms, n. stipulations, conditions; terminology, nomenclature.

terrace, n. esplanade, plateau.

terrible, adj. dreadful, formidable, shocking, horrible, frightful, dire.

terrify, v. appall, intimidate, daunt, horrify, alarm, shock, frighten.

territory, n. province, region, district.

terror, n. alarm, consternation, dismay, panic, fright, affright.

test, n. trial, ordeal; standard, touchstone, criterion; crucible.

test, v. try, prove, assay.

testify, v. depose, attest, asseverate, verify.

testimonial, n. credential, certificate, voucher, recommendation.

testimony, n. attestation, deposition, corroboration; witness, evidence.

testy, adj. irritable, choleric, captious.

text, n. book, manuscript; passage; subject, topic, theme.

texture, n. fabric, web; grain, structure, contexture.

thankful, adj. grateful, appreciative.

thankfulness, n. gratitude, appreciation. Antonym: ungratefulness.

thankless, adj. trying, difficult, unappreciated.

theater, n. playhouse; lyceum; arena, stage.

theatrical, adj. dramatic, histrionic, scenic; stagy, artificial.

theory, n. hypothesis, conjecture, speculation, assumption, premise, philosophy, concept, scheme.

thick, adj. broad, fat, wide, chunky, bulky, solid; dense, bushy, copious, heavy, concentrated; unintelligent, dim, dense, obtuse; syrupy, gooey, viscous; indistinct, slurred.

thicken, v. coagulate, condense, curdle, congeal, solidify, set, gel.

thickness, n. denseness, density, compactness; grossness.

thick-skinned, adj. obtuse, dull, insensitive, unconcerned, callous, impervious, hard. Antonym: sensitive.

thief, n. robber, pilferer, filcher, peculator; embezzler, defaulter.

thievery, n. theft, larceny; embezzlement, peculation; shoplifting.

thievish, adj. light-fingered, pilfering, predatory; stealthy, sneaking.

thin, adj. emaciated, slim, bony, lean, skeletal, lanky, slender, skinny, gaunt; fine, narrow, threadlike, delicate, fragile; sheer, gauzy, diaphanous, light; watery, diluted, insipid; reedy. Antonyms: fat, concentrated, resonant, thick, substantial.

thin, v. dilute, weaken, water down.

thing, n. object, article.

things, n. clothes, furniture, appurtenances, belongings, goods, luggage, accessories.

think, v. meditate, cogitate, ponder, contemplate, brood, reflect, muse.

thinkable, n. conceivable, imaginable, presumable.

thinking, adj. rational, pensive, reflective, contemplative, cogitative, introspective.

thinking, n. cogitation, meditation, contemplation, thought.

thinness, n. emaciation, slenderness.

thirst, n. dryness, aridity, drought, dehydration; desire, hunger, craving, yearning.

thorough, adj. complete, profound. Antonyms: superficial, cursory, partial.

thought, n. reflection, cogitation, reverie, musing, meditation, consideration.

thoughtful, adj. contemplative, meditative, reflective, cogitative, wistful, pensive, introspective; considerate, empathetic.

thoughtless, adj. inconsiderate, careless, unmindful, remiss, rash, inadvertent, indiscreet.

threat, n. menace, threatening, fulmination, intimidation.

threaten, v. menace; augur, portend; impend, be imminent.

threshold, n. doorsill, sill, entrance, entry; verge, brink, edge, dawn, beginning, onset, inception; ceiling, maximum, upper limit.

thrift, n. frugality, economy, thriftiness, providence; prosperity.

thrifty, adj. sparing, economical, provident, frugal; thriving, prosperous; luxuriant.

thrill, n. excitement, adventure, delight, pleasure, kick.

thrill, v. excite, delight, stimulate, electrify.

thrilling, adj. moving, exciting, sensational.

thrive, v. flourish, prosper.

thriving, adj. flourishing, thrifty, prosperous, successful, blooming.

throb, n. beating, pulsation, palpitation.

throb, v. palpitate, pulsate, beat.

throw, v. pitch, hurl, fling, cast, toss, sling, heave.

throw away, v. discard, dump, scarp, ditch; squander, waste; reject, decline.

throw-away, adj. off-the-cuff, incidental, offhand.

throw out, v. expel, evict, oust, reject; emit; discharge. Antonym: retain.

thrust, v. push, force, impel, shove, stab, pierce, protrude.

thunder, v. detonate, roll, boom.

thunderstruck, n. dumfounded, astounded, amazed.

tickle, v. titillate; please, delight, gladden.

ticklish, adj. difficult, critical, delicate.

tidy, adj. orderly, neat, trim.

tie, v. secure, fasten, bind, tether, leash.

tie, n. knot, fastening; bond, obligation; draw, dead heat.

tight, adj. taut, tense; snug, close-fitting.

till, v. cultivate, plow, dig.

tilt, v. slant, slope, incline, tip, cant.

time, n. duration; while, spell, season, interval, interim, lapse.

timely, adj. appropriate, opportune; punctual. Antonyms: untimely, inopportune.

timid, adj. timorous, shy, diffident, meticulous, faint-hearted, cowardly.

timidity, n. diffidence, shyness, timorousness, cowardice.

tip, v. incline, lean, cant, tilt; careen, capsize; pour, empty.

tip, n. pointer, suggestion, word of advice, hint; gratuity; point, end, top, head.

tire, v. fatigue, weary, jade, bore, tucker, exhaust.

tiresome, adj. irksome, wearisome, fatiguing, tedious,

tissue, n. fabric, stuff, cloth, texture, web, network; handkerchief.

together, adv. united, jointly, concertedly, simultaneously, collectively.

together, adj. composed, organized, self-possessed.

toil, v. labor, drudge, sweat.

toil, n. work, labor, drudgery. Antonym: relaxation.

token, n. sign, symbol, index, indication.

token, adj. symbolic, nominal, perfunctory.

tolerable, adj. bearable, sufferable, endurable; mediocre, so-

so, ordinary.

tolerance, n. endurance, toleration, sufferance. Antonym: intolerance.

tolerant, adj. indulgent, forbearing, charitable. Antonym: intolerant.

tolerate, v. endure, suffer, brook; allow, permit, admit.

toleration, n. tolerance, endurance, sufferance; allowance, permission.

tone, n. sound, note; cadence, modulation; force, vigor, energy.

tone down, v. subdue, moderate, soften.

tool, n. implement, utensil, instrument.

top, n. summit, crest, apex, vertex, pinnacle, zenith.

topic, n. subject, theme; division, head, subdivision.

torment, n. pain, anguish, distress, torture; bane, infliction.

torment, v. persecute, hector, tease, tantalize, harry; torture.

torn, adj. rent, lacerated, ripped.

tornado, n. hurricane, cyclone, whirlwind.

torpid, n. numb, benumbed, unfeeling; lethargic, dull.

touch, v. meet, impinge; graze.

touch, n. touching, contact, contiguity, osculation.

touching, adj. pathetic, affecting, moving, tender.

touching, prep. respecting, concerning, regarding.

touchy, adj. irascible, irritable, petulant, testy, choleric, snappish.

tough, adj. tenacious, unyielding;

cohesive, adhesive, obdurate, refractory, stubborn.

tour, n. journey, trip, excursion, expedition.

tousled, adj. disordered, disheveled.

tower, n. steeple, campanile, minaret, spire, belfry.

tower, v. overtop, rise above.

toy, n. gimcrack, plaything, trinket, amusement.

track, n. trace, vestige, footprint, footmark.

trade, n. commerce, barter, traffic, business; handicraft.

trade, v. exchange, barter, traffic, swap.

trader, n. trafficker, dealer, merchant, tradesman, monger.

tradesman, n. trader, merchant; artisan, craftsman, mechanic, journeyman, handicraftsman.

trail, n. train; track, spoor, trace, path, footpath.

trailing, adj. procumbent, prostrate. Antonyms: upright, erect.

train, v. discipline, nurture, drill; accustom, habituate, familiarize.

trained, adj. skilled, practiced, disciplined. Antonym: untrained.

training, n. discipline, nurture, drilling, exercise.

traitorous, adj. perfidious, treasonable, recreant, faithless.

tramp, n. vagrant, vagabond, nomad, hobo, derelict.

trample, v. crush; scorn, spurn, disregard.

transaction, n. procedure, affair, deal, business.

transform, v. transfigure, metamorphose; transmute.

transformation, n. transfiguration, metamorphosis; transmutation.

transgress, v. violate, infringe, disregard.

transgression, n. violation, infringement infraction.

transient, adj. fleeting, transitory, temporary, impermanent.

translate, v. construe, render, interpret.

translation, n. rendering, interpretation.

transparency, n. diaphaneity, translucency. Antonym: opacity.

transparent, adj. diaphanous, translucent, pellucid. Antonym: opaque.

trap, n. snare, springe; pitfall, booby trap; artifice, stratagem.

trap, v. entrap, ensnare, catch.

trash, n. rubbish, refuse, trumpery.

travel, v. journey, itinerate, peregrinate.

traveler, n. wayfarer, itinerant, voyager, pilgrim, tourist.

traveling, adj. wayfaring, itinerant, wandering, peripatetic.

travesty, n. burlesque, parody, caricature, take-off.

tray, n. salver, waiter, plateau, server.

treacherous, adj. traitorous, perfidious, faithless, deceitful.

treachery, n. treason, perfidy, disloyalty.

treat, v. regale, feast; negotiate; behave toward, deal with.

treaty, n. covenant, agreement, compact, concordat, pact, protocol.

tree, n. young sapling, seedling.

tremble, v. quake, quiver, shudder, dodder, quaver, totter, vibrate, oscillate.

trembling, n. tremor, quivering, quaver, trepidation, rigor, oscillation.

trend, n. tendency, drift; fad, craze, vogue.

trespass, v. encroach upon, infringe, intrude.

trial, n. test, experiment, proof, essay, examination; probation; ordeal.

trick, n. ruse, artifice, stratagem, sleight, hoax, maneuver.

trick, v. deceive, cheat, defraud, cozen, impose upon.

trickery, n. deception, chicanery, artifice, duplicity.

trickster, n. rogue, cheat, imposter, scoundrel.

tricky, adj. difficult, complicated, problematic, thorny, complex; devious, knavish, unprincipled, treacherous, sly, cunning, crafty.

trifle, n. triviality, bagatelle.

trifling, adj. trivial, paltry, piddling, insignificant, piffling, frivolous.

trim, adj. spruce, smart; neat, tidy.

trim, v. adjust, arrange; decorate, adorn, garnish, embellish.

trip, n. jaunt, journey, excursion, expedition, outing, voyage;

trip, v. lapse, slip, stumble.

triumph, n. victory, conquest; exultation, ovation.

triumph, v. overcome, prevail, succeed; exult, rejoice.

triumphant, adj. exultant, jubilant; victorious.

trivial, adj. trifling, frivolous, insignificant, unimportant.

troop, n. company, battery, squad, band, throng, crowd.

trouble, v. vex, disturb, distress, inconvenience, incommode, pester, worry.

trouble, n. tribulation, adversity, reverses, affliction, calamity, misfortune.

troublesome, adj. vexatious, burdensome, afflictive, harassing, galling, wearisome.

trousers, n. pants.

true, adj. correct, exact, accurate, veritable, authentic, real, genuine.

true-blue, adj. incorruptible, loyal, true.

trump, v. outrank, outdo.

trumpet, v. broadcast, proclaim, announce, declare.

trust, n. credence, confidence, belief, reliance, affiance, faith; credit. Antonyms: distrust, doubt.

trust, v. depend upon, rely upon; give credit to; entrust, commit.

trustee, n. fiduciary, regent.

trustful, adj. unsuspicious, confiding, credulous, confident.

trusty, adj. trustworthy, faithful, reliable.

truth, n. veracity, truthfulness; accuracy, precision, exactness, correctness.

truthful, adj. veracious, honest, ingenuous, veridical.

try, v. test, examine, prove; attempt, essay, endeavor.

try, n. attempt, essay, trial, experiment.

trying, adj. severe, distressing, hard, irksome, afflictive, ordeal.

tug, n. trace; pull, effort.

tumble, v. heave, toss, roll, pitch; topple.

tumult, n. commotion, hurly-burly, turbulence.

tumultuous, adj. disorderly, turbulent, noisy, riotous.

tune, n. air, melody; order, harmony, unison, concord, accord.

tune, v. attune, modulate, harmonize.

tuneful, adj. melodious, harmonious.

tuneless, adj. inharmonious, discordant, dissonant.

turmoil, n. commotion, uproar, tumult, turbulence, agitation.

turn, v. revolve, spin, gyrate, rotate, wheel, veer.

turn, n. bend, winding, meander, curve, detour, deflection.

turning, n. rotation, revolution, spinning, gyration; extroversion.

turning, adj. revolving, rotary, rotating, gyratory, winding.

turning point, n. crisis, crossroads; pivot.

turtle, n. tortoise; terrapin.

twig, n. spray, branch, sprig, switch.

twilight, n. dusk, evening.

twine, v. entwine, encircle, wreathe.

twinkle, v. blink, wink; flash, sparkle, scintillate.

twinkling, n. sparkling, scintillation, flash, twinkle.

two, n. couple, pair.

twofold, adj. double, duplicate.

type, n. symbol, token, representation; model, exemplar, prototype, archetype. Antonyms: atypical, abnormal, variant, unique.

typical, adj. emblematical, representative, indicative. Antonyms: atypical, abnormal, variant, unique.

typify, v. represent, prefigure.

tyrannical, adj. despotic, arbitrary, autocratic, imperious, absolute.

tyrannize, v. domineer, persecute, oppress.

tyranny, n. despotism, absolutism, oppression, rigor, severity.

tyrant, n. despot, autocrat; oppressor, persecutor, usurper.

U

ubiquitous, adj. omnipresent, global, universal.

ugly, adj. repulsive, unsightly, loathsome, hideous, gruesome, frightful.

ultimate, adj. final, farthest, extreme.

ultimately, adv. finally, eventually, at last.

ultra, adv. especially, particularly, very, mega.

umpire, n. referee, judge, arbitrator, arbiter.

unabated, adj. undiminished.

unable, adj. incapable, powerless, inept.

unacceptable, adj. objectionable, unwelcome, undesirable.

unaccountable, adj. incomprehensible, inexplicable, inscrutable.

unaccustomed, adj. unfamiliar, unwonted, unused.

unacquainted, adj. unfamiliar, strange.

unadulterated, adj. unsophisticated, unalloyed, pure.

unadvised, adj. imprudent, unwise, indiscreet, inconsiderate.

unaffected, adj. unmoved, untouched, unimpressed; artless, naive, sincere, natural, unfeigned.

unafraid, adj. fearless, bold, confident, courageous, undaunted, unabashed, undismayed.

unalterable, adj. immutable, unchangeable.

unanimity, n. unison, accord, agreement.

unanswerable, adj. irrefutable, incontrovertible.

unappeasable, adj. insatiate, insatiable, unquenchable, implacable.

unappreciable, adj. imperceptible.

unapproachable, adj. inaccessible, distant.

unarmed, adj. defenseless, unguarded, unprotected.

unasked, adj. unsolicited, voluntary, free-will.

unassailable, adj. impregnable, invincible, secure, invulnerable.

unattainable, adj. unachievable, impracticable, impossible.

unauthentic, adj. spurious, supposititious.

unavailing, adj. futile, nugatory, ineffectual, vain, pointless, fruitless.

unavoidable, adj. inevitable, unpreventable, inescapable, inevitable, manifest, necessary.

unaware, adj. unconscious, unmindful, insensible.

unbearable, n. intolerable, insufferable, unendurable.

unbecoming, adj. inappropriate, unseemly, unsuitable, indecorous.

unbelievable, adj. incredible, fabulous, amazing, astonishing, mind-boggling; implausible, far-fetched, unlikely.

unbeliever, n. doubter, skeptic, infidel, free-thinker, nonbeliever, atheist. Antonym: adherent.

unbelieving, n. incredulous, doubtful, skeptical.

unbend, v. relax; straighten, release, loosen.

unbending, adj. inflexible, unyielding, rigid, resolute, incompliant.

unbiased, adj. unprejudiced, impartial, neutral, disinterested.

unbidden, adj. unasked, uninvited; spontaneous, voluntary, volitional.

unblushing, adj. shameless, unabashed, brazen-faced, indecent, immodest.

unbounded, adj. illimitable, boundless, unlimited, limitless, immeasurable, vast, infinite, immense.

unbreakable, adj. inviolable, indestructible, strong, permanent, indissoluble, resilient. Antonym: fragile.

unbridled, adj. unrestrained, uncurbed, uncontrolled, licentious, immoderate.

unbroken, adj. whole, intact, continuous; inviolate; undisturbed, sound.

uncanny, adj. weird, eerie.

unceasing, adj. incessant, perpetual, perennial, ceaseless.

unceremonious, adj. informal, unconstrained; bluff, blunt.

uncertain, adj. distrustful, hesitating; dubious, precarious, problematical, insecure.

uncertainty, n. distrust, hesitation, doubt, dubiousness, dubiety, incertitude.

unchangeable, adj. immutable, invariable, changeless, stereotyped, unalterable.

unchanging, adj. unvarying, permanent.

uncharitable, adj. illiberal, intolerant, ungenerous, bigoted, censorious.

unchecked, adj. unbridled, unrestrained, unhampered, untrammeled, uncurbed.

uncivil, adj. discourteous, rude, churlish, boorish, brusque, impolite.

uncivilized, adj. savage, barbarous, crude, oafish, loutish.

unclean, adj. soiled, dirty, foul, filthy, nasty.

uncommon, adj. unusual, singular, rare, unique, queer, strange, odd, scarce.

uncommunicative, adj. reserved, taciturn, reticent, secretive.

uncompelled, adj. voluntary, spontaneous, gratuitous, unconstrained, volitional.

uncomplaining, adj. resigned, patient, forbearing, long-suffering, meek.

uncomplimentary, adj. unflattering, derogatory, blunt.

uncompromising, adj. inflexible, irreconcilable, intransigent, firm.

unconcerned, adj. indifferent, nonchalant, cool, apathetic, disinterested, carefree, blithe. Antonym: anxious.

unconditional, adj. absolute, unqualified, unrestricted, carte blanche.

unconscionable, adj. unreasonable, inordinate, exorbitant, excessive.

unconscious, adj. unaware, artless, naive; insensible, out cold, down for the count; automatic, mechanical, instinctive, involuntary, reflex.

unconsciousness, n. insensibility; coma, oblivion.

unconstrained, adj. spontaneous, uncompelled, voluntary, natural.

uncontrollable, adj. ungovernable, irrepressible.

unconvincing, adj. inconclusive, unpersuasive, lame.

uncouple, v. disconnect, detach, disjoin, loose.

uncouth, adj. awkward, clumsy, rude, ungainly, loutish, gawky, ungraceful.

uncover, v. disclose, reveal, expose, show.

uncultivated, adj. untilled, fallow.

uncultured, adj. unlettered; ignorant; philistine.

undecided, adj. unsettled, pending; wavering, irresolute, dubious, controvertible.

undecipherable, adj. illegible, unreadable, inexplicable, mysterious.

undefined, adj. vague, indefinite, obscure; boundless, limitless.

undemonstrative, adj. staid, quiet, demure, phlegmatic, sedate.

undeniable, adj. incontestable, indisputable, unquestionable, indubitable, irrefutable.

under, prep. beneath, below, subordinate, inferior, subject to.

underbrush, n. undergrowth, jungle.

underground, adj. subterranean, subterraneous.

underhanded, adj. surreptitious, clandestine, covert, sneaky, devious, deceitful, scheming.

underline, v. underscore, emphasize, highlight.

underling, n. subordinate, inferior, understrapper.

underlying, adj. fundamental, basic.

underrate, v. underestimate, undervalue.

understand, v. comprehend, apprehend, grasp, discern.

understandable, adj. comprehensible, intelligible.

understanding, n. comprehension, discernment, apprehension; accord.

undervalue, n. depreciate; underrate, underestimate.

underwrite, v. insure; subscribe.

undeserved, adj. unmerited, unjust, unfair.

undeserving, adj. unworthy.

undeveloped, adj. in embryo, embryonic, immature, abeyant.

undignified, adj. unseemly, unbecoming, groveling, servile, obsequious.

undiminished, adj. unabated, entire, whole, intact.

undisputable, adj. incontrovertible, incontestable, indisputable, undeniable.

undo, v. reverse, annul, nullify, abrogate, neutralize, invalidate.

undoing, n. reversal, annulment, invalidation, abrogation; impoverishment, ruin.

undoubted, adj. indubitable, unquestioned, unchallenged, undisputed.

undoubting, adj. sure, confident, sanguine, implicit.

undress, v. disrobe, strip, divest.

undressing, n. disrobing, stripping.

undue, v. unreasonable, immoderate, exorbitant, excessive, disproportioned.

undying, adj. unending, neverending, endless, perpetual, eternal, everlasting, abiding.

unearth, v. uncover, disclose, ferret out.

unearthly, adj. weird, supernatural, preternatural, eerie.

uneasiness, n. restlessness, inquietude, perturbation, anxiety, agitation, malaise.

uneasy, adj. restless, restive, anxious, perturbed, impatient.

uneducated, adj. illiterate, unschooled, ignorant.

unemotional, adj. detached, impassive, cold; phlegmatic.

unendurable, adj. intolerable, insufferable.

unequal, adj. unmatched, uneven, disparate; ill-balanced, disproportioned.

uneven, adj. jagged, rugged, rough.

unexcelled, adj. unequaled, unsurpassed, superior, supreme.

unexcitable, adj. imperturbable,

phlegmatic.

unexpected, adj. unforeseen, unanticipated, unlooked for, sudden, surprising, startling, out of the blue.

unfading, adj. perennial, amaranthine, permanent, enduring.

unfailing, adj. sure, certain, constant, inexhaustible, infallible, inevitable.

unfair, adj. unjust, partial, unconscionable, inequitable, disingenuous.

unfairness, n. injustice, inequity, partiality.

unfaithful, adj. disloyal, faithless, perfidious, undutiful.

unfaithfulness, n. disloyalty, perfidy, apostasy, inconstancy, treachery.

unfaltering, adj. steadfast, unwavering, unswerving.

unfamiliar, adj. unaccustomed, strange, novel; unacquainted.

unfavorable, adj. adverse, inimical, unpropitious, inauspicious, derogatory, hostile.

unfeeling, adj. insensible, insensate, insentient, numb, apathetic.

unfeigned, adj. genuine, sincere, unaffected, real.

unfinished, adj. incomplete, in progress, partial.

unfit, adj. unsuitable, ineligible, inappropriate, unqualified, incompetent, inapt, inept.

unfit, v. disqualify, incapacitate, disable.

unflattering, adj. uncomplimentary, derogatory, frank.

unflinching, adj. resolute, steadfast, fearless.

unfold, v. unfurl, expand, evolve, unroll; disentangle, unravel, resolve.

unforced, adj. spontaneous, voluntary, optional, unconstrained.

unforgivable, adj. unpardonable, inexcusable.

unforgiving, adj. implacable, relentless.

unfortunate, adj. unlucky, unsuccessful, disastrous, ill-starred, ill-fated.

unfounded, adj. baseless, groundless.

unfriendliness, n. enmity, hostility, disfavor, antipathy.

unfriendly, adj. hostile, inimical, aloof, distant, frosty, inhospitable.

ungainly, adj. awkward, gawky, ungraceful, lumbering, loutish.

ungenerous, adj. illiberal, narrow, sordid, uncharitable, stingy.

ungodly, adj. godless, impious, irreverent, profane, unrighteous.

ungovernable, adj. unruly, unmanageable, refractory, intractable, mutinous, impotent.

ungraceful, adj. awkward, clumsy, uncouth, lumbering, ungainly.

ungrateful, adj. unthankful, unappreciative; disagreeable, offensive.

ungratefulness, n. ingratitude, thanklessness.

ungrateful person, n. ingrate.

unguarded, adj. defenseless, unprotected; incautious, unwary.

unhallowed, adj. unsanctified, profane.

unhandy, adj. inconvenient; clumsy, awkward. maladroit.

unhappiness, n. infelicity, misery, distress, sorrow, woe.

unhappy, adj. infelicitous, unfortunate; miserable, wretched, sad, sorrowful:

unharmed, adj. unscathed, inviolate uninjured, unhurt, intact.

unhealthy, adj. unwholesome, insalubrious, unsanitary, unwell, sick.

unheeded, adj. disregarded, ignored, unnoticed.

unholy, adj. unhallowed, unconsecrated, profane, impious, evil, ungodly.

unvarying, adj. invariable, constant, undeviating; consonant, consistent. Antonyms: diverse, variant, heterogeneous, variable.

uniform, adj. consistent, standardized, unvarying, regular.

uniform, n. costume, dress, garb, outfit, attire.

uniformity, n. sameness, consistency, standardization, regularity; invariability, equableness. Antonyms: diversity, variation, anomaly.

unimaginative, adj. matter-of-fact, prosaic, literal, practical, unromantic.

unimportance, n. immateriality, insignificance, triviality, paltriness.

unimportant, adj. immaterial, insignificant, trivial, paltry.

unimpressive, adj. unimposing, mediocre, average.

unintentional, adj. accidental, unpremeditated, fortuitous.

union, n. coalition, combination, merger, fusion, unification, incorporation. Antonym: disunion.

unique, adj. unmatched, exclusive, distinctive, matchless, rare.

unite, v. join, combine, annex, associate, link, couple, yoke, slice.

united, adj. combined, incorporate, federated, confederate, affiliated, unified.

unity, n. oneness, singleness; concord, harmony, agreement, uniformity.

unjust, adj. unfair, inequitable, iniquitous, unmerited.

unjustifiable, adj. indefensible, inexcusable, unwarrantable.

unkind, adj. cruel, harsh, austere, rigorous, uncompassionate.

unkindness, n. cruelty, brutality, severity, incivility, disfavor.

unknowable, adj. incomprehensible, enigmatic, mysterious, indecipherable, inexplicable, inscrutable.

unknown, adj. obscure, inglorious, nameless; unidentified, anonymous.

unlawful, adj. illegal, illicit, contraband, illegitimate, unlicensed.

unlike, adj. dissimilar, different, diverse, sundry, variant.

unlikely, adj. improbable; unpromising.

unlimited, adj. limitless, illimitable, infinite, absolute, unbounded.

unload, v. disburden, unlade, relieve.

unlovely, adj. homely, plain, unattractive, repulsive.

unlucky, adj. unfortunate, luckless, ill-starred, unhappy.

unmanageable, adj. ungovernable, intractable, refractory, fractious.

unmannerly, adj. impolite, discourteous, boorish, uncivil, rude.

unmelodious, adj. discordant, harsh, dissonant, inharmonious, unmusical.

unmerciful, adj. cruel, pitiless, merciless, inclement, unsparing, stern.

unmindful, adj. unaware, careless, oblivious, inadvertent, inattentive, heedless.

unmistakable, adj. distinctive, unique; manifest, palpable, obvious, patent, evident, unambiguous.

unmovable, adj. fixed, stable, immobile.

unmoved, adj. calm, dispassionate, indifferent, unstirred, impassive.

unnatural, adj. abnormal, monstrous, anomalous, aberrant, variant.

unnecessary, adj. superfluous, useless, needless, uncalled for, expletive, redundant.

unnoticed, adj. unheeded, unnoted, surreptitious.

unobtainable, adj. unprocurable, unattainable, inaccessible.

unobtrusive, adj. unpretentious, unassuming, modest.

unorthodox, adj. unconventional, nonconformist, heretical, untraditional.

unpaid, adj. outstanding, payable, due.

unpardonable, adj. inexpiable, unforgivable.

unpleasant, adj. disagreeable, uncongenial.

unpopular, adj. disliked, obnoxious, odious, offensive.

unpretentious, adj. modest, unassuming, unaffected, natural, humble, down-to-earth.

unpreventable, adj. unavoidable, inevitable.

unprincipled, adj. unscrupulous, dishonest, corrupt, amoral, unethical.

unproductive, adj. unfruitful, barren.

unprofessional, adj. amateurish, incompetent, inexpert, shoddy.

unprofitable, adj. profitless; futile, fruitless, unavailing, losing, unsuccessful. Antonym: lucrative.

unpromising, adj. unlikely; inauspicious, unpropitious.

unqualified, adj. incompetent, ineligible; absolute, unconditional.

unquestionable, adj. incontrovertible, irrefutable, incontestable, indubitable, obvious, indisputable.

unravel, v. disentangle, extricate, ravel; decipher, unfold.

unreachable, adj. inaccessible, remote, unapproachable, out-of-the-way.

unreadable, adj. illegible.

unreal, adj. fanciful, imaginary, visionary, unsubstantial, shadowy.

unreasonable, adj. irrational, absurd, unwise, preposterous, senseless; excessive.

unrecognized, adj. ignored, disregarded, unacknowledged.

unrelenting, adj. relentless, implacable, inexorable, remorseless pitiless, unmerciful.

unreliable, adj. untrustworthy, undependable, uncertain.

unremitting, adj. indefatigable,

persevering, unceasing, constant, continuous, chronic, unrelenting.
unrest, n. anxiety, restlessness, uneasiness, disquiet; turbulence, strife, conflict, disturbances, fighting, disorder, instability.
unrestrained, adj. unbridled, ungoverned, uncurbed, riotous, impotent.
unrestraint, n. freedom, liberty, license, abandon.
unrestricted, adj. unlimited, unfettered, clear, open, unobstructed, unhindered, unhampered, at liberty, limitless.
unruly, adj. turbulent, ungovernable, refractory, insubordinate, fractious.
unsafe, adj. insecure, risky, perilous, dangerous, hazardous.
unsatisfactory, adj. disappointing, insufficient.
unsavory, adj. offensive, rank, unpleasant; insipid, savorless.
unscrupulous, adj. unprincipled, dishonest, dishonorable, knavish.
unseasonable, adj. inopportune, ill-timed, untimely, premature.
unseemly, adj. unbecoming, improper, indecorous.
unseen, adj. invisible, unperceived, secret, unnoticed, unobserved.
unselfish, adj. magnanimous, generous, altruistic, charitable.
unsentimental, adj. matter-of-fact, prosaic, pragmatic, practical.
unsettle, v. disorder, derange, upset, unhinge, disconcert.
unsettled, adj. undetermined, dubious, controvertible, disputable.
unsightly, adj. offensive, repulsive.

unskilled, adj. inexpert, amateurish, untrained, inexperienced.
unsociable, adj. antisocial, hostile, cold, unfriendly, shy, standoffish.
unsophisticated, adj. unadulterated; innocent, guileless, gullible, ingenuous.
unsound, adj. defective, impaired; sophistical, fallacious, illogical.
unsparing, adj. liberal, generous, bountiful, openhanded, magnanimous, ungrudging, profuse.
unspeakable, adj. disgusting, awful, appalling, revolting, horrifying; indescribable, inexpressible, beyond words.
unstable, adj. insecure, unsteady, unbalanced, uneven, unhinged, rickety, insecure; volatile, unpredictable, erratic.
unsteady, adj. inconstant, precarious, wavering, variable, vacillating.
unstudied, adj. extemporaneous, extempore, impromptu, offhand.
unsuccessful, adj. unfortunate, unlucky, fruitless; ineffective, failed, vain.
unsuitable, adj. inappropriate, incongruous, incompatible.
unsurpassed, adj. peerless, transcendent, superior, unrivaled, matchless.
unsuspecting, adj. unsuspicious, gullible, naive, unsophisticated.
unsustainable, adj. untenable, controvertible.
untangle, adj. unravel, disentangle.
unthankful, adj. ungrateful.
untidy, adj. disorderly, slatternly,

littered.

untimely, adj. premature, unseasonable, inopportune, ill-timed, malapropos.

untiring, adj. indefatigable, unceasing, tireless, unremitting, unwearied.

untrue, adj. mendacious, false, untruthful, unfaithful, incorrect, fictitious, imaginary; cheating, disloyal, two-faced.

untruth, n. falsehood, fiction, fabrication, lie, fib, deceit.

untruthful, adj. mendacious, lying, dishonest, deceptive, fabricated.

untwist, v. unravel, disentangle, uncoil.

unused, adj. unaccustomed, unfamiliar.

unusual, adj. uncommon, curious, rare, odd, unique, extraordinary.

unvarying, adj. invariable, monotonous, uniform.

unveil, v. expose, uncover, reveal, disclose.

unwavering, adj. steadfast, resolute.

unwholesome, adj. baneful, insalubrious, unpleasant, distasteful, nasty, noxious.

unwieldy, adj. ponderous, cumbersome, clumsy.

unwilling, adj. reluctant, indisposed, loath, disinclined, averse.

unwind, v. disentangle, unravel.

unwise, n. imprudent, injudicious, inexpedient, indiscreet.

unwittingly, adv. unknowingly, innocently, accidentally, inadvertently.

unworthy, adj. unmeritorious, undeserving, despicable, contemptible.

unyielding, adj. inflexible, stiff, unbending, incompliant, indomitable.

upgrade, v. improve, promote, advance, raise.

upgrade, n. improvement, promotion, advance, raise.

uphill, adj. ascending, acclivitous, rising.

uphold, v. support, sustain, vindicate, defend.

upkeep, n. maintenance.

upper hand, n. advantage, mastery, dominion, control.

upright, adj. erect, perpendicular, vertical; honorable, honest.

uproar, n. turmoil, fracas, clamor, tumult, commotion.

uproot, v. displace, evacuate, relocate; pull up, dig up, deracinate.

upset, v. overturn, overset, capsize, invert, overthrow; disconcert.

upside down, adj. upturned, inverted, reversed; disordered, topsy-turvy, messy, untidy.

upward, adv. uphill, aloft.

upward, adj. rising, increasing, growing, ascendant.

urge, v. importune, exhort; impel, force; incite, instigate.

urgency, n. importance, exigency; determination.

urgent, adj. pressing, imperative, insistent, exigent.

usage, n. treatment; custom, practice, use.

use, n. employment, application, service, utilization, exploitation; necessity. Antonyms: disuse, obsolescence, desuetude, inutility.

use, v. employ, apply, utilize, exploit; treat, behave toward.

useful, adj. serviceable, advantageous, available.

usefulness, n. utility, advantage.

useless, adj. unserviceable, futile, worthless, unavailing.

usher, v. show to a seat; introduce, forerun, precede, escort.

usual, adj. ordinary, general, accustomed, conventional, prevailing, everyday.

usually, adv. ordinarily, generally, customarily, commonly.

usurp, v. arrogate, seize, appropriate, take, commandeer.

utility, n. usefulness, helpfulness, value, efficacy, service.

utilize, v. use, employ, exploit.

utmost, adj. farthest out, extreme, last; greatest, maximum, uttermost.

utter, v. speak, pronounce, express.

utter, adj. complete, absolute, perfect; unconditional, unqualified, peremptory.

utterance, n. speech, articulation.

utterly, adv. entirety, completely, wholly, unconditional, altogether.

uttermost, adj. extreme, utmost, farthest.

V

vacancy, n. emptiness; space, vacuum, chasm, gap.

vacant, adj. empty, unfilled, void, uninhabited, untenanted. Antonyms: full, filled, occupied.

vacate, v. empty, evacuate, resign, abdicate, annul.

vacation, n. holiday, break, retreat, trip; evacuation; invalidation.

vaccinate, v. inoculate.

vacillate, v. fluctuate, waver, veer, oscillate.

vacillating, adj. irresolute, changeable, wandering, undecided, inconstant.

vagabond, n. vagrant, tramp, mendicant, beggar; rascal, rogue.

vagrant, n. tramp; beggar, vagabond, rascal.

vagrant, adj. wandering, nomadic, vagabond.

vague, adj. indefinite, ambiguous, obscure, uncertain, groundless, hazy, indistinct.

vagueness, n. indefiniteness, ambiguity, obscurity, uncertainty.

vain, adj. conceited, arrogant, egotistical, overweening, narcissistic.

valid, adj. cogent, logical, justifiable, efficacious, well-grounded.

validity, n. strength, cogency, soundness, force. Antonym: invalidity.

valley, n. vale, hollow, bottom, dale, ravine.

valuable, adj. costly, precious, rare, expensive: esteemed, worthy.

valuable, adj. precious, costly, priceless; beneficial, worthwhile.

valuable, n. treasure.

valuation, n. appraisement, appraisal.

value, n. worth, excellence.

value, v. appraise; prize, esteem, appreciate.

vandal, n. destroyer, hooligan,

ruffian.

vanishing, adj. evanescent, disappearing, transient.

vanity, n. pride, narcissism, self-importance, conceit, egotism; futility, emptiness, uselessness, pointlessness, worthlessness, ineffectuality.

vanquish, n. overcome, defeat, subjugate, subdue, rout.

vapor, n. gas, haze, fog, fume.

vaporize, v. evaporate; disintegrate.

variability, n. variableness, mutability, inconstancy, unpredictability, inconsistency, changeability. Antonym: predictability.

variable, adj. mutable, changeable. Antonyms: invariable, unchangeable.

variance, n. change, alteration; dissension, disagreement, difference, nonconformity.

variation, n. mutation, change; deviation, diversity, discrepancy, diversification.

varied, adj. various, diversified, different.

variety, n. diversity, diversification, multiplicity; assortment.

various, adj. manifold, diverse, sundry, numerous, multifarious.

varnish, v. lacquer, enamel, glaze, stain; gloss over.

varnish, n. finish, glaze, polish, patina, gloss.

vary, v. diversify, variegate, modify; deviate, depart.

vast, adj. spacious, immense, monstrous, huge, extensive, immeasurable.

vault, v. leap over, spring, bound, jump; tumble.

vegetate, v. sprout, grow, germinate, pullulate; rusticate, hibernate.

vehicle, n. conveyance, carriage; medium, instrument.

veil, n. disguise, pretense, cloak, mask.

veil, v. cover, conceal, mask, shroud, hide, obscure.

venerate, v. reverence, revere, honor, esteem.

veneration, n. reverence, honor.

vengeance, n. retribution, avengement, revenge.

venial, adj. pardonable, excusable, forgivable.

vent, v. emit, utter, say, discharge.

venture, n. chance, risk, hazard, contingency.

venture, v. dare, hazard, risk.

venturesome, adj. daring, bold, intrepid, undaunted, temerarious.

veracious, adj. truthful, honest.

veranda, n. porch, piazza, terrace.

verbal, adj. oral, spoken, vocal.

verdict, n. finding, decision.

verification, n. confirmation, corroboration, authentication, attestation, proof.

verify, v. corroborate, confirm, attest, authenticate, prove.

verse, n. poetry, rhyme, versification. Antonym: prose.

versed, adj. acquainted, skilled, proficient, conversant.

version, n. rendition, translation.

vertical, adj. upright, perpendicular, plumb. Antonyms: horizontal, flat, level.

very, adj. veritable, true, real, actual, unquestionable, identical, same.

very, adv. exceedingly, highly, greatly, extremely, excessively, surpassingly, incredibly, awfully, exceptionally.

vestibule, n. hall, lobby.

vex, v. tease, plague, harass, torment, tantalize.

vexatious, adj. annoying, troublesome, irritating, provoking, aggravating.

vibrate, v. shake, quiver, tremble, shudder, throb.

vibration, n. oscillation, swinging, vacillation, libration.

vice, n. sin, iniquity, licentiousness, immorality; defect, fault.

vicinity, n. neighborhood, nearness, propinquity, proximity.

vicious, adj. immoral, evil; defective, faulty, imperfect.

victorious, adj. triumphant, conquering, successful, exultant.

victory, n. triumph, conquest, mastery.

vie, n. contend, compete, emulate.

view, n. scene, landscape, vista, perspective, panorama.

vigilance, n. watchfulness, circumspection, attention, caution.

vigilant, adj. watchful, attentive, circumspect, wakeful.

vigor, n. strength, force, lustiness, energy, endurance, virility.

vigorous, adj. strong, lusty, robust; energetic, cogent, forcible, luxuriant.

vile, adj. base, depraved, vicious, iniquitous, felonious, atrocious.

villainous, adj. unprincipled, knav-

ish, arrant, depraved, atrocious.

vim, n. activity, energy, spirit, life. Antonyms: lifelessness, languor.

vindicate, v. justify, exonerate, absolve.

vindication, n. justification, defense.

vindicator, n. justifier, champion, advocate.

vindictive, adj. revengeful, implacable, malevolent, rancorous.

violate, v. break, disobey, transgress, contravene, profane, desecrate.

violation, n. transgression, infringement, breach, infraction, contravention. Antonyms: inviolability, keeping, obedience.

violence, n. force, impetuosity, vehemence, intensity, severity.

violent, adj. passionate, vehement, impetuous, fierce, brutal, aggressive, vicious.

virile, adj. masculine, vigorous, strong; potent.

virtual, adj. potential, energizing; practical, essential.

virtually, adv. practically, really, substantially, potentially.

virtue, n. excellence, worth, goodness, purity, morality, integrity.

virtuous, adj. good, exemplary, moral, pure continent, upright.

visible, adj. perceivable, perceptible, discernible, apparent, evident, manifest. Antonyms: invisible, imperceptible.

vision, n. sign; apparition, dream, phantasm, specter.

visionary, adj. dreamy, imaginative, romantic, fanciful.

voice, n. utterance, speech; vote, choice, election, suffrage.

void, adj. vacant, empty, vacuous; destitute, devoid, lacking.

void, n. emptiness, abyss, space, nothingness.

void, v. cancel, annul, reject.

volume, n. book, tome; dimensions, compass, size, bulk, mass.

voluntary, adj. free, volitional, unforced, spontaneous.

voracious, adj. rapacious, ravenous, insatiable, fierce, gluttonous.

voracity, n. rapacity, voraciousness, greediness.

vote, n. suffrage; ballot, ticket.

vote, v. declare, choose.

voter, n. elector, suffragist, constituent.

vouch, v. attest, corroborate, warrant.

voucher, n. coupon, ticket, receipt.

vow, n. pledge, promise, oath.

vow, v. swear, promise, declare.

vulgar, adj. rude, offensive, unrefined, low-born, coarse, inelegant; bad-mannered, uncouth, boorish; tasteless, common, outlandish. Antonyms: refined, dainty, pure, chaste.

vulgarity, n. crudeness, offensiveness, impropriety; bad manners, uncouthness, boorishness; tastelessness,; expletive.

W

waddle, v. toddle, totter.

wage, v. stake, bet, wager.

wager, v. bet, stake, pledge, hazard, speculate.

wages, n. compensation, pay, earnings, hire, salary.

wagon, n. vehicle, wain, cart; caravan, van.

waif, n. urchin, orphan, stray.

wait, v. tarry, stay, linger, await, abide; delay, postpone.

wait, n. waiting, delay, halt, stop; ambush.

waiter, n. attendant, server.

waiting, n. tarrying, lingering, delay; abeyance, suspension, quiescence.

waiting room, n. station, depot.

waive, v. relinquish, forego, surrender.

wake, v. awake, waken; arouse, rouse, revive.

wakeful, adj. sleepless, restless, insomniac; vigilant, watchful, alert.

wakefulness, n. sleeplessness, insomnia, vigilance, watchfulness.

walk, n. stroll, promenade, constitutional; gait, step,

walk, v. stroll, tramp, stride, plod, trudge, tread.

walker, n. pedestrian, perambulator, hiker, rambler.

wall, n. foundation; partition, barrier, divider, fence; barricade, fortification.

wallow, v. welter, flounder; grovel.

wander, v. ramble, range, rove, stroll, roam, stray.

wanderer, n. nomad, vagrant, rover, rambler, stroller.

wandering, n. rambling, ranging, roving, strolling.

wandering, adj. nomadic, migratory, itinerant, vagrant, vagabond.

wane, v. decrease, diminish, fade, decline.

want, n. deficiency, lack, dearth, scarcity, need, default, absence.

want, v. need, require; desire, wish, crave.

wanting, n. absent, missing, deficient, defective, needy, destitute.

wanton, adj. unrestrained, uncontrolled, unchecked, unbridled, undisciplined.

war, n. hostilities, warfare, strife, battle.

war, v. contend, fight, combat, militate, battle.

ward, n. district, region, constituency; charge, responsibility, dependent.

warden, n. keeper, custodian, curator, warder.

warehouse, n. storehouse, depot, magazine, repository, depository.

wares, n. merchandise, commodities.

warfare, n. war, hostilities; crusade, struggle, strife, militancy.

warlike, adj. military, martial, belligerent.

warm, adj. lukewarm, tepid, thermal; zealous, ardent, fervent.

warm, v. heat, thaw, cook, swelter.

warmth, n. heat; ardor, fervor, passion, earnestness, fervency.

warn, v. admonish, caution, notify, apprise, advise, forewarn, signal.

warning, adj. cautioning, monitory, monitorial, ominous.

warped, adj. twisted, bent, bulging, protuberant, distorted.

warrant, v. guarantee, assure, insure; justify, defend, affirm, attest, vouch.

warrant, n. commission, authority; guaranty, surety; voucher, attestation.

warranty, n. guaranty, guarantee, security, warrant.

wary, adj. guarded, cautious, circumspect, careful, vigilant.

wash, v. lave, bathe, foment, rinse; launder.

waste, v. squander, misspend, fritter away, dissipate, dawdle.

waste, adj. refuse, rejected, unused, unproductive, untilled.

waste, n. wasting, squandering, dissipation, decrement, prodigality; wilderness.

wasteful, adj. extravagant, prodigal, unthrifty, improvident, lavish, thriftless.

waster, n. spendthrift, prodigal, squanderer.

watch, n. vigil, outlook, attention; watcher, patrol, watchman.

watch, v. keep vigil, be on the lookout, keep guard.

watchful, adj. vigilant, heedful, attentive, alert, circumspect, wary.

watchtower, n. observatory, crow's nest.

waterfall, n. cascade, cataract.

wave, n. undulation, surge, swell, billow, breaker.

wave, v. undulate, float, flutter; flourish, brandish, beckon, signal.

waver, v. vacillate, fluctuate, veer, oscillate, hesitate.

wavering, adj. vacillating, fluctuating, oscillating, unstable, irresolute, uncertain.

way, n. manner, method, mode,

fashion, style, guise, custom.

wayward, adj. disobedient, perverse, willful, intractable, headstrong.

weak, adj. feeble, infirm, debilitated, fragile, delicate, invalid.

weaken, v. debilitate, enfeeble, enervate, unnerve, emasculate, incapacitate.

weakening, adj. deteriorating, failing, waning, fading, declining, dwindling.

weakening, n. deterioration, decline, damage, undermining.

weakness, n. flaw, fault, limitation, drawback, Achilles' heel.

wealth, n. riches, fortune.

wealthy, adj. opulent, affluent, rich, capitalistic, independent.

wearied, adj. tired, fatigued, exhausted.

weary, adj. tired, fatigued, worn, exhausted, spent.

weave, v. entwine, interlace, mat, plait, braid.

wedding, n. nuptials, marriage, espousals.

weep, v. sob, cry.

weight, n. heaviness, ponderousness. gravity, poise.

weighty, adj. heavy, ponderous, massive, onerous; momentous, important.

welcome, n. greeting, salutation.

welfare, n. prosperity, happiness, weal, success, well-being.

well, adj. good, desirable, fortunate, expedient, favorable, beneficial, advantageous.

wet, adj. damp, moist, humid, soaked.

wet, v. moisten, dampen, soak, imbrue, saturate.

whimsical, adj. fanciful, fantastic, fictitious, imaginary.

whine, n. whimper, puling, complaint,

whine, v. whimper, pule, complain.

whip, v. lash, beat, thrash, flog, drub, punish, chastise.

whipping, n. chastisement, castigation, punishment, scourging.

whirl, v. spin, revolve, twirl, rotate, gyrate, wheel, pirouette.

whirling, n. spinning, rotation, gyration, pirouette.

whirlwind, n. cyclone, typhoon, twister.

whisper, n. susurrus, susurration, whispering; innuendo, suggestion, intimation.

white, adj. blanched, bleached, etiolate, pale.

whole, adj. all, total, entire; intact, complete, inviolate.

whole, n. sum, total, totality, all, aggregate, gross. Antonyms: part, portion, fraction, disintegration.

wholeness, n. entirety, completeness, integrity.

wholesome, adj. healthy, salubrious, salutary, nutritious, beneficial.

wicked, adj. sinful, iniquitous, evil, immoral, depraved, vicious.

wickedness, n. iniquity, depravity, immorality, sinfulness, vice.

wide, adj. broad; extensive, vast; comprehensive.

wide-awake, adj. alert, keen, vigilant, watchful, wary, attentive.

widespread, adj. prevalent, extended, extensive.

wife, n. spouse, consort, helpmate, partner.

wiggle, v. squirm, wriggle.

wild, adj. untamed, undomesticated, feral, natural; rowdy, riotous, disorderly, uncontrollable; fierce, violent; outrageous, madcap, crazy, foolish; stormy, tempestuous, blustery.

will, n. determination, resolve, willpower; volition, preference, choice; command, wish, behest, order; testament, devise.

will, v. want, desire, wish.

willful, adj. refractory, headstrong, perverse, disobedient, inflexible.

willing, adj. disposed, voluntary, eager, keen, enthusiastic, ready, agreeable.

willingness, n. readiness, disposition, alacrity.

wily, adj. crafty, artful, intriguing, designing, tricky, insidious, politic.

win, v. achieve, attain, succeed, triumph, prevail; gain, earn, attain, accomplish.

win, n. victory, success, triumph. Antonym: defeat.

wince, v. shrink, flinch, recoil.

wind, n. breeze, zephyr; draught; gale, squall; hurricane.

wind, v. coil, twine, twist, encircle, curl; snake, meander, bend, curve.

winding, n. convolution, labyrinth, zigzag, snaky, snaking, meandering. Antonym: straight.

windy, adj. blustery, gusty, tempestuous.

winning, n. achievement, gaining.

winning, adj. charming, captivating, winsome, engaging.

winter, v. hibernate.

wipe, v. swab; expunge, efface, obliterate, erase.

wisdom, n. lore, learning, sapience, erudition, knowledge, enlightenment.

wise, adj. erudite, sapient, learned, philosophical, enlightened.

wisely, adv. prudently, judiciously, sagaciously.

wish, v. desire, aspire; invoke, imprecate; congratulate.

wish, n. desire, longing, aspiration, hankering.

wit, n. sense, understanding; repartee, drollery, facetiousness.

witch, n. sorceress, enchantress; hag; siren.

witchcraft, n. sorcery, enchantments, necromancy, black art, conjuration.

witchery, n. witchcraft, sorcery; fascination, spell, charm, entrancement.

withdraw, v. retire, retreat, quit; recall, retract, recant, disavow.

withhold, v. refrain, abstain; refuse, deny.

witness, v. testify, bear witness, confirm, corroborate, attest.

witness, n. attestation, testimony, evidence; eye-witness, deponent.

witty, adj. facetious, droll, sharp.

wizard, n. wonder-worker, magician, conjurer, sorcerer, enchanter.

wolf, v. devour, gulp down, consume.

woman, n. dame, matron, lady, female.

wonder, n. surprise, astonishment, amazement, awe, marvel.

wonderful, adj. marvelous, wondrous, phenomenal, miraculous, portentous.

wood, n. forest, grove, woodland, timberland.

woods, n. forest, copse, thicket.

word, n. term, etymon, root; derivative; signal.

work, v. toil, labor, strive; drudge, slave; operate, manipulate. Antonyms: shirk, idle, dabble, loaf.

work, n. industry, toil, labor, employment, occupation; effort. Antonyms: idleness, dalliance, sloth.

worker, n. employee, hand, artisan, artificer, craftsman, journeyman. Antonyms: idler, drone, dabbler, sluggard, truant.

working, adj. industrious; operational, functioning, effective, running.

workman, n. artisan, artificer, craftsman, journeyman.

world, n. earth, creation, universe, cosmos; globe, planet.

worldly, adj. terrestrial, earthly, mundane, terrene; secular, temporal.

worn, adj. damaged, shabby, dog-eared, tattered.

worn out, adj. tired, pooped, exhausted, depleted.

worry, v. harass, vex, annoy, torment, tease, fret.

worry, n. anxiety, fretting, apprehension, concern, solicitude. Antonym: unconcern.

worrying, adj. anxious, distressing.

worship, v. adore, revere; idolize, deify, apotheosize, glorify.

worst, v. defeat, vanquish, conquer, overcome, overthrow, discomfit.

worth, n. worthiness, excellence, virtue, merit, integrity, honor, value.

worthless, adj. valueless, good-for-nothing, futile, trashy, unworthy.

worthy, adj. meritorious, excellent, estimable, deserving, reputable, exemplary, upright.

wound, n. hurt, injury, gash, lesion, trauma, abrasion.

wound, v. injure, damage, hurt, maim, disable.

wrangle, n. altercation, dispute, squabble, brawl, bickering, quarrel.

wrap, n. enfold, swathe, envelop.

wreck, v. demolish, destroy, ruin, shatter.

wretch, n. outcast, pariah, vagabond, knave, rogue.

wretched, adj. miserable, unhappy; contemptible, abject, despicable, paltry.

wrinkle, n. corrugation, pucker, crease, furrow.

write, v. inscribe; note, record, jot down; compose, create; correspond.

writer, n. scribe, scrivener, penman, secretary, correspondent, essayist.

writing, n. handwriting, chirography, penmanship, calligraphy.

wrong, adj. immoral, bad, wicked, sinful, dishonest, improper, criminal; incorrect, mistaken, erroneous; amiss, unsuitable, incorrect, improper. Antonyms: right, suitable.

wrong, n. sin, crime, injustice, inequity, oppression, disservice, trespass, transgression, injury.

wrong, v. insult, injure, wound, harm; cheat, defraud, maltreat, abuse.

wrongdoer, n. sinner, criminal, culprit, delinquent, offender.

wrongdoing, n. misdemeanor, malfeasance, malpractice, dereliction, iniquity.

wrought, adj. shaped, fashioned, twisted, formed.

wry, adj. twisted, distorted, awry; ironic, cynical, sardonic.

Y

yank, v. pull, jerk, twitch.

yap, n. bark, yelp.

yard, n. enclosure, court, area, courtyard.

yawn, v. gape; drowse.

yearbook, n. annual, almanac.

yearly, adj. annual, anniversary.

yearly, adv. annually.

yearn, v. long, desire, hanker after, pine.

yearning, n. longing, hankering, pining.

yell, n. outcry, scream, shriek, howl, yowl, vociferation.

yell, v. scream, shriek, screech, bawl, howl, yowl.

yellow, adj. golden, sallow, tawny, amber; blonde, fair; scared.

yelp, n. bark, yap.

yield, v. produce, pay, return; submit, surrender, succumb, give up. Antonyms: resist retain, withhold, refuse, withstand.

yield, n. product, crop, harvest.

yielding, n. production, bearing; surrender, relinquishment, submission, compliance.

yielding, adj. compliant, tractable submissive, amenable, unresisting.

yoke, v. couple, join, unite, link, hitch together; subject, enslave.

yokel, n. bumpkin, boor, rustic.

young, adj. juvenile, youthful, immature, adolescent.

young, n. offspring, brood, children, babies.

younger, adj. junior.

youth, n. juvenility, youthfulness; adolescence, teens, minority.

youthful, adj. immature, juvenile, adolescent, boyish. Antonyms: adult, manly, mature.

Z

zany, adj. madcap, wacky, screwball.

zeal, n. fervor, ardor, zealotry, intensity, passion, devotion, devotedness.

zealot, n. enthusiast, partisan, devotee, fanatic.

zealous, adj. ardent, eager, strenuous; fervent, passionate, intense, devoted, impassioned.

zenith, n. culmination, pinnacle acme, summit, apex. Antonym: nadir.

zero, n. cipher, nothing, naught.

zest, n. relish, flavor, taste, enjoyment, gusto.

zip, v. fasten, close; go fast, zoom, rocket, whoosh.

zip, n. energy, vigor; nothing, zilch.

zone, n. clime, region, district, precinct, sector, neighborhood.